RETHINKING LUXURY BUSINESS

5-7, rue de l'École-Polytechnique ; 75005 Paris

http://www.editions-harmattan.fr

ISBN : 978-2-343-19418-9
EAN : 9782343194189

RETHINKING LUXURY BUSINESS

L'Harmattan

Marché & Organisations/Market & Organizations

SUMMARY

RETHINKING LUXURY BUSINESS AND THE ECONOMY IN THE EXPERIENTIAL AND DIGITAL ERA GENERAL PRESENTATION

Dr. Wided BATAT
Associate Professor
American University of Beirut
wided.batat@bnc-consulting-group.com

This special issue seeks to expand on the research conducted to date, and approach the relationship between luxury businesses, digital, and customer experience. Despite being one of the most traditional industries, the luxury sector is highly dynamic and rapidly changing influenced by new ideas, technologies and generations. One of such influences is the prevalence of digital technology and social media (Denegri-Knott & Molesworth, 2010). It challenges a number of fundamental premises of luxury brands, including exclusivity (Tom et al., 1998), status, authenticity (Berry, 1994; Chaudhuri, 1998) and sensory experience (Holbrook & Hirschman, 1982). Digital luxury experiences (Batat, 2019a, 2019b, and 2017) are different from their offline counterparts (Tran & Voyer, 2013). In the luxury literature, specific phrases like "luxurious webmosphere" or "luxemosphere" were developed, indicating the need to adapt traditional conceptualizations (Kapferer, 2008; Atwal & Williams, 2009) to the digital context (Henning et al., 2012; Okonkwo, 2009, 2010). Descriptive accounts have highlighted that luxury in a digital environment involves different approaches to storytelling (Kretz & de Valck, 2010), and consumer-brand relationships (Okonkwo, 2009). However, little is known about the underlying mechanisms manifested in these new phenomena. Luxury is a well-researched area in the domain of business, marketing, and economy but most extant luxury research still focuses almost exclusively on luxury goods (Lipovetsky & Roux, 2003), ignoring luxury services, luxury experiences, how consumers construct their own moments of luxury and the new emerging economy of luxury experiences.

This special issue explores luxury consumption and production in a digital and experiential era. In line with the prior research in marketing on luxury experience and digital transformation (Batat, 2019a, 2019b), this special issue takes a multidisciplinary and holistic perspective to explore the role of digital and customer experience in rethinking the luxury industry in the future. The objective of this special issue is to advance knowledge on luxury by bringing together international scholars (research in French and English) from different disciplines and practitioners working in the field of luxury. This special issue integrates a multidisplinary research and works that go beyond the focus on goods and prestige to address issues including the experiential economy of luxury, innovation for luxury brands, and new concepts to better understand luxury consumers. In the line with this logic, the ten papers selected for this special issue address digital and experiential aspects related to the luxury industry.

The first research in this special issue by Batat and De Kerviler relies on multidisciplinary luxury literature to define French art of living (*art de vivre*) and the way it contributes to make the French luxury industry unique and competitive. The French art of living, although an abstract concept, is strongly connected to the luxury goods industry. Yet, although the French art of living is what can enhance the competiveness and the uniqueness of French luxury businesses, the concept of *art de vivre* is not defined in the literature and remains very abstract. In this conceptual article, Authors define the concept of the French art of living and identify the five pillars, namely, culinary art and tasting, beaux arts (fine arts), haute couture, French literature, and the art of perfume that French luxury businesses can implement in developing a competitive advantage that is embedded in the French luxury culture and experience.

A digital and heritage luxury theme follows in the second paper by Duma and colleagues in which attention turns to mastering the digital transformation as a heritage luxury fashion brand. Authors refer to digital transformation as the world of fashion and luxury with new challenges. Especially the relationship between luxury brands, digital technology and the Internet is an intricate one. For authors, disruptive innovations driven by information technology are forcing luxury fashion brands to adapt and future-proof business models must make use of digital technologies and e-business concepts in order to adapt to changing consumer behavior. However, what might be seen as obvious for large, multinational companies or for recent start-ups does come with various challenges in the case of small and medium-sized heritage luxury brands with decades, or, in some cases, centuries of history and a culture as well as a reputation tied to it. The present case study examines how a traditional Swiss heritage luxury fashion brand chose to react to the digital transformation and derives insights and recommendations for similar companies.

The issue of luxury and social media is featured in the third paper, by Track and colleagues. In their paper, the authors explore the building process of luxury brand on Instagram. This case study examines Delvaux's Instagram marketing activities using Kim and Ko's (2012) conceptual framework of five dimensions of social media marketing activities, namely entertainment, interaction, trendiness, customization, and word of mouth. More specific, based on a survey among 195 luxury consumers, a structural equation model is developed to explore how these dimensions affect customer brand equity and purchase intentions. Specifically, the study demonstrates a positive impact of trendiness, entertainment and word of mouth on customer brand equity. Moreover, entertainment and word-of-mouth enhance purchase intention, while trendiness had a significant negative effect on purchase intention. Furthermore, it was found that the effect of consumer's overall impression of Delvaux's Instagram marketing activities on purchase intention is partly mediated by customer brand equity. These findings suggest that luxury brands' investments in Instagram could have significant positive effects on customer brand equity and consequently purchase intention and thus provide further support for social media marketing as an important and cost-effective marketing tool for luxury brands in the digital age.

Luxury connoisseurs and Twitter is a continuing theme in the fourth paper, by Talukdar. This study investigates the effect of marketers' use of Twitter on the stock prices of luxury brands. Using stock return response modeling, this study fits three regression models that use tweet volume from luxury brands, retweet volume of brands' tweets, and their ratio to predict the variability in their stock price returns, after accounting for market returns. The results show that there are negative correlations among Twitter variables and stock returns of luxury brands, after accounting for market returns. The research findings have implications for advancing the understanding of the link between social media marketing and financial interface.

In the fifth paper, Brun and Karaosman explore sustainability in the luxury fashion supply chain from the millennials' perception. The research aims at exploring millennials' opinions about sustainability in luxury fashion and its scope is threefold. First, it evaluates the perceived coherence between luxury fashion and sustainability at a conceptual level, assesses the centrality of sustainable principles, and clarifies the role of luxury fashion brands within the green trend. The second purpose adopts a higher level of detail, testing young adults' awareness and perceived relevance of specific sustainability elements within the luxury fashion industry. Eventually, the study explores the causes of the discrepancy between a pro-environmental attitude and actual sustainable purchasing in luxury fashion, as well as the post-purchase justifications for unsustainability. The topics are explored through focus group discussions involving the Millennials and results include a strong coherence between luxury fashion and sustainability, accompanied by consumers' challenging expectations from companies. The predominance of social sustainability and the attention to basilar unsustainable practices emerge, together with the relevance of supply chain monitoring. The research also provides an overview of the causal relationships between the barriers that contribute to an attitude-behavior gap, and an indication of the justifications that facilitates it. In the sixth paper, Zhiqing and Shin propose a conceptual framework on the influence of authenticity and rarity on luxury brand value. The conceptual framework illustrates the internal relations of luxury brand authenticity, rarity and brand behavior. It emphasizes that in post-scarcity world, the nature or technical scarcity will tend to zero. The gap in the quality and functional value between each brand will diminish or even disappear. Intangible value generated by brand authenticity became the brand kernel, thus placing a price tag and attracting consumers, especially for luxury brand. Authenticity becomes the dominant factor distinguishing a luxury brand from others and whether the brand behavior reflects its authenticity consistently, continuously and individually determines how consumers judge this brand.

The seventh paper by Mosca and Chiaudano focuses on digital channels and distribution in the luxury market. Authors explore distribution strategies in the luxury brand market and digital channels. With the evolution of new technologies and new devices such as smartphones and tablets, companies that operate in the high-value market started to embrace digital channels as a part of their distribution strategies. However, little research has been done regarding luxury brand companies and the new distribution patterns available online. By analyzing the distribution strategies implemented online by well-known luxury brand companies, this paper aims to demonstrate that companies operating in the luxury brand market have overcome their skepticism about the use of digital technologies for selling products via online channels. In fact, thanks to the new digital technologies luxury firms are able to recreate online the same distribution models available offline, thereby responding effectively to new consumption patterns and the needs of luxury brand consumers.

In the eighth paper, Magnelli and colleagues examine innovative in-store ICT marketing solutions for an enhanced luxury shopping-experience. For authors, the new challenge facing the luxury sector is how to reconcile the potential offered by technology while preserving the sense of exclusivity in brand names and their accompanying heritage. In the meantime, however, there is a unique opportunity to form new and lasting relationships with clients by focusing not only on the product but also on an in-store shopping experience making the "customer journey" ever more dynamic through conceptual changes that have distinguished experience design in recent years. In the ninth paper, Vaileanu and colleagues examine the luxury value in the AI (Artificial Intelligence) era. Authors argue that the high prices associated with quality are a permanent barrier for the majority to access high quality and luxury, as the two concepts "democratization of luxury" and "luxury as quality and rarity" seemed to be contradiction in terms. But a new growth paradigm was identified if we apply quantic approach and functional economy approach to the analysis of the potential new "forms of luxury" ("luxury functionalities), which could be in the same time "not luxury quality" and "luxury quality" depending on the "observer", after the analogy with "the cat and the paradox of Schrodinger". But in the digital world, the "observer" is demultiplexed, the observation is in real time and continuously). Luxury domain could inspire and generalize the "augmented value creation" by "open valorization strategies" and scaled-up by national regulatory support (for example, the Law PACTE in France, the country where fashion and luxury adds to more than 42 milliards and 86% exports). New research will be conducted on this potential "augmented quality growth paradigm" inspired by the luxury new business model.

The final paper, by Kolenc and Bounaouas uses a qualitative study to explore the valorization of experiences perceived as luxurious by young consumers (26 biographical stories). Four main categories have been identified. 1) The luxury offer: In the two cases (direct and indirect experience), the respondents described components of mix marketing (product, price, place and promotion). However, the luxury experience is not always produced or controlled. 2) Feelings: experiential living implies individual emotions and feelings described by respondents during the consumption experience. The authors noticed that negative emotions were likely to appear when the contact employees seem unpleasant. 3) Individual representations: Luxury representations make consumers able to evaluate their own experience. However, positive or negative experience can affect individual representations. 4) Consumer values: They appear to be more generated by the experiential context than luxury products possessions. They also seem to be closely linked to individual representations. The findings provide first insights about the understanding of the luxury experience and highlight the role of individual representations in its valorization.

REFERENCES

ATWAL, G. & WILLIAMS, A., 2009, Luxury Brand Marketing – The Experience is Everything!, *Journal of Brand Management*, 16, 5/6, pp. 338-346.

BATAT, W., 2017, *Luxe et Expérience client*, Dunod, Paris.

BATAT, W., 2019a, Experiential Marketing: Consumer Behavior, Customer Experience and The 7Es, Routledge, London.

BATAT, W., 2019b, The luxury experience: Creating the ultimate customer experience, Springer, New York.

BERRY, J.W., 1994, Acculturation and Psychological Adaptation. In A.-M. BOUVRY, F.J.R. VAN DE VIJVER, and P. SCHMITZ (Eds.), Journeys into Cross-cultural Psychology (pp. 89-125). Lisse, Netherlands: Swets and Zeitlinger.

CHAUDHURI, A., 1998, Product Class Effects on Perceived Risk: The Role of Emotion, *International Journal of Research in Marketing*, 15(2), pp.157–168.

DENEGRI-KNOTT, J. & MOLESWORTH, M., 2010, Digital Virtual Consumption: Concepts and Practices, *Consumption, Markets & Culture*, 13 (2): 109–132.
KRETZ, G., & DE VALCK K., 2010, 'Pixelize me!': Digital storytelling and the creation of archetypal myths through explicit and implicit self-brand association in fashion and luxury blogs in RUSSELL W. Belk (ed.), Research in Consumer Behavior, 12, 313 – 329.
GRIGORIAN, V. & PETERSON, F. E., 2014, Designing Luxury Experience, *European Business Review*, forthcoming.
HENNINGS, N., WIEDMANN, K.-P., KLARMANN, C., 2012, Luxury Brands in the Digital Age – Exclusivity versus Ubiquity, in: *Marketing Review St. Gallen*, 29 (1): 30-35
HOLBROOK, M. B. & HIRSCHMAN, E. C., 1982, The experiential Aspects of Consumption: consumer fantasies, feelings and fun, *Journal of Consumer Research*, September, 9(2) 132-140.
KAPFERER, J-N, 2008, The new strategic brand management. London: Kogan.
KIM, A. J., & KO, E., 2012, Do social media marketing activities enhance customer equity? An empirical study of luxury fashion brand, *Journal of Business Research*, *65*(10), 1480–1486.
LIPOVETSKY, G. & ROUX, E., 2003, Le Luxe Eternel - De L'âge du Sacré au Temps des Marques, Paris: Le Débat, Gallimard.
OKONKWO, U., 2009, Sustaining the Luxury Brand on the Internet, in: *Journal of Brand Management*, 16, 5/6, pp. 302–310.
OKONKWO, U., 2010, Luxury Online – Styles, Systems, Strategies, London.
SHARMA, P., CHAN, R., 2011, "Counterfeit proneness: Conceptualization and scale development", *Journal of Marketing Management*, Vol. 27, Issue 5/6, pp. 602-626
TOM, G., GARIBALDI, B., ZENG, Y., PILCHER, J., 1998, "Consumer demand for counterfeit goods", *Psychology & Marketing*, Vol. 15, Issue 5, pp. 405-421.
TRAN, V. & VOYER, B. G., 2013, Teaching note: Chanel: Should the icon of timeless fashion catch up with its time and sell its clothes online? The Case Centre, 12p, Case n° 313-290-8

HOW CAN THE ART OF LIVING (*ART DE VIVRE*) MAKE THE FRENCH LUXURY INDUSTRY UNIQUE AND COMPETITIVE?

Dr. Wided BATAT
Associate Professor
American University of Beirut
wided.batat@bnc-consulting-group.com

Dr. Gwarlann DE KERVILER
IÉSEG School of Management, Paris
LEM-CNRS 9221
g.dekerviler@ieseg.fr

ABSTRACT

The French art of living (*art de vivre*), although an abstract concept, is strongly connected to the luxury goods industry. We refer to "French luxury" as a sector of excellence that merges culture, lifestyle, and historic luxury brands. Yet, although the French art of living is what can enhance the competiveness and the uniqueness of French luxury businesses of both old and emerging young brands, the concept of *art de vivre* is not defined in the literature and remains very abstract. In this conceptual article, we define the concept of the French art of living. We identify the five pillars, namely, culinary art and tasting, beaux arts (fine arts), *haute couture*, French literature, and the art of perfume that French luxury businesses can implement in developing a competitive advantage that is embedded in the French luxury culture.

Keywords: French art of living, *art de vivre,* pillars of French art of living, luxury businesses, French luxury, marketing
JEL codes: M30, M31.

INTRODUCTION

The French art of living (*art de vivre*) is a combination of several elements that take root in the history and culture of France, and that signify taste, aesthetics, a sense of detail, and the discipline in all its forms (cultural, social, intellectual, courtesy, artisanal work, etc.). This art of living combines different components that cannot be separated and are all grounded in the logic of the French art of living, which refers to the ideology of living surrounded by these different aspects, to perpetuate habits, and to favor environments that allow this *art de vivre* to continue. Furthermore, the French art of living, although an abstract concept, is strongly connected to the luxury goods industry (Bastien, 2013). Everywhere across the world, we refer to the French luxury as a sector of excellence that merges French culture, lifestyle, and historical luxury brands and houses. Luxury brands, with their capacity to provide multi-dimensional experiences, serve as a rich resource to enrich consumers' personal meaning and to enlarge their perspectives (De Kerviler and Rodriguez, 2019).

In fact, French luxury goods and services, such as leather goods, clothes, hotels, perfumes, gastronomy, and artists are highly regarded all over the world. For more than several decades, France has established itself as the international leader in luxury thanks, in particular, to François 1st and Louis XIV, who wanted to improve the image of France. Nowadays, tourists as well as investors seek these centuries-old traditions and know-how. Thus, the French art of living is about luxury and is enhanced by the way luxury houses highlight their stories, which are embedded within the local history and culture. French luxury culture and know-how are often linked to craftsmanship. All these elements circulate and reflect a dream of experiencing the French art of living. Beyond consumers, French luxury also fascinates international students who come to learn the roots of luxury in France to apply them in their country. Luxury is the embodiment of France and is connected to the French art of living, making the French luxury industry competitive. To be competitive, luxury businesses should tell the story of their country and its culture.

Therefore, a French luxury brand is a brand that was born in France, nourished by French culture, based on know-how, expressing a French style and taste whose creation is made in France, and that promotes the French art of living and French heritage. French fashion brands and accessories, wines, spirits, jewelry, watchmaking, and gastronomy are highly rated, and all of them promote a certain French art of living that makes French luxury exceptional, unique, and competitive. Yet, although the French art of living is what makes French luxury businesses competitive at the international level, the concept of *art de vivre* is not clearly defined in the literature. Thus, the questions that come to mind are as follows: What do we mean by French art of living (*art de vivre*)? How can this concept make the French luxury industry unique and competitive? In this conceptual article, we propose a definition of the concept and identify the main pillars that French luxury businesses can implement in their international strategies as well as in the development of competitive luxury goods that are embedded in the French art of living.

1. THE ART OF LIVING (*ART DE VIVRE*) FOR THE FRENCH LUXURY INDUSTRY: DEFINITION AND FOUNDATIONS

The French art of living is composed of a multitude of elements that comprise both material and immaterial heritage. It is the pinnacle of what makes people dream when they think of France and those who live there. But what is it exactly? What are its main pillars? And how does it contribute to make the French luxury economy model successful, unique, and competitive? We answer these questions in the next section.

1.1. The rise of the French art of living

Although the art of living (*art de vivre*), French style, is a widespread concept across the world, it is difficult to find a conceptual definition of the concept (Thomas, 2013) due to its complexity and its tangible (material) and intangible (immaterial) dimensions. Indeed, what are the characteristics of the French art of living or the French way of life? What exactly do we know about the French art of living and its relationship to the French luxury industry and identity construction?

A brief answer to these questions is not easy as this well-known French lifestyle encompasses various aspects. What can we take for granted is the fact that French culture and the French luxury sector are often introduced as a model when it comes to tableware, gastronomy, aesthetics, refinement, or elegance. The French art of living is strongly connected to luxury and cannot be defined otherwise than by the affirmation of very French qualities such as know-how, artisanal craftsmanship, refined beauty, description, and family education, and values (Batat, 2018). According to Batat (2018, 2019a), French luxury is strongly related to a French institutional perspective and, thus, to local regulation.

Following this perspective, we argue that the art of living is a major characteristic of the way French luxury is defined within the French culture where public organizations define luxury according to economic and social criteria. As stated by Batat "while the economic delimitation of luxury is difficult to grasp, the French regulations have solved this problem by proposing a definition based on the logic of activity categorization. In France, the luxury sector has always been strictly regulated since the decree of January 29, 1945, which distinguishes luxury from other segments of the same activity. The decree defines 17 activities related to luxury that include all industries, craftsmanship, and creative activities, ranging from art, floral art, and leather to music, publishing, and throughout fashion as well as jewelry." (2019a, p. 15).

French luxury is specific as it is embedded in a unique sociocultural, economic, and political context, and refers first to the French art of living. French luxury products respond to the expectations of traditional (old consumers of luxury mainly European and American) and modern consumers (new emerging countries such as China, Russia, Middle East, etc.). The question is about how to combine and gather different meanings and perspectives in one integral and comprehensive framework. The uniqueness and the excellence of the French luxury contribute to promoting and disseminating the "French art of living," a real economic capital for the French luxury industry and a reference to promote small and large luxury businesses.

The French style (which could be the equivalent of what the Anglo–Saxons refer to as the "French touch") is inseparable from the three following elements: *savoir-faire*, *savoir-vivre*, and *savoir-être* that make the French art of living internationally renowned.

The French word *savoir-faire* might be similar to the English word "know-how" but it does not carry the same meaning. While know-how indicates the capabilities of individuals to behave or express themselves properly in social settings, the French word *savoir-faire* refers to competencies acquired and developed by individuals through living social experiences within different cultural contexts. In the case of the French art of living, the *savoir-faire* is related to the artisanal and ancestral dimension of luxury. According to Batat (2019a), "the craftsmanship perspective has a definition of luxury that is rooted in the ground of its application. For example, in France, becoming an artisan, it is necessary that the profession should be listed in the official ranking of craftsmanship established by the local administration. This list includes various trades, ranging from a taxi driver and plumber, who are both artisans, to luxury craftsmanship, such as a leather tanner. Faced with this divergence of professions, 'Artisanat, the first company in France,' has created another category—appellation—to distinguish the best artisans, those, who by their search for excellence, are naturally between art and crafts, distinguished from other professions that do not require know-how, tradition, and excellence, such as electrician" (p. 18). Therefore, the best artisans have an ancestral know-how and can be classified in the "Artisanat," a recognized but very small group of market actors who collaborate with luxury brands, have superior quality products, target a wealthy clientele, and practice high prices that are justified by a traditional and ancestral know-how (Batat, 2018, 2019a).

The second element that makes the French art of living unique and contributes to the promotion of French luxury across the world is *savoir-vivre*, which refers to what in English we define as good manners in society. In the French culture, *savoir-vivre* is more about knowing how one can get more from life such as knowing how to take time to enjoy a meal or a nap. It is about spending few "quality moments" with loved ones and make a pause within a heavy agenda to fully go through an experience with others. In relation to the French art of living that makes the French luxury unique and iconic, we can cite the French gastronomy and French people's relationships to foods and drinks, thus showing that French eating behaviors are a real *savoir-vivre*. French gastronomy and the way of eating are a reference in the world as well as an example of healthy eating behaviors to achieve dietary well-being (Batat et al., 2018; Batat, 2019b; De Kerviler, 2019). Following the logic of French gastronomy as a unique *savoir-vivre* that characterizes the French art of living, De Kerviler (2019) argues that French gastronomy is, in fact, the result of a unique combination of historical, sociological, political, cultural, geographical, and social dimensions and the main challenge today is for French gastronomy to remain attractive for a wide global audience.

The third element that makes the French art of living unique is the *savoir-être* that reflects one's interpersonal skills and personal qualities. This component indicates an individual's ability to produce actions and reactions adapted to human social interactions within a particular cultural setting. For instance, the French art of living requires certain behaviors and attitudes that individuals are expected to display in order to socialize and define a social role within the French society. It is linked to a social capital dimension. In fact, the French luxury business requires more than purchasing luxury items; to succeed, individuals in the French luxury culture should also demonstrate that they know the history of the luxury houses, their iconic products, and their symbolic dimensions embedded within the French culture. In other words, what does the luxury brand tell about the individual in the social context, is it a French luxury or other luxuries? For French people, a luxury brand is born in France, nourished by culture, based on know-how, expressing a unique style and taste, and thus should reflect a French art of living that brings together luxury houses which aim to promote the French heritage, celebrate the French culture across the world, and make French people proud of their identity. Therefore, through these three elements, namely, *savoir-faire*, *savoir-vivre*, and *savoir-être*, the French art of living offers a way of life and a way of seeing the world that are by definition elegant, luxurious, refined, and expressing good taste.

1.2. The five pillars of the French art of living: The basis for a distinctive and competitive French luxury economy

France and its rich history linked to the spirit of the Enlightenment, home of writers, artists, philosophers, architects, creators among the brightest in the world, has special features: a rich cultural heritage that includes countless buildings and unique architecture (e.g., Renaissance castles of the Loire, Versailles, the Eiffel Tower), many museums (e.g., the

Louvre), theater halls (e.g. Opera Garnier, Comédie Française), bookstores, and art galleries, etc. Thus, the French way of living is a combination of material and immaterial elements that take root in the history of France, which convey taste, aesthetics, and attention to details. The analysis of the multidisciplinary literature related to the emergence and the growth of the French luxury and its art of living, including history, sociology, economics, and marketing allowed us to define five core pillars (see Figure 1) of the French *art de vivre.*

Figure 1: Five pillars of the French art of living

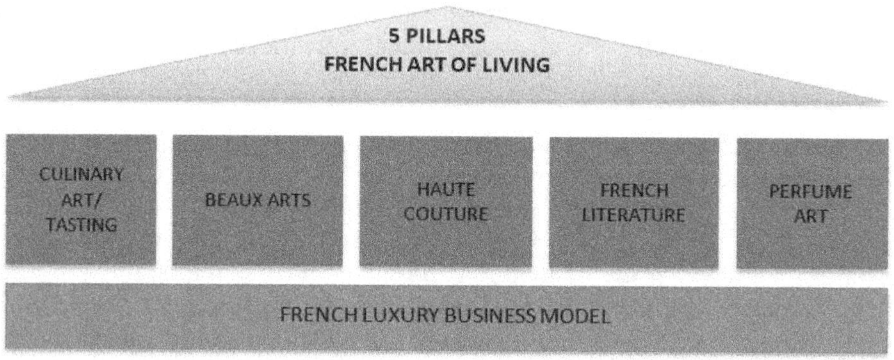

As shown in Figure 1, the five pillars are part of a unique French art of living that makes the French luxury business model exclusive and competitive across the world. The five pillars are explained and discussed in the next section.

1.2.1. Culinary art/tasting

French gastronomy, or French *haute cuisine*, is generally perceived from abroad as an elite art intimately associated with luxury. The French art of living has as its ambassador a privileged gastronomy, inscribed on the World Heritage of UNESCO which highlights France and its culinary customs. Gastronomy is inseparable from the French way of life. It is not only the content of the plate but also the importance given to the meal and the conviviality, which are so unique. In France, the meal is a moment that requires attention and time (De Kerviler, 2019). Welcoming guests, decorating a room with talent, making a perfect match between food and wine, or setting a table with taste are priorities for the majority of French people. French cuisine is distinguished by its refinement and creativity which contributes to make the French art of living shine in the world. In the art of gastronomy for instance, the French chefs, such as Anne Sophie Pic, Yannick Alléno, or Pierre Hermé, achieve excellence through their unequaled know-how, their technical and aesthetic qualification as well as their creativity. French gastronomy can be termed as a social and historical phenomenon that has led to a distinctive cultural practice. Similar to other social practices, gastronomy as a field draws on a combination of social, economic, and cultural conditions. This includes abundant, various, and readily available foods and experienced craftsmen (local producers and chefs) in a culturally specific site (the restaurant), both of which are supported by knowledgeable consumers (diners) and a secular culinary tradition (Ferguson, 1998).

Luxury hotels and the Michelin-starred restaurants welcome famous chefs and attract tourists from all over the world, including the United States and Russia, in search for refined culinary experiences. In the late 19th century, new luxury hotels such as the Negresco in Cannes (1912) and Ritz in Paris (1898) flourished. Horses were replaced by cars, which allowed the bourgeoisie to easily discover regional culinary and artistic treasures. The French coasts were thriving with new palaces, casinos, and theaters where French cooks and Maîtres d'hôtel celebrated the French cuisine. The bourgeoisie who previously ate in their private homes were welcomed by the restaurants in Cannes or Paris. The aspirations of both affluent and ordinary clientele of the Belle Epoque took wing when they were able to enjoy palaces and fine restaurants as public places that retained ostentatious and sophisticated references specific to the Versailles nobility and also avoided an expensive house brigade (Ory, 1998).

French *haute cuisine* was transformed under the reign of Louis XIV at Versailles, where the culinary rules were highly codified. Depending on the number of guests, at each service, the appropriate dishes were arranged symmetrically, with a center dish, four medium dishes, and four small and eight smaller dishes. This allowed diners to select from different dishes served simultaneously. The art of placing guests around the table and serving them meals symbolized the "etiquette" (unwritten rules) of Versailles, underlining their positions in the tiered pyramid of the French society. For presenting the visual and aromatic pleasures, the table was arranged in a proportionate set to give it a harmonious and symmetrical appearance. Haute cuisine was originally meant to serve the court and the aristocracy. However, the French Revolution witnessed the exit of the aristocracy and chefs moved on to showcase their culinary talents to the general elite public. Hence, a new class of consumers that enjoyed rich fine food emerged that was derived from the ancient practices of fine dining.

French cuisine was also strengthened by the culinary discourse, transcending the realms of immediate culinary production to a broader cultural arena. The spectacular development of a culinary discourse during the age of Enlightenment in France transformed the act of eating into an art linked to taste and refinement. Grimod de la Reynière, Carême, and Brillat-Savarin were the pioneers of the culinary discourse. These critics established and popularized a cultural hierarchy, helping ordinary customers to appreciate taste. Cooks are deemed to be unable both to arrive at a broader theorization of their own individual taste and to lack sufficient access to the public. Therefore, culinary discourse acts as a mediator between producers and consumers of cultural objects and as a determinant of symbolic value (Lane, 2013). George Auguste Escoffier Culinary Guide (1903) codified "Classical Cuisine" in terms of culinary practices and menus. Then, in the late 1960s and early 1970s, renowned chefs, such as Paul Bocuse, coined the term "Nouvelle Cuisine" to describe lighter dishes, experimenting with ingredients and flavors. Often referred to as the "Pope of French cuisine," Paul Bocuse was also a tireless pioneer and the first chef to blend the art of cooking with savvy business strategies.

Furthermore, French know-how includes the arts of setting the table (selection of porcelain, the silver cutlery, the glasses adapted to each drink), the art of serving the wine and makes dining a unique cultural experience.

Taste can be defined as the capacity to recognize and differentiate among various objects or experiences. Pierre Bourdieu claimed that every unique style of inhabiting a world originates in the internalized standards of a social milieu. Bourdieu (1986) locates taste in a specific social site and ties it to a social class. Taste is an instrument of aesthetic sensitivity and intellectual discernment (Ferguson, 2011). Taste can be considered as judgment power and individuals can be distinguished on the basis of their tastes. Thus, taste can be conceptualized in two ways: (1) an endowment associated with higher social positions or (2) a resource to win a struggle that is gained from exercise of taste. For Bourdieu, cultured families exhibit different patterns of cultural consumption. If an individual was raised in a setting filled with paintings and sculpture, then he or she would be endowed with a greater amount of cultural capital and would have the capacity to exercise the sort of taste in cultural activities expected and respected among fellows who already held a high socioeconomic position.

To make an educated choice, one must accept the efforts to taste different options and discern his or her preferences. Institutions can facilitate opportunities for learning and cultural environment can foster individual curiosity and willingness to appreciate good food. Discerning and discriminating taste can be taught at schools if meals are a quintessential part of children's education. Each year in France, the "Semaine du goût" (Taste Week) motivates youngsters to discover a large "palette" of savors by being served very different meals. Guy Savoy, Three Michelin Star Chef of the restaurant La Monnaie de Paris, underlined that if you have not tried eating a large variety of apples, you will never be able to appreciate the taste of a succulent one. One must have tried and discovered many different tastes to fully appreciate good food.

The natural resources of France represent a constant source of creativity, inspiration, and expertise around cooking practices. "*Terroir*" is a unique concept that represents the extraordinary confluence of land, culture, tradition, and climate. There is no appropriate alternative English term for the French word "*Terroir.*" Historically, *terroir* refers to a small region whose soil and climate imparts distinctive qualities to food products (Barham, 2003). Figuratively, *terroir* can also specify a region considered to have a marked influence on its inhabitants. In this interpretation, products of terroir result from long commitment of the same area and represent the interplay of human ingenuity and curiosity with the natural givens of a place. Products of terroir are synonymous with cultural diversity, reflections of the evolution of a society, of its attachment to certain habits of consumption. The concept of an origin designation for a food product involves the unique characteristic roles of soil, climate, and the specialized knowledge that are associated with generations of food producers bound to a particular location; it is the raw material of the food ingredient that is valued.

What might be unique about the French approach to *terroir* is the perspective that it is not human actions that dictate what is produced and how, but rather that natural phenomena constrain human practices. *Terroir* is a given, which was existing before human beings who only revealed its potential. Food production becomes a complex dance with nature with the goal of interpreting or translating the local ecology, displaying its qualities to its best advantage. Through observation of nature and dedication to excellence, French producers and cooks created a unique heritage of French gastronomy. This is visible, for instance, with the Chardonnay wine: passionate craftsmen observed that depending on the climate, soil, and location of the land, a specific type of wine would best develop. Chefs have gained the knowledge through hard work and experience to benefit from French natural richness to create multisensory delights, arousing all senses at once. The richness of the markets, providing a multitude of diverse meats, fishes, fruits, and vegetables, awakens the palate of French customers.

1.2.2. Les beaux arts (fine arts)

The French *art de vivre* can also be linked to the fine arts, which are fully embedded in the culture and lifestyle of French people. The French *art de vivre* is linked to the attention devoted in France to "les beaux arts" and includes the fine arts developed primarily for aesthetics or beauty. It is distinct from applied art, which serves a more practical function, such as pottery. "Les beaux arts" are judged according to their perceived beauty and aesthetic qualities, which requires a refined judgment usually referred to as having good taste. It encapsulates an important element of the French *art de vivre*, revolving around the appreciation of art as a source of personal enhancement and of soul elevation. The importance of Arts in France started to thrive in the 16th century during the Renaissance and the reign of François 1st (1515-1547). In 1648, Cardinal Mazarin, Chief Minister to the kings of France Louis XIII and Louis XIV, created the "Academie des Beaux Arts" to educate the most talented students in drawing, painting, sculpture, engraving, and architecture. Louis XIV was known to select graduates from the school to decorate the royal apartments at Versailles. Many of the most famous artists in Europe were trained here; to name but a few, they include Géricault, Degas, Delacroix, Fragonard, Ingres, Moreau, Renoir, Seurat, and Sisley. Rodin, however, applied on three occasions but was refused entry. In 1699, the Academy mounted its first exhibition at the Louvre, where it continued to show for 100 years. From 1725 onwards, exhibitions were held in the Salon Carré, and became known simply as "salons." The art presented in the salons dictated national and international tastes and formed the basis of what we have come to know today as traditional European art. Training for aspiring artists is still provided at the prestigious École des Beaux Arts in Paris today.

Nowadays, education to the arts is compulsory for French children through what is called "Le parcours d'éducation artistique et culturelle (PEAC)." The education for fine art has three pillars: (1) artistic education, (2) meetings with artists, and (3) practice of arts. The objective is to allow everyone to develop an intellectual curiosity through personal access to the arts. Practically, a "culture referent" is appointed to develop partnerships with cultural institutions to encourage the understanding of various artistic domains and organize visits to museums. As such, it is at the heart of French education to perpetuate an interest for and knowledge of the arts. Major art exhibits are held regularly, mainly in Paris, educating French people to become attentive to aesthetic, harmony, and beauty even in their daily life. French deeply appreciate owning a masterpiece from a painter, listening to a piano concert, or designing a modern interior for their apartment. This is part of the French culture to enlarge one's perspective through experiencing various arts. As Marcel Proust, famous French author, would say in his book "Un amour de Swann", listening to music allows one to explore emotions and feelings, to have memories coming back, and distant oneself from the everyday.

1.2.3. The art of perfume

French women have a natural taste for and knowledge of which perfume fits their style and personality. Choosing perfume is a very personal, intimate, and identity-revealing act. A perfume has to connect not only with one's style but also to trigger associations with one's story and memories. Moreover, well-known brands of perfume bring a strong heritage and a rich story (i.e. how the fragrance was created, when the name was chosen and in reference to whom, etc.) that enhance the ties between a consumer and his/her chosen brand of perfume (Ardelet,

Slavich and De Kerviler, 2015). Many of the greatest names in the perfume industry—Chanel, Christian Dior, and Givenchy—are French. France was maybe not the first country in the world to invent perfumes but, nowadays, in terms of international perfume sales, France is the leading producer country, with 30% of the world market. LVMH, one of France's flagship companies in the luxury industry, is the greatest luxury goods company in the world, and French perfumes and cosmetics are among its most important brands (Givenchy, Guerlain, Kenzo, Dior, etc.).

The art of perfumery can be traced back to the origins of Western civilization in Mesopotamia. Then, at the Renaissance, perfumes became particularly popular in Europe as Catherine de Medicis, wife of King Henri II (1519 – 1559), introduced a fashion for perfumes into France and boosted the local industries of essences in Montpellier and Grasse in the south of France. She was fanatical about gloves to protect her white hands and she brought with her Renato the Florentine, her trusted perfumer. The true turning point of elevating perfumery from alchemy into full-blown artistry came with scent-obsessed King Louis XIV (1638–1715). Moving his court from Paris to Versailles, Louis XIV was determined to elevate every activity up to the pinnacle of elegance. Inside the palace, "faire la toilette quotidienne," or "daily grooming of oneself," involved applying cosmetics to the body and face, dusting scented powders on hair wigs, and sprinkling fragrant waters on fresh linen. The King's minister of finance, Jean-Baptiste Colbert, set out to grant privileges to the guilds of "perfumers and glove-makers" on the basis of excellence, encouraging the development of this delicate craft and securing France as the center of the European perfume industry. From the courts of France to international globetrotters today, fragrance continues to express femininity in the most glamorous and elegant way.

The heart of the French perfume industry is the small town of Grasse, in the Alpes Maritimes department, northwest of Nice. Grasse enjoys a mild Mediterranean climate that is particularly suited to horticulture, notably the production of jasmine, one of the most important natural aromas used by the perfume industry. But Grasse is also famous for its production of many other natural fragrances, including lavender, myrtle, roses, and mimosa. In recent years, the natural fragrances extracted from flowers and other plants have been largely replaced by chemically produced scents that can be mass-produced anywhere in the world. However, in the production of top-of-the-range high quality perfumes made from natural extracts of plants, nothing can replace the acquired skills of France's master perfume producers. Knowledge about perfume art is perpetuated in various schools (Isipca, Ecole de chimie de Montpellier, Ecole supérieur du parfum), drawing from the French heritage and its "Osmothèque" (world's largest scent archive, a leading international research institution tracing the history of perfumery, based in Versailles). A perfume, although ephemeral or short-lived, is the result of long work, a long initiation.

The perfumer exposes and reveals himself. It is an empirical art based on observation, memory, proportions, and feelings. The young perfumer, like a musician, learns to recognize and memorize raw materials, which will be his tools to perfume words, colors, forms, and ideas and aim toward what is beautiful. By dint of hard work and patience, he acquires the necessary technique and becomes a composer able to imagine and materialize an odor. He makes of his recorded creations a means of expression that will highlight his personality. The perfumer's work is a question of experience, culture, and taste. When the taste of a wine or the smell of a perfume evokes personal moments in a consumer's life, the person is more likely to prefer that wine or perfume as it fosters a stronger connection between the self and the product or brand (e.g., Belk, 1988). When products foster self-referencing narratives in-store, consumers become distracted and do not undertake an analytical evaluation of the objective characteristics of the product, focusing instead on the symbolic benefits associated with product consumption (Ardelet, Slavich and De Kerviler, 2015).

1.2.4. *Haute couture* and La Parisienne style

Haute couture has always been an integral part of the French fashion and luxury sector as well as one of the most important pillars that make the French art of living distinctive. Louis Vuitton, Hermès, Givenchy, Dior, Chanel, Lanvin, Christian Lacroix, Pierre Cardin, and Saint Laurent are some of the most prestigious French *haute couture* houses. The taste for details is also obvious, of course, in the creations of the great French fashion designers who have given French *haute couture* high status, which alone has a strong appeal as French chic is exported all over the world. French *haute couture* is an ancestral know-how. The profound respect of craftsmanship is the cornerstone of this universe. In this respect, we can mention two iconic products from one of the most famous French luxury houses, "Hermès," due to their monumental success: the Kelly bag and the Carré or Square. The Kelly leather bag was launched in 1935.

Today, the bag remains entirely handmade, on order, in Paris, and it comes in various materials such as crocodile skin. The Kelly owes its name to Princess Grace of Monaco. While her pregnancy was not yet official, the Princess used her Hermès bag to hide the roundness of her belly when she appeared on the cover of *Time* magazine alongside her husband. This photo changed the destiny of the bag forever: it became the emblem of French glamor. The myth is not touched. Only 60 Kelly bags are created each season. The second iconic item is the Hermès Square (Carré Hermès). Created in 1937 by Robert Dumas, this silk twill scarf is inspired by the colored silks of Longchamp jockeys. Since 1937, artists such as Philippe

Ledoux and Pierre Peron have created more than 2,000 drawings for the square. Hermès does not import silk from China but instead owns her own silk farm in Brazil. Once transported to Lyon, the yarn is woven into a silk twice as thick and heavy as for the normal production of high-end scarves. The colors are deposited one by one on a layer stencil—a process that requires hundreds of hours.

Moreover, French chic woman, is the embodiment of freedom and elegance. *La Parisienne* is a key characteristic of what makes French fashion and luxury unique. From the tradition of Versailles emerged the pleasure of shopping in an elegant environment for the latest trends. This heritage of elegance at the royal court and tradition of fashion in France has been perpetuated and progressively reshaped to give birth to the Parisian style. The Parisian woman today has a unique chic. She is an authentic "BCBG (Bon Chic Bon Genre)" or "Right Chic Right Style," associating trendiness and a bourgeois heritage. Authenticity in fashion derives from intrinsic motivations to create new outfits as opposed to extrinsic motivations to attract attention (Audrezet et al., 2018). This authenticity allows the Parisian woman to be a real trend-setter and followed by so many "would-be-fashionistas." Her approach to life is linked to a unique *savoir-vivre* and a delicate taste for harmony and beauty. According to Ines de La Fressange, co-author of the book "La Parisienne" (2012), the Parisian woman is "anti-show-off" and searching for original brands producing beautiful pieces and not for conspicuous consumption. She has an aesthetic eye, knowing how to mix and match pieces of clothes with style and elegance. For instance, she will assemble a cocktail dress with sneakers or a masculine shirt on a sexy black dress. The Parisian woman focuses on sobriety and on feeling both comfortable and beautiful in her clothes. She is about striving to find the perfect elegance while giving the impression that it is so natural and effortless. She adopts a "*faussement négligée*" ("falsely untidy") allure, with the right balance between casual and chic together with a subtle touch of glamorous. The Parisian woman has this unique art of transforming her old-fashion, boring and conventional heritage into timeless style and good taste. How does she manage to convert flat classic into fun trends? She re-builds from her heritage, re-inventing the traditional "bourgeois" style to create a new art of living, rooted in inherited values but with added trendiness and innovation. Thanks to her open-minded spirit, traveling the world, and connected life, she receives inspiration from everywhere to revisit her "classics," bringing a trendy touch. She adds modernity and happiness to timeless pieces, such as the little black dress, by adding small details like fancy buttons, modern shapes, or eco-friendly fabrics. She does all that but also a little mysterious something that she keeps secret, on purpose, because as the famous French writer Alexandre Dumas used to say, "God has invented Parisian woman so that foreigners cannot understand French people."

1.2.5. The French art of literature

French writers and poets. France is the country of writers, philosophers of the Enlightenment and existentialists who frequented Saint-Germain-des-Prés and the Café de Flore. Indeed, The French conception of education gives room to critical thinking and reflection. For instance, the French rhetoric art was an integral part of young French education toward defining a social role within the society by developing and structuring the intellect and the art of the debate. Gustave Flaubert defines rhetoric as an art of "using beautiful expressions for pretty poor subjects." (1845, p. 102). Rhetoric, therefore, is the art of eloquence and persuasion, a definition that corresponds, in its broadest sense, to that given in ancient times. Rhetoric discourse, initially conceived as an oral speech and not as a text, is intended to lead the audience to examine the facts in the light of a particular point of view, i.e., the speaker's. In other words, the primary function of rhetoric was not so much to represent the world as to bring it to a specific angle (e.g., Lamy, 2010). Texts of judicial eloquence - indictments and pleadings- are as far as possible from the neutral presentation of facts. It is the weight of this story that explains that rhetoric could be described as manipulative and insincere (Reboul, 2013). The essence of French rhetoric was as an oratory art. The French art of rhetoric manifests itself well in the two components of memory (techniques of remembrance of the discourse) and of the action (art, essential for the speaker and gestures).

Theater. The Comédie-Française is one of the four French "National Theatres" (la Comédie française, le Théâtre national de La Colline, l'Odéon Théâtre de l'Europe et le Théâtre National de Strasbourg). Comédie Française is the epitome of the French art of theater and the oldest active theater in the world with its own actors. Created in 1680 by **King Louis XIV** to compete with the Italian comedies, Comédie-Française allowed Molière - one of the greatest writers in the French language and universal literature - and his actors to play in front of the French nobility. The Comédie-Française today has a repertoire of 3,000 works and three theaters in Paris. The names of nearly all the great actors and dramatists of France have, at some time in their career, been associated with that of the Comédie-Française. Since 1995, the Comédie-Française has been defined as a public body and receives a grant from the Ministry of Culture. With the legacy of Comedie Française and that of the many famous writers of classical theater plays, including Moliere, Racine, Corneille, Musset, Guitry, Feydau, and Marivaux, French people are very fond of theaters. Classical plays are being showcased frequently to the enjoyment of families, kids, and adults. There have been almost 50,000 theatrical performances generating 6.4 million tickets sold in 41 theaters in 2016 in Paris. More than just an entertaining activity in France, going to the theater is viewed as an important part of culture in France. Indeed, through a play, spectators can be taught about history, society, and morality in an indirect and sometimes more approachable and embodied manner than only through books.

2. THE FRENCH ART OF LIVING AND ITS CONTRIBUTIONS TO THE LUXURY ECONOMY AND BUSINESS

The major French luxury brands are now grouped together in an organization whose name directly refers to the monarchical roots of luxury in France: the Comité Colbert. This association, made up of 80 luxury houses and 15 major French cultural institutions, and considered as the main influence group of the luxury sector, also celebrated its 60th anniversary at the Palace of Versailles. This aristocratic symbolism of luxury, considered as a real asset by French luxury houses—the foreign clientele being particularly sensitive to this historical aspect—is a strong competitive advantage that differentiates French luxury from other luxuries. It is then easy to understand why the defense of the sector by French political actors is a real challenge to enhance the attractiveness of French luxury across the world. If the French luxury shines today at an international level, it is because French culture, with its art of living, provides fertile ground and an ecosystem comprising various craftsmen and crafts that sustain the sector and support leading luxury brands.

Under the Second Empire, the rise of department stores, such as the Bon Marché (1838), offered not only customers goods, but also dreams. As presented earlier, French luxury and the French art of living with its five pillars are interconnected and contribute to enhance the uniqueness of the French luxury industry by providing luxury brands a successful French model capable of penetrating international markets where the French art of living represents a sustainable competitive advantage. The history of French luxury and its art of living is intimately linked to the historical legacy of its country of origin and more particularly to its aristocratic past. Luxury houses, such as Hermès, Chanel, and Louis Vuitton take advantage of this rich history like for instance Dior, which used the Palace of Versailles for its commercials to connect luxury with the French art of living and, thus, enhancing its uniqueness.

According to a 2018 survey "Global Powers of Luxury Goods" by Deloitte, France is positioned as the leading country in terms of sales of luxury goods. This is mainly due to four successful national champions among the top companies in luxury: LVMH (ranked 1st), Kering (ranked 5th), L'Oréal Luxe (ranked 6th), and Hermès (ranked 11th), which all together represent more than 5 billion yearly sales. These players have managed to adapt in order to attract millennials and the highly connected Chinese population. In particular, French *haute couture* remains highly attractive with a growth of 17% in 2018.

French companies also benefit from the growth of airport sales through increasing travel tourism. The 6% increase in France's tourist numbers in

2018, especially from Asia, benefits goods expressing the French *art de vivre*, which is well showcased in airport duty free shops. In 2018, Louis Vuitton opened a new flagship store at Charles de Gaulle Airport, highlighting the importance of this tendency.

French *horlogerie* remains successful in selling "Made in France" watches to the domestic market as well as the UK, Italy, and Germany. It is currently the fifth-ranked exporter of watches in the world. For instance, in 2018, Florian Chosson successfully launched the brand "Routine," 86% made in France and using 13 French companies to produce it, outperforming his forecasts. In the furniture and design industry, French *art de vivre* is attractive. The example of Roche Bobois, a French family business founded in 1960, is illustrative. The group embodies the Art de Vivre à la Française through a collection of stylish pieces of furniture designed by talented creators like Jean Nouvel and Christophe Delcourt. More than 50% of its sales are made outside of France, particularly in the US, Canada, and the UK (Roche Bobois Annual Report).

The sales of French *art de vivre* are also manifested through the hotel and restaurant industries, taking advantage of the unique "Patrimoine" of France. Beyond the romanticism of Paris, French delights are symbolized by fairy tale castles, such as Versailles or Châteaux de la Loire, soaring cathedrals like Notre Dame de Paris or Cathedral of Reims, amazing landscapes like Le Mont Saint Michel and Courchevel, or romantic villages in the French Riviera. As a result, France is the first-ranked tourist destination in the world with more than 90 million foreign tourists in 2018 and the aim is to reach 100 million in 2022. Moreover, the luxury hotels (five-star hotels and Palaces) are in a growth phase, experiencing a 60% increase between 2012 and 2017 centered around Paris, Côte d'Azur, and the ski resorts.

CONCLUSION

The French *art de vivre* cannot be understood without a detour through French history in order to grasp its roots and deep meaning. As detailed in this paper, the French art of living has its foundations in a strong cultural heritage stemming from the Renaissance and the reign of Louis XIV, when arts and literature flourished. Continuously evolving since then, it has managed to maintain a timeless touch by paying tribute to and being inspired by its magnificent past while embracing the constant transformation of the French society. The French art of living is still strongly tied to *savoir-faire*, *savoir-vivre*, and *savoir-être*, which combine an intellectual dimension through knowledge of luxury traditions and craftsmanship, an emotional dimension through a hedonic and witty approach to life as well as a behavioral dimension through an adoption of good manners and politeness in social settings.

More specifically, we have established five important pillars on which French *art de vivre* is founded, namely, culinary arts, beaux arts, haute couture, French literature, and perfume arts. Under each of these pillars, France has developed a unique and original touch, perpetuated, enriched over ages, and established a clear differentiation with other countries. As noted by the French Ministry of Education, there is a strong belief in France that arts and culture lead to the world and lead the world to France. As such, the French *art de vivre* is attractive, distinct, and unique, and creates competitive advantage for France in the global battle for cultural, social, and economic influence. Education in France is attentive to preserve this *art de vivre*, by allowing French people to continuously develop their sensitivity to the arts and the national history. The passion of the French people for their "Patrimoine" is exemplified by the continued success of the "Journée du Patrimoine," which nurtures the strong cultural focus in France that bridges the past and the present.

REFERENCES

ARDELET, C., SLAVICH, B., & DE KERVILER, G., 2015, Self-referencing narratives to predict consumers' preferences in the luxury industry: A longitudinal study. *Journal of Business Research*, 68(9), 2037-2044.

AUDREZET, A., DE KERVILER, G., & MOULARD, J. G., 2018, Authenticity under threat: When social media influencers need to go beyond self-presentation, *Journal of Business Research, (in press).*

BARHAM, E., 2003, Translating Terroir: The Global Challenge of French AOC Labeling, *Journal of Rural Studies,* 19,127-138.

BASTIEN, V., 2013, Le luxe « à la française," un marché porteur, ou une stratégie originale et dominante? *Annales des Mines–Réalités industrielles*, (4) novembre, 55-61.

BATAT, W., 2018, Luxe et expérience client, Dunod, Paris.

BATAT, W., 2019a, Experiential Marketing: Consumer Behavior, Customer Experience and The 7Es. Routledge, London.

BATAT, W., 2019b, The luxury experience: Creating the ultimate customer experience. Springer, New York.

BATAT, W., PETER, P., MOSCATO, E., CASTRO, I., CHAN, S., CHUGANI, S., & MULDROW, A., 2018, The experiential pleasure of food: A savoring journey to food well-being, *Journal of business Research.* (in press).

BELK, R. W., 1988, Possessions and the extended self, *Journal of consumer research, 15*(2), 139-168.

BOURDIEU, P., 1986, *The forms of capital.* In J. Richardson (Ed.) Handbook of Theory and Research for the Sociology of Education (New York, Greenwood), 241-258.

DE KERVILER, G. (2019). The Food gastronomy experience: A French perspective on food well-being. In *Food and Experiential Marketing: Pleasure, Wellbeing and Consumption*, 1st Edition, BATAT, W. (Ed). Routledge, New York. (in press).
DE KERVILER, G. & RODRIGUEZ, C., 2019, Luxury Brand Experiences and Relationship Quality for Millennials: The Role of Self-Expansion, *Journal of business Research* (in press).
ESCALAS, J.E., 2004, Imagine yourself in the product: Mental simulation, narrative transportation, and persuasion, *Journal of advertising, 33*(2), 37-48.
ESCOFFIER, A., 1903, Le Guide culinaire. 1st Edition, (Ed) Flammarion.
FERGUSON, P.P., 1998, A Cultural Field in the Making: Gastronomy in 19th Century France, *American Journal of Sociology*. 104, 3, 597–641.
FERGUSON, P. P., 2011, The Senses of Taste, *The American historical review*, 116(2), 371-384.
FLAUBERT, G., 1845, L'éducation sentimentale, Première Edition, Paris.
DE LA FRESSANGE, I. & GACHET, S., 2012, La parisienne, Première édition, Flamarion.
LAMY, B., 2010, Rhétorique ou l'art de parler, Kessinger Publishing.
LANE, C., 2013, Taste makers in the "fine-dining" restaurant industry: The attribution of aesthetic and economic value by gastronomic guides, *Poetics*, 41(4), 342-365.
ORY, P., 1998, Le discours gastronomique français des origines à nos jours, Gallimard/Julliard, Paris.
REBOUL, O., 2013, Introduction à la rhétorique, PUF, Paris.
THOMAS, P., 2013, L'art de vivre à la française: délocalisation, ou disparition? *Annales des Mines–réalités industrielles*, 4(novembre), 10-13.

MASTERING THE DIGITAL TRANSFORMATION AS A HERITAGE LUXURY FASHION BRAND

Dr. oec. HSG Fabio DUMA
ZHAW School of Management and Law
fabio.duma@zhaw.ch

Florence LABATI, MBA
Arcs-en-Ciel Suisse
labatiflo@gmail.com

Gianluca BRUNETTI, BSc
ZHAW School of Management and Law
brunegia@students.zhaw.ch

Maya GADGIL, MLaw
ZHAW School of Management and Law
maya.gadgil@zhaw.ch

ABSTRACT

Digital transformation presents the world of fashion and luxury with new challenges. Especially the relationship between luxury brands, digital technology and the Internet is an intricate one. Disruptive innovations driven by information technology are forcing luxury fashion brands to adapt and future-proof business models must make use of digital technologies and e-business concepts in order to adapt to changing consumer behavior. However, what might be seen as obvious for large, multinational companies or for recent start-ups does come with various challenges in the case of small and medium-sized heritage luxury brands with decades, or, in some cases, centuries of history and a culture as well as a reputation tied to it. The present case study examines how a traditional Swiss heritage luxury fashion brand chose to react to the digital transformation and derives insights and recommendations for similar companies.

Keywords: business model transformation, digital transformation; luxury fashion; luxury fashion management; customer orientation; cross-channel strategy; omnichannel strategy; heritage luxury brand management
JEL codes: M30, M31

INTRODUCTION

The fashion industry is a major driver of the global economy. Luxury companies or groups represent a significant portion of the 20 « super winners » of the industry and combine around 24% of total economic profit in the fashion industry in 2017 (BoF & Mc Kinsey, 2018, p. 96). Although the majority of labels have stationary distribution channels, a growing percentage of luxury purchases is made via online channels (Deloitte, 2017, p. 8). A study by Bain & Company states that seven out of ten customer transactions are already influenced by at least one digital interaction with the company before a product is purchased in the physical store (D'Arpizio & Levato, 2017, p. 1).

The digital transformation presents the luxury and fashion world with new challenges (Laudon, Laudon & Schoder, 2016, p. 73). Disruptive innovations driven by information technology are forcing companies to further develop their business models. Isolated retail solutions and distribution and communication channels are at odds with customer expectations. The consumers obtain information via a large number of touchpoints and actively participate in shaping their customer journey (i.e. their information and purchasing process) (Lay, 2018). For luxury fashion companies, this means that they must adapt their corporate strategies, visions and resources to the changing environmental and competitive conditions (Remy et al., 2015, p. 5). While this might be an obvious move for newer and/or larger brands, the digital transformation confronts small and medium-sized luxury heritage companies with many challenges. They not only have to change strategies, processes and resources, but also the mindset of owners and employees and a company culture that has often evolved over decades, if not centuries.

In general, the relationship between luxury brands and digital technology has long been complicated for various reasons. Kapferer describes the relationship of the luxury industry to the World Wide Web as rather reserved and conservative (2015, p. 113). The Internet represents almost the exact opposite of what the concept of luxury stands for or used to stand for. By definition, the digital sphere is accessible to all and detached from social hierarchies. It changes rapidly and stimulates only two sensory perceptions: seeing and hearing. In contrast, luxury is multisensory. It is about social differentiation and exclusivity (cf. e.g. Vigneron & Johnson, 1999). Luxury in its traditional sense embodies longevity in the form of exceptional quality and craftsmanship (Okonkwo, 2009, p. 304). And moreover, luxury is more than just a product, a service or a lifestyle. Rather, as Okonkwo further explains, it is a philosophy and a culture (2009, p. 302), based on a series of values and convictions that set it apart from the premium and mass markets. In all cultures, luxury has always been there to help a few people stand out from others, and it still is today. Thus for a long time it was believed not to be suitable for the digital domain (Okonkwo, 2009, p. 303).

However, as evidenced by changing consumer habits, luxury companies can no longer ignore the massive change and ever-growing power of the online universe. The holistic experience, which usually goes hand in hand with a luxury object or a luxury service, has been staged and controlled solely by the luxury brand for a very long time. In other words, the brand dominated its customers (Kapferer, 2012). In a world where the masses have the power to influence the marketing communication and messages of companies (Okonkwo, 2009, p. 306), this is no longer possible.

Against this background, it is not surprising that independent, privately owned SMEs, who have been nurturing their heritage luxury brand for decades and with their often limited resources, face major challenges in this age of rapidly advancing digitalization and changing customer behavior. Even though there is no long-term data on successful digital strategies for luxury brands yet, there are balanced approaches that take into account the nature and uniqueness of a luxury brand while at the same time exploiting the enormous potential of e-business. In view of the fact that every industry and every company has to undergo a different type of digital transformation, the aim of the study was to identify approaches that are suitable for and promise sustainable success to small and medium-sized companies (SMEs) with a heritage brand in the luxury fashion sector. In the literature, respective scientific and at the same time practice-oriented contributions are still rather hard to find, hence the case study followed an exploratory approach and examined a traditional Swiss heritage luxury fashion house that is internationally renowned and, despite its over a century old history, has pioneered digital transformation.

In the following section, the applied methodology is briefly described and the theoretical foundations of the case study are then explained, whereby the topic of digital transformation in the luxury context is illuminated from different perspectives. The empirical part describes the case mentioned above and concludes with recommendations on the digital transformation of small and medium-sized heritage luxury companies.

METHODOLOGY

The case study has been chosen as a suitable research design in order to illustrate the challenges and possibilities of the digital transformation with regards to the change of a business model in the context of the heritage luxury fashion sector. In a case study, one or more cases are examined, using suitable methods and data (Punch, 2014, p. 120; Flick, 2014, p. 121). The empirical data included in the present case study are publicly available on the website of the chosen company, as well as internal information shared by company executives in semi-structured expert interviews. It is part of the classic approach within qualitative social research at an early stage to talk with representatives who have experience with the research problem under study (Rubin & Rubin, 2012, p. 3; Kubicek, 1977, p. 23). Qualitative interviews are particularly suitable if the research project aims at a detailed description of the researched subject, at the integration of different perspectives into a holistic overall picture, and at process descriptions (Weiss, 1994, p. 9 ff.; Seidman, 2006, p. 10; Schostak, 2006, p. 9 ff.).

The research question in the present case is: How can an SME with a heritage brand in the luxury fashion sector successfully meet the challenges associated with the digital transformation of the business model? The aim of the case study is therefore to develop a deeper understanding of the case under study, taking into account the specific complexity and context in which the company operates. A case study has a holistic focus; it aims to capture and understand the case in its entirety. Although, by definition, the findings of a case study are not generalizable, it is important to bear in mind that while each case is unique, it can be compared with other cases in many ways (Punch, 2014, p. 123). In deriving conclusions from the following case study, the authors have therefore not only described the approach of the specific Swiss heritage luxury fashion brand to digital transformation, but have also looked at possible common elements of companies of similar size and positioning in the fashion industry.

THEORETICAL BACKGROUND

The theoretical framework is based on three pillars, which are intended to describe the core of the concept of luxury, as well as the use of the Internet and digital technology, and to generate an understanding of the peculiarities of the relationship between luxury brand and digital technology:

- The first pillar is the existing literature on luxury management in general, the peculiarities of luxury branding and, related to this, the challenges for luxury brands in dealing with the digital space and new customers;

- The second pillar encompasses the existing knowledge on the success factors of digitalization and digital transformation; and
- The third pillar combines the first two and places the state of knowledge in the context of digital transformation in the luxury fashion segment.

These pillars were chosen to bridge the still existing gap between the luxury world and the fast-changing world of new technologies or what Kapferer calls the "double myopia" (2015), double short-sightedness: luxury managers lack insight and the courage to act, while "techies" do not understand the essence of luxury. According to Kapferer, this situation can pose a real threat to a luxury company (p. 115).

LUXURY BRAND & LUXURY STRATEGY: A BALANCE OF TRADITION & INNOVATION

"Luxury begins where necessity ends", as simple as Coco Chanel's (in Wiedmann & Hennings, 2017, p. 163) quote may sound, the countless definitions of luxury are multifaceted, dynamic and context-dependent (Kapferer & Bastien, 2012, p. 45). The term luxury originally stems from the Latin word "lux" and means as much as light or brightness. "Luxuria", on the other hand, stands for prosperity, opulence or splendour. Despite its partly negative connotations, luxury as a social phenomenon has been inspiring mankind for thousands of years (Duma, Hallier-Willi & Steinmann, 2015, p. 10). Luxury is often associated with wealth, exclusivity and individuality. People define their personal status and social belonging to a particular social group through their possessions (Duma et al., 2015, p. 5). Kemp (1998), on the other hand, states that luxury is characterized, above all, by its relative and subjective character. Perceptions and sensations are dynamic, differ from individual to individual and are decisively influenced by the context and social environment of a person (p. 604).

Duma et al. (2015) summarize numerous luxury definitions and describe luxury with the following core attributes: social differentiation, limited availability, exclusivity, rarity, exceptional quality, high price, embodiment of a status symbol as well as relativity (p. 12). Kapferer and Bastien, on the other hand, describe luxury with the following core attributes: origin, culture, unique know-how and price that exceeds functional value, quality, hedonistic experience as well as restrictive, controlled distribution and finally personalized service and social privileges (2012, p. 47). Finally, Wiedmann and Hennings define luxury with aesthetics, history, exclusivity, perceived price, excellent quality, selective availability, brand awareness and non-essentiality (2017, p. 165). What becomes clear is, that there is no general definition that can conclusively grasp the concept of luxury with all its cultural, economic, social and historical functions. Rarity and exclusivity can, however, be classified as two of the core characteristics of luxury goods, as are the high price range and excellent product quality. A luxury brand is therefore a brand that is charged with the corresponding attributes (internally defined brand identity) or described by the target groups or the general public with these characteristics (brand image or reputation perceived from the outside).

Kapferer & Bastien (2012) have pointed out that luxury is not an absolute category; it is a relative concept and depends on the social, economic, and political structure of the time in question. Hence, as luxury consumption changes over time, the definition of a luxury strategy may change as well. Kapferer & Bastien define a luxury strategy as "a very specific business model", one different from fashion or premium business models, due to its "strict rules of use".

To clarify this initially vague definition, they identify six qualities that constitute luxury today:

- A hedonistic experience or a product made to last
- A price that far exceeds what the mere functional value would command
- A brand tied to a heritage, unique know-how, and culture
- A product available in purposefully restricted and controlled distribution
- A good offered with personalized accompanying services
- An object that represents a social marker, making the owner or beneficiary feel special, with a sense of privilege.

These qualities are all necessary, but may be weighted differently depending on the type of luxury good. The management of a luxury brand always moves in the positioning cross between accessibility and exclusivity as well as between tradition and innovation (cf. Kapferer & Bastien, 2012). Any imbalance in this respect endangers the value of the luxury brand in the perception of the target groups in the medium- to longterm. Especially at a time when technology and online channels are increasingly dominating all spheres of life, careful consideration must be given here without missing the signs for change.

While for many large international luxury brands many of the above mentioned aspects of a classic luxury strategy might have become relative, especially when taking into account their premium and entry level luxury offerings and the increasing pace at which the business is moving, for heritage luxury firms operating in market niches these defining attributes are still of value. However, their business models too have to be adapted to the new expectations and behavior of luxury customers around the world, who are to an increasing extent getting their information, sharing their opinions and even purchasing their products online. Heritage and tradition need to be balanced with innovation and creativity.

DIGITALIZATION & DIGITAL TRANSFORMATION OF BUSINESS MODELS

In contrast to the phenomenon of luxury, digitalization is a phenomenon of modern times. From a technical point of view, it is understood as the transformation of analogue data into digital data so that they can be managed and stored electronically (Loebbecke, 2006, p. 360). This definition, however, falls short in many respects. Rather, digitalization stands for a continuous process of change that links both the economy and society by means of information technologies (Laudon et al., 2016, p. 73). The intelligent networking and automation of systems, processes and people creates new business models. Digital value creation processes generate new sources of income for companies, promote interaction with customers and also offer the opportunity to achieve competitive advantages through data know-how (BMWi, 2015, p. 3). Digitalization can be summarized as often with disruptive change, driven by technological innovations and forcing traditional organizations, structures and cultures to adapt (BMWi, 2015, p. 3).

The graph below shows not only the accumulation of channels and forms of interaction with customers, but also the increasing speed at which companies have to adapt to new challenges. (Abtan et al., 2016, p. 5).

Figure 1: Accumulation of Technological Opportunities and Challenges (illustration based on Abtan, et al., 2016)

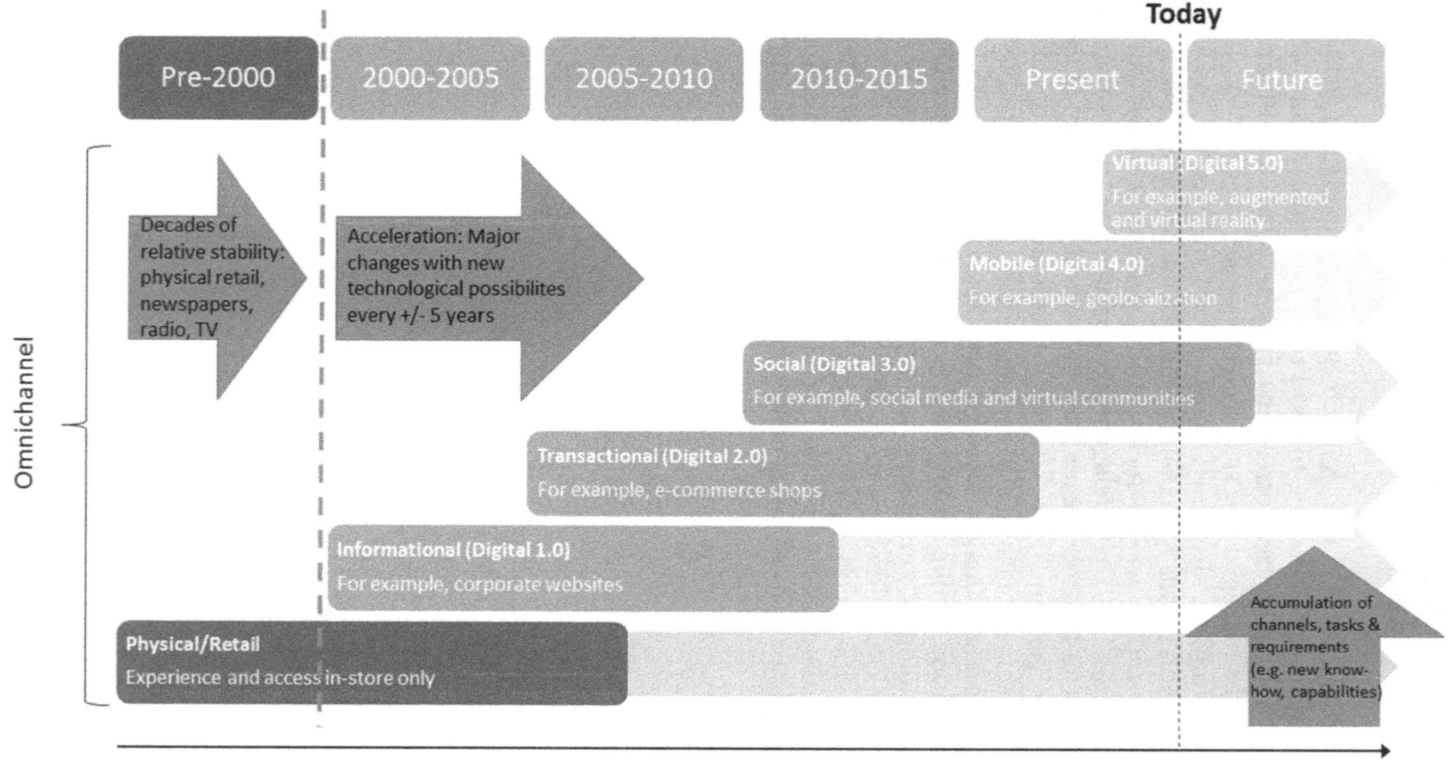

Technology is only one part in the equation, the necessary changes also influence the way in which to interact with customers, the control of the company over the brand and the culture of the company that is increasingly forced to transform from a closed entity mode to an ecosystem and network mode, in which the company plays a role, but has to rely on external partners in order to keep up with the accelerating speed at which its surroundings change (Achille et al., (2013).

TWO WORLDS, ONE FUTURE: DIGITAL TRANSFORMATION IN LUXURY AND LUXURY FASHION

Luxury is a relative and dynamic phenomenon, subject to gradual change as a result of the cultural and social evolution in history and the values of people that may shift over the course of their lives. Luxury companies have always been among the most innovative in their field, while at the forefront of their respective industries, they cultivate a culture of excellence and perfection. Dramatic changes, however, have so far not been part of the evolution of the luxury segment. The balance between innovation and tradition has always been a priority. It is therefore not surprising that many luxury companies show difficulty with the disruptive nature of digital technology and the Internet. Especially for smaller, traditional family businesses, which rely on the outstanding quality of their products and services and uphold craftsmanship and heritage, entering the digital world can lead to major distortions. The company may, for example, be interacting directly with end customers for the first time in its history; their products might be strongly defined by their haptics, and therefore must be advertised differently, made "tangible" and emotionally charged; and finally the interface to the Internet requires new skills and ways of thinking on the part of employees, which – taken together – creates many challenges the management has to overcome and in an ever increasing speed.

With digitalization and luxury fashion (to distinguish clearly from fast fashion which almost by definition goes hand in hand with technology), two at first sight opposing worlds meet. Being digital stands for omnipresence, availability and dynamism. Luxury, on the other hand, embodies long-term principles based on tradition, culture and timelessness, at least in the classical sense (Kapferer & Bastien, 2012, p. 247). Although the concepts differ fundamentally, the interface between the two topics is now more in focus than ever (HavasLuxHub, 2015a). Digital technologies and smartphones are increasingly becoming an integral part of our society. The consumption of luxury fashion is partly shifting from the boutique to the Internet. Networked consumers are increasingly exchanging information via mobile devices and obtaining information online. The newly created communication channels are making customers an increasingly powerful market player (Remy et al., 2015, p. 7).

As differing the nature of luxury might be, the Internet offers the luxury fashion industry the opportunity to create a 360 degree experience for its customers and to present the brand universe using the vast possibilities and reach of the digital sphere. Nonetheless, luxury fashion companies explicitly refrained from premature imitation of mass strategies (Kapferer & Bastien, 2012, p. 247). Due to the above-mentioned contrasts, digital strategies were often delayed and implemented only if there was clear added value and insignificant risk of brand dilution. Own websites and the presence in the social media are regarded as first steps into a digital future. However, the technological possibilities are far greater, as technologies can be used in almost all stages of the value chain. These range from automated procurement systems through product development to the point of sale (Okonkwo, 2010, p. 291). The use of artificial intelligence as well as virtual and augmented reality can also redesign the entire shopping experience (Deloitte, 2017, p. 8).

In recent times, we have seen brands (often subsidiaries of large luxury groups) that are expanding worldwide and have made significant digital progress. On the other hand, there are as well some smaller niche luxury brands that have recognized the enormous potential of technology, the Internet and social media, either because they can source and produce more efficiently, reach a global audience via new channels or because they can cultivate personal interaction with their customers much more intensively. The luxury industry has definitely opened up and realized that new technologies, platforms and channels are not the enemy, but rather offer countless opportunities - if they are implemented appropriately. It is not a question - as Kapferer (2015) criticises - of embracing the Web unconditionally. As always, the right approach for luxury brands lies in the balance. The question that naturally arises is: Where is the right balance for an individual heritage luxury fashion brand? Kapferer (2015) notes, that although the Internet has led to a major paradigm shift, the organizational structure of luxury companies has not changed significantly and it is therefore time for luxury brands to carry this revolution into their organizations and take it into account when recruiting junior staff (p. 115).

Just as there are few examples of small or medium-sized heritage luxury fashion companies that have already gone through a digital transformation, there is hardly any literature that deals with the question of how such a luxury brand can take advantage of the opportunities offered by new technologies, the Internet and social media without putting its perceived exclusivity at stake.

The next section is devoted to the description of the theoretical framework underlying the analysis of the case study. Its aim is to identify key aspects and potential success factors of the digital transformation process for luxury fashion SMEs with a heritage brand.

DIGITAL TRANSFORMATION IN LUXURY FASHION: A THEORETICAL FRAME OF REFERENCE

The theoretical framework described below (Figure 2, The Luxury Temple) summarizes the most important elements of a digital transformation while taking into account the specific challenges faced by managers in the luxury segment. The theoretical aspects mentioned above as well as the authors' practical experiences with the digital transformation of fashion companies form the basis of the framework.

Figure 1 below shows the framework that combines strategic management issues in the luxury context with structural aspects and operational processes (marketing, logistics, IT, accounting and HR). The challenge in the digital transformation of a luxury company is clearly to integrate the digital strategy into the existing structures (some of which have grown organically over decades, if not centuries) and also into the often still analogue processes.

However, a successful digital transformation also affects the company's employees with their attitudes, skills and habits; corporate culture as well as relationships with suppliers and, last but not least, with customers. This last point is crucial for a heritage luxury fashion company. While the company should adapt to the changing expectations and behavior of its customers to stay relevant, it should at the same time be careful not to lose the source of its mystique and social cachet. Finally, an important aspect of its mission is to provide customers with exceptional experiences and to create lasting emotional impressions that go beyond the mere purchase of the product.

The goal is therefore a structured approach that integrates the various pillars of digitalization. The four pillars of the model are the stationary retail trade, the online business, the relationship with the customer and the relationship with the partners. The roof of the temple is another crucial point: data consolidation. Customer relationship management as well as surveys and analysis of "big data" provide the opportunity to identify and understand customers, adapt to changing needs, expectations and behaviours and improve the overall process involving all key partners and suppliers.

It should also not be overlooked that a digital transformation is almost always preceded by consistent legacy data cleansing and an inventory of existing processes in order to create the basis for a careful and structured integration of new digital processes.

Figure 2: The Luxury Temple - Digital Transformation of Luxury Fashion Companies (own illustration, 2017)

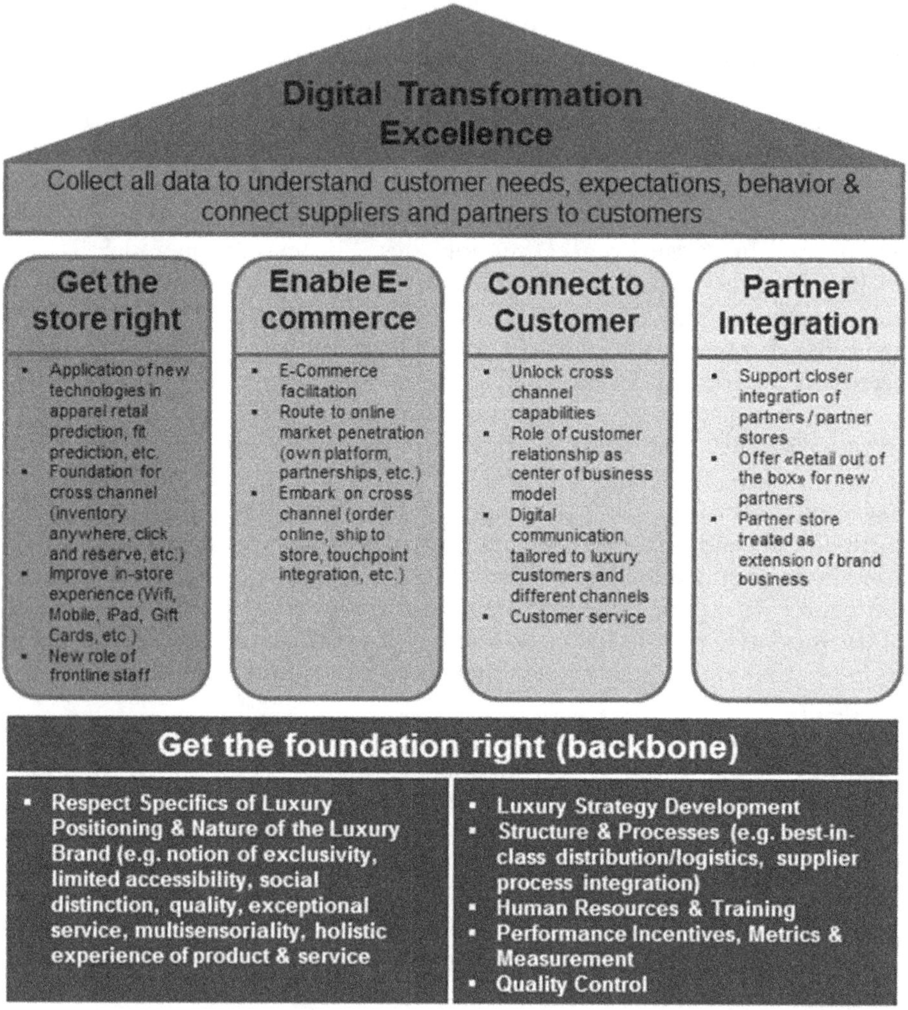

Last but not least, everything described above must have a solid foundation to support the adequate and successful digital transformation of the heritage luxury brand. Among other things - always assuming that the company wants to maintain its luxury positioning and not expand into the premium or mass segment - it is important to understand and respect the special features of the luxury positioning. These include concepts such as perceived exclusivity and limited offerings, social differentiation, the exceptional quality of the overall customer experience and the consistency of communication and touchpoints, i.e. all points of contact with customers.

These special features must be taken into account in the corporate strategy, in the design of structures and processes, in the human resource policy, in the performance management and in the quality control, supply chain management as well as in the customer orientation. Only in this way can the luxury company ensure that its most important asset, the luxury brand with its image and reputation, is not diluted or even damaged.

CASE STUDY: DIGITAL TRANSFORMATION OF A SWISS HERITAGE LUXURY FASHION COMPANY

Company History & Background Information

The history of Zimmerli of Switzerland is a history of entrepreneurship, of commitment to quality and perfection in craftsmanship, design and choice of materials, but also a history of innovation. The claim of the traditional Swiss company, which produces "the finest underwear in the world since 1871", illustrates its claims. These claims are still being pursued just as purposefully today as they have been in the last 100 years.

A history of tradition through innovation

The history of the brand began as early as 1866, when Isaac William Lambs invented the hand-operated single needle knitting machine, for which he received a gold medal at the 1867 World Fair in Paris. When Johann Jakob Zimmerli's dye works went bankrupt in 1871, he reads an article in the newspaper about the new knitting machine. He sends his wife, Pauline Zimmerli, to Basel, where she is trained by Lamb's agents and is soon able to knit the finest stockings and men's socks. Pauline quickly became a competent businesswoman and sold her products far beyond regional borders. As a result of her success, new employees had to be hired as early as 1874. And not enough: Inspired by the success and the desire for new products, Pauline invented a new knitting machine and sent her plans and ideas to the USA. In the same year, the first twin needle knitting machine was delivered to Switzerland and Pauline began manufacturing ribbed fabric and underwear. This not only laid the foundation for a successful company, but for an entire industry.

This was followed by a success story and international expansion. Until today, highly qualified seamstresses in Ticino, the southern part of Switzerland, produce some of the most prestigious undergarments in the world under the name Zimmerli of Switzerland S.A.. Zimmerli pursues a development strategy from a premium to an international luxury brand. As part of this strategy, the first flagship store in Rue St. Honoré in Paris and a shop-in-shop in KaDeWe Berlin opened in 2012 with the aim of further promoting brand awareness and prestige in the best locations in the world. Then in 2013 Zimmerli gave a further boost to its growth and repositioning strategy. This also included a redesign of the visual brand identity, which should reflect the established values of the brand today. In the same year Zimmerli achieved the highest turnover in its history. At the same time, the new store concept was implemented in new monobrand spaces at the Jelmoli department store in Zurich and in brand boutiques in Moscow and Taipei. In 2014, the brand further increased its international presence by opening a second boutique in Moscow, one in Interlaken, one of Switzerland's major tourist centers, as well as in Salzburg, Macau and Basel. In 2016, the subsidiary Zimmerli Shanghai Trading Co Ltd. was founded in Shanghai, China, and shortly afterwards the first boutique was opened in Plaza 66 in Shanghai. Further boutiques were opened in Mendrisio, Berlin and Geneva, as well as a shop-in-shop in the Harrods department store in London.

To increase productivity, Zimmerli merged the two previously separate cutting and sewing departments in Mendrisio, Switzerland. With its focus on the highest quality and craftsmanship "Made in Switzerland" as well as re-branding and a greater presence in the international retail market, Zimmerli wants to be able to offer its customers the best possible service. The next paragraphs show the role of Zimmerli's digital transformation in reaching this goal.

Analysis of the digital transformation approach

The analysis of the approach to digital challenges is, based on our case study, divided into four main aspects, all of which are related to the temple model (Figure 2) presented above: Digital Awareness, Digital Project Management Approach, Team Competencies, Results of the Company.

Digital Awareness

Only in 2013, the Swiss heritage luxury fashion brand decided to invest in digital transformation in order to reach new international target groups. At the same time, the brand was positioned as contemporary and could benefit from the possibilities of storytelling that were previously not available in traditional business (e.g. videos, looking behind the scenes, etc.). However, as haptics are very important for understanding these kind of products, the company continued to open new businesses in parallel with its digital efforts, eg. testing a new physical store concept, the so-called Touchpoint. Customers were able to view, touch and try on the entire collection, although not all styles, colours and sizes. They could order the products on a screen. It turned out that 50% of the customers (average male, 50-52 years old) would have preferred to shop directly in the store, while the other half appreciated being able to have the goods delivered anywhere.

"We are aware that we cannot tell customers that they need to go to a store. They decide for themselves where to buy their underwear. Many still go to a shop and want to be advised by a salesperson. But once they have found their preferred quality and material, they order online in the future. That's why we offer them all sales channels." (Baumann, personal communication, 2018).

In addition to winning new customers, management wanted them to perceive the brand not only as traditional, but also as innovative and contemporary. With the external help of consultants and agencies in the field of digital transformation, the company went online with its own web shop in autumn 2014. Further steps followed, which were carefully evaluated before new processes and touchpoints were integrated into the corporate structure.

The company describes itself as small and agile, which is also reflected in its pragmatic but thoughtful way of digitizing. While they had previously strategically focused on selective distribution in order to secure their luxury image, they now had to adapt their approach to the new environment, online distribution. This decision went hand in hand with a clear policy to ensure that the company's online presence as a whole is consistent with the positioning of the brand as a luxury product and continues to be perceived as such worldwide.

Digital Project Management Approach

In order to create digital awareness and ensure the necessary know-how, the company invested in an internal team with extensive experience (including in content management and digital storytelling) and in a selected external team of various experts. The digitization team was led by a dedicated external project manager who was able to motivate, coach and guide the team members. In addition to external support, specific skills in logistics, design, Google advertising and other "new" activities related to digital transformation were integrated into the team.

Communication and the availability of information were considered important: all activities, plans, resource integration and project status were available online for the project team, regardless of whether they concerned the internal or external team. This fostered the cultural development of the internal team and the company as a whole. With each change, the employees concerned were involved from the outset enabling them to contribute their know-how and avoid conflicts and resistance.

In addition, great efforts were made to inform the entire workforce of the company's plans and upcoming changes and to give them the opportunity to voice concerns, exchange ideas or participate in the evaluation of solutions. It was made clear that the employees and their input are crucial for an SME in the digital transformation process, that the knowledge and experience of all is needed and that every contribution counts. This was also necessary because quality and excellence are key aspects of a luxury brand that depend heavily on the right workforce. The company was not afraid to take courageous steps and also to get help from outside.

Team Competencies

The company made sure that all employees of the company could actively participate in the digital transformation project right from the start. A blog was set up to integrate the individual employees into the brand and enable them to engage with the brand. Employees were able to present their favorite piece from the collection and thus became part of the process. At the beginning of the digital transformation, all employees were given a « digital identity » that enabled them to receive all the company's news and information online, while at the same time making it easier for them to access private data such as salary information or holiday requests.

In addition to involving the existing workforce and internal skills development, the company decided to create a new job and hire a digital technical specialist.

Results of the Company

The e-boutique, which was set up as a first step, enabled the company to establish more direct contact with end customers and thus better understand their needs. This digitalization exercise showed to what extent the end users are using the online opportunities both directly in the B2C business and in the B2B business. However, it also turned out how important haptics are and that around 50% of existing customers still prefer physical touch points where they can touch the products and buy them directly.

The company has seen a significant RoI (return on investment) from the process of digital transformation. The increased digital presence has measurably increased brand awareness, a key goal. The e-commerce business continues to grow and the company continues to invest in online communication and distribution as well as in the offline presence of its touchpoints.

The various channels of digital transformation open up exciting opportunities and initiatives not only for the regular offering, but also for new forms of sales (shop-in-shop, corner or touchpoints), some of which have already been implemented and others are well on their way. The physical sales concepts are linked to the digital processes on both the customer and company sides. The company not only digitized the interface to the customers, but also internal processes (e.g. from design to production) in order to increase efficiency and accelerate time-to-market.

SUMMARY AND CONCLUSION

Zimmerli of Switzerland showed a high level of digital awareness and the company's vision for its digital future is strong and clear. The brand has a solid credibility in the market. The company's customers are loyal and choose the brand for its high quality and elegance. But thanks to digitization, customers are becoming more knowledgeable and sophisticated. The online channels, combined with a growing number of physical touchpoints, enable the company to tell its story convincingly and appealing to all the senses. In addition, the company can present its product range or a selection of it to customers wherever they prefer to shop.

What becomes clear from the analysis of the digital transformation approach at Zimmerli of Switzerland is a set of implementation principles and of facilitators leading to its success in the digital sphere.

The following implementation principles have been identified at Zimmerli:

- Customer Centricity
- Operational Efficiency
- Channel Integration
- Consistent & Adequate Design

Firstly, the customer is the main protagonist in the digital transformation approach of the company (e.g. physical pop-up touchpoint at Zurich mainstation). Secondly, the company practices the integration of technology in all business fields from manufacturing, communication and administration, to supply chain management and customer relationship managment (CRM) in order to boost operational efficiency. Thirdly, at Zimmerli « high tech » is balanced with « high touch » and thus online and offline channels are integrated for a consistent omnichannel experience speaking and including the important role of haptics in the case of the Zimmerli products. And last, but not least the company translated its heritage & values into all channels to ensure one consistent «design language» across the channels and distribution partners.

The facilitators of the successful digital transformation process where the following:

- Proactive Management
- Change Management
- External Knowledge Transfer

The Zimmerli management saw changes in consumer behavior etc. early and moved quickly and in a pragmatic way. This is, as mentioned earlier, not always the case in traditional, privately owned companies of the same size. Additionally, the Zimmerli workforce has been involved from the beginning. This, and the open communication and close collaboration with existing distribution partners, minimized resistance, maximized agency and commitment and fostered a culture mutation based on old Zimmerli values. And finally, additional support and new know-how came from an external project manager who accompanied the digital transformation where needed. Moreover, Zimmerli established a couple of new functions and hired people with know-how in the digital communication field, that was previously not to be found in the company. Looking at the organizational changes at the company, what becomes evident is, that no «digital silo» has been created. Existing employees, new hires and external experts work together and learn from each other.

In the below section, key findings are mentioned which can be of relevance for any luxury fashion brand, especially those with a heritage brand and small- to medium size:

- **No exclusive focus on the technical side of the digital transformation**: Particular attention should be paid to cultural development within the company in order to give impetus, avoid or reduce fears and resistance. The employees concerned should be involved in the project from day one.

- **The power of the luxury brand** (e.g. its tradition, its history, etc.) must be reconciled with the power of the customer/market. The exclusivity of the brand and how its particular history is perceived must be taken into account. The effects of the digital transformation of the business model or parts thereof on brand image and reputation should be carefully weighed and considered. The brand is an important value in the material and immaterial sense, especially in the luxury segment.

- **E-commerce** is growing rapidly and, if properly used and embedded in a professional communication strategy that links online and offline, can be a great opportunity for a SME in the luxury fashion industry to update its image, gain worldwide recognition and reach new audiences where they are most likely to shop. For SMEs, the art lies in the creative and sometimes unconventional use of available channels and platforms (e.g. social media) in order to compensate for the existing resource disadvantage compared to larger competitors and to gain awareness among the relevant target groups or to advertise the digitally available offer.

- **A proactive approach pays off**: No waiting until business partners and customers demand a stronger digital presence. Identification of the key drivers of change and adaptation to the dynamic environment in good time is key.

- **Combine external support and internal skill development**: One should not be afraid to request external support for specific questions of digital transformation. However, it is advisable to make sure that the necessary knowledge and new skills also flow into the internal team in order to guarantee long-term success.

And finally it is important not to see digital transformation as just another project, but an ongoing process. The digital development and the adaptation of the corporate culture are essentially ongoing and never completed as new channels and better technology keep emerging and changing the competitive landscape and customer behavior and expectations. The art of leading a heritage luxury fashion brand through these unchartered and, at times, unpredictable waters, seem to lie in the ability to maintain the balance between tradition and innovation. By re-defining and re-conciling company heritage and the specific values and culture that come with the changing circumstances, a small- or medium sized company like Zimmerli of Switzerland seems to have a fair chance of success even in uncertain and volatile times like these.

LIMITATIONS & FURTHER RESEARCH

The present study is based on one single case study and, while based on additional literature on the topic under research, the insights gained are not intended to be generalized. However, a transferability is given in the case of similar companies and when the individual context is adequately taken into consideration.

Research in the field of digital transformation of luxury brands has been fairly general and often focused on large, international brands. Furthermore, it often fails to consider the interdependence of the technical, the strategic, the operational and last, but not least also the cultural or human consequences of digitaliziation in a company. Given the opportunities, but on the other hand also the major challenges that arise from the digitalization of luxury and luxury fashion, we however suggest more research directed towards small and medium-sized, privately owned or family owned luxury companies in general and specifically those with a long standing tradition, a company culture grown over decades or centuries and thus a heritage brand of high value. Such brands and their organizations need to be carefully transformed for success in the digital era, while at the same time not losing touch with their fascinating roots. Challenges to be addressed are can be found in the fields of cultural change, internal and external know how transfer, customer orientation, process re-engineering or supply chain management to name just a few.

REFERENCES

ABTAN, O., BARTON, C., BONELLI, F., GURSKI, H., MEI-POCHTLER, A., PIANON, N., and TSUSAKA, M., 2016, *Digital or die: The choice for luxury brands.* [White Paper]. The Boston Consulting Group.

ACHILLE A., BELLAICHE J-M., LUI V., 2013, *Luxury Ecosystems: Controlling Your Brand while Letting It Go.* The Boston Consulting Group.

BMWi, 2015, *Industrie 4.0 und Digitale Wirtschaft: Impulse für Wachstum, Beschäftigung und Innovation.* München: PRpetuum GmbH.

BOVENSIEPEN, G., RUMPUFF, S., & BENDER, S., 2015, *Store 4.0: Zukunft des stationären Handels.* PricewaterhouseCoopers AG.
BUSINESS OF FASHION & MCKINSEY, 2018, The State of Fashion 2019.
BÜTTNER, M., HUBER, F., REGIER, S., & VOLLHARDT, K., 2008, Phänomen Luxusmarke: Identitätsstiftende Effekte und Determinanten der Markenloyalität. In: K. BELLMANN, R. BRONNER, F. HIMPEL, D. SCHMIDT-GALLAS & K. J. SRNKA (Hrsg.): *Spektrum wirtschaftswissenschaftliche Forschung.* S. 1-160. Wiesbaden: Gabler.
D'ARPIZIO, C., & LEVATO, F., 2017, *The Millennial State of Mind: Digital is reshaping how luxury is purchased across generations.* Bain & Company.
DEDERL, M., KANITZ, C., & MEI-POCHTLER A., 2017, Vom Haben zum Sein – die Zukunft der globalen Luxusindustrie. In: W. M. Thieme (Hrsg.): *Luxusmarkenmanagement: Grundlagen, Strategien und praktische Umsetzung.* S. 147-162. Wiesbaden: Springer Gabler.
DELOITTE, 2017, *Global Powers of Luxury Goods 2017: The new luxury consumer.* Abgerufen von https://www2.deloitte.com/content/-dam/Deloitte/global/Documents-/consumer-industrial-products/gx-cip-global-powers-luxury-2017.pdf.
DUMA, F., HALLIER-WILLI, C., & STEINMANN, C., 2015, *The Business of Luxury.* Zürich: vdf Hochschulverlag AG.
FLICK, U., 2014, *An Introduction to Qualitative Research (5. Aufl.).* London: SAGE
GOLDSTON, N., 2017, *What You Need To Know About Luxury Consumer Trends For 2018.* Abgerufen von https://www.forbes.com/sites/njgoldston/2017/12/29/what-you-need-to-know-about-luxury-consumer-trends-for-2018/#6a1bfa8a21eb.
HavasLuxHub (2015). *Where To Invest in Fashion Technology?.* Abgerufen von https://www.havasluxhub.com/where-to-invest-in-fashion-technology/.
KAPFERER, J.-N., 2018, *Luxury brands and emotions.* Keynote speech given at the Monaco Symposium on Luxury, April 12, 2018.
KAPFERER, J.-N., 2015, *Kapferer on Luxury. How Luxury Brands Can Grow Yet Remain Rare.* London: Kogan Page.
KAPFERER, J.-N. & BASTIEN, V., 2012, *The luxury strategy – break the rules of marketing to build luxury brands.* London: Kogan Page.
KEMP, S., 1998, Perceiving luxury and necessity. *Journal of Economic Psychology, 19(5),* S. 591-606.
KUBICEK, H., 1977, Heuristische Bezugsrahmen und heuristisch angelegte Forschungsdesigns als Elemente einer Konstruktionsstrategie empirischer Forschung. In R. Köhler (Hrsg.), *Empirische und handlungstheoretische Forschungskonzeptionen in der Betriebswirtschaftslehre* (S. 3-36). Stuttgart: Poeschel.
LAUDON, K. C., LAUDON, J. P., & SCHODER, D., 2016, *Wirtschaftsinformatik: Eine Einführung.* 3. Auflage. Hallbergmoos: Pearson Studium.

LOEBBECKE, C., 2006, *Digitalisierung: Technologien und Unternehmensstrategien.* Berlin: Springer.
OESCHER, G., 2018, *Omni-Channel-Management.* Abgerufen von https://wirtschaftslexikon.gabler.de/definition/omni-channel-management-54201.
OKONKWO, U., 2010, *Luxury Online: Styles, Systems, Strategies.* Basingstoke: Palgrave Macmillan.
OKONKWO, U., 2009, Sustaining the luxury brand on the Internet. *Brand Management, 16, 5/6,* p. 302-310
PIANON, N., ARNAULT, B., & BONELLI, F., 2017, *The True-Luxury Global Consumer Insight.* 4. Auflage. Milano: The Boston Consulting Group & Fondazione Altagamma.
PUNCH, K. F., 2014, *Introduction to Social Research. Quantitative & Qualitative Approaches (3. Aufl.).* London: SAGE.
REMY, N., CATENA, M., & DURAND-SERVOINGT, B., 2015, *Digital inside: Get wired for the ultimate luxury experience.* McKinsey & Company.
REPPA, R. & HIRSH, E., 2007, The Luxury Touch. *Strategy & business,* Ausgabe Nr. 46.
RUBIN, H. J. & RUBIN, I. S., 2012, *Qualitative interviewing: the art of hearing data.* Thousand Oaks: SAGE Publications.
SALESFORCE, 2016, *Ist Omni-Channel Marketing das neue Multi-Channel Marketing?.* Abgerufen von https://www.salesforce.com/de/blog/2016/10/ist-omni-channel-marketing-das-neue-multi-channel-marketing-.html.
SEIDMAN, I., 2006, *Interviewing as Qualitative Research. A Guide for Researchers in Education and the Social Sciences* (3. Aufl.). New York: Teachers College Press.
SCHOSTAK, J., 2006, *Interviewing and Representation in Qualitative Research.* Maidenhead: Open University Press.
THIEME, W. M., 2017, Das Wesen der Luxusmarke. In: W. M. Thieme (Hrsg.): *Luxusmarkenmanagement: Grundlagen, Strategien und praktische Umsetzung.* S. 1-34. Wiesbaden: Springer Gabler.
VIGNERON, F. & JOHNSON, L. W., 1999, A Review and a Conceptual Framework of Prestige-Seeking Consumer Behavior. *Academy of Marketing Science Review, 1999 (1),* pp. 1-15.
WEISS, R. S., 1994, *Learning from strangers: the art and method of qualitative interview studies.* New York: The Free Press.
WIEDMANN, K.-P., & HENNINGS, N., 2017, Die steigende Nachfrage nach Luxusmarken: Ein globales Phänomen mit lokalen Besonderheiten. In: W. M. THIEME (Hrsg.): *Luxusmarkenmanagement: Grundlagen, Strategien und praktische Umsetzung.* S. 163-176. Wiesbaden: Springer Gabler.

LIST OF FIGURES

BUILDING A LUXURY BRAND ON INSTAGRAM: THE CASE OF DELVAUX

Ineke TACK
Ghent University
ineke.tack@hotmail.com

Marijke DE VEIRMAN
Ghent University
marijke.deveirman@ugent.be

Liselot HUDDERS
Ghent University
liselot.hudders@ugent.be

ABSTRACT

This case study examines Delvaux's Instagram marketing activities using Kim and Ko's (2012) conceptual framework of five dimensions of social media marketing activities, namely entertainment, interaction, trendiness, customization, and word of mouth. More specific, based on a survey among 195 luxury consumers, a structural equation model is developed to explore how each of these dimensions affect customer brand equity and purchase intentions. Specifically, the study demonstrates a positive impact of trendiness, entertainment and word of mouth on customer brand equity. Moreover, entertainment and word-of-mouth enhance purchase intention, while trendiness had a significant negative effect on purchase intention. Furthermore, it was found that the effect of consumer's overall impression of Delvaux's Instagram marketing activities on purchase intention is partly mediated by customer brand equity. These findings suggest that luxury brands' investments in Instagram could have significant positive effects on customer brand equity and consequently purchase intention and thus provide further support for social media marketing as an important and cost-effective marketing tool for luxury brands in the digital age.

Keywords: luxury, social media marketing, Instagram, customer brand equity, fashion industry, sponsored content.
JEL codes: M30, M31

INTRODUCTION

Today, brands like Louis Vuitton are posting videos of their catwalk shows on social media to offer all fans the opportunity to view the show online. Moreover, whereas in the past only professional photographers recorded fashion shows, today this behavior is displayed by practically every guest present, including fashion bloggers and high-end social influencers. As a result, many designers have changed the look of their shows to make sure they are being shared online. For instance, in February 2014, Karl Lagerfeld transformed his set into a Chanel supermarket (Blanks, 2014), and in 2017 he simulated a space launch (Menkes, 2017). This shows that not only the way fashion brands exhibit their products has been adjusted, but also the way fashion is consumed and shared has changed.

Social media have become an important source of inspiration for consumers and it has been widely recognized that a thoughtful social media strategy may impact consumers' brand preferences and purchase decisions. Although luxury brands have long been hesitant in adopting social media (Chevalier & Gutsatz, 2012; Kapferer & Bastien, 2012; Okonkwo, 2010), most luxury brands are now present on social media and even managed to build large followings. Burberry for instance, was one of the first premium brands to use Facebook, Twitter and YouTube to offer its customers a new and interesting experience. Partly because of this, the brand succeeded in repositioning itself as a trendy brand with a fresh look, which resulted in positive outcomes in terms of growth, revenue and brand advocacy (Phan, Thomas & Heine, 2011).

Because of the channel's omnipresence, an increasing amount of luxury fashion brands are now using Instagram as a legitimate and important marketing tool. Instagram in its turn, is doing its utmost to attract the fashion industry. The social networking site has hired Eva Chen, former style editor of Lucky, as head of 'fashion partnerships'. Chen and her team advise models, designers and stylists on the use of Instagram. Instagram, a visual storytelling and discovery platform with over 1 billion monthly active users, lends itself perfectly for luxury brands to showcase their aesthetically appealing products. According to Tennille Kopiasz, Dior Perfume's Senior Vice President of Marketing, luxury brands always aimed to inspire consumers using storytelling, therefore, Instagram is a natural fit. Luxury brands are well-known for their highly polished print and TV campaigns, a strategy they can perfectly translate to Instagram. Today, Chanel is the leading luxury brand on Instagram with 37.8 million followers, followed by Gucci with 38.1 million followers, Louis Vuitton with 35.7 million followers and Dior with 28.7 million followers. Other high-end luxury brands including Dolce & Gabbana, Prada, Michael Kors, and Burberry also have a strong presence in the platform, all having over fifteen million followers on Instagram. Moreover, luxury brands can leverage their exposure by partnering with high-end luxury influencers who directly appeal to their target audience by posting aspirational content, including their lifestyle and luxury experiences and may transfer their images to the brand (De Veirman, Cauberghe & Hudders, 2017; Mc Cracken, 2005). By following luxury brands and influencers, consumers may fill their news feed with inspiration for new trends and collections, holiday destinations and purchases in high-quality photos.

The purpose of this study is to identify how Instagram marketing activities affect customer brand equity, which is an important indicator of brand success, and consequently purchase intention. First, we discuss how luxury brands may use social media for marketing purposes and in what way Instagram in particular may be valuable for luxury brand communications in terms of customer brand equity. Next, we focus on five types of social media marketing activities of luxury fashion brands (entertainment, interaction, trendiness, customization, and word of mouth) as proposed by Kim et al. (2012). We elaborate on the relationship between these specific activities, customer brand equity and purchase intention and we report the results of the empirical case study. We conclude with a discussion on practical implications.

1. LUXURY BRANDS' SOCIAL MEDIA MARKETING ACTIVITIES

For a long time, luxury brands avoided the internet and social media in particular for promotion purposes as they were regarded incompatible in nature (Kapferer et al. 2012; Hennings, Wiedmann & Klarmann, 2012). However, in order to stay relevant in a dynamic and volatile landscape marked by shorter brand lifecycles, traditional luxury firms were forced to develop innovative strategies and change track (Ko, Phau & Aiello, 2016). Moreover, to reach the new luxury consumers, who are younger and important, reachable through social media (Kapferer, 2015), luxury brands started embracing these digital touchpoints (Kim et al., 2012). Today's luxury sector recognizes the importance of social media, and brands have become aware of the opportunities these channels offer to reach consumers and build brand awareness, which consumers are likely to use in their purchase decisions (Kelly, Kerr & Drennan, 2010; Bernoff & Li, 2011, Rambourg, 2014). Social media now play a central role in the success of a brand (Phan et al., 2011) and luxury brands actively use them for advertising and marketing purposes (Kim et al. 2012). Moreover, research shows that this strategy pays off (Godey et al., 2016; Kim et al., 2010, 2012;

Phan et al., 2011). Still, a field of tension remains in that social media on the one hand makes luxury approachable for mass markets, which contrasts with the exclusivity and rarity that defines it (Kastanakis and Balabanis 2014). Luxury brands need to balance between answering to the democratization of luxury and expanding their markets, while constructing and maintaining images of exclusivity and superiority in the head of consumers, which helps them justify spending a premium for products that fulfil needs beyond utility (Kapferer, 2015 ; Atwal & Williams, 2009; De Souza & Ferris 2015). One way to do so is by using visual communication via social media to convey this image to consumers, for instance through Instagram (Lee, Hur & Watkins, 2018).

Kim et al. (2012) developed a framework, including five dimensions of luxury brands' social media marketing activities, namely entertainment, interaction, trendiness, customization, and word of mouth (WOM). In the next section we elaborate on each of these dimensions and apply them to the specific context of Instagram.

Entertainment

Entertainment can be described as the result of the pleasure one derives from a social media experience (Agichtein, Castillo, Donato, Gionis & Mishne, 2008) and is considered a strong motive for social media use (Goldsmith & Horowitz, 2006; Kaye, 2007; Muntinga, Moorman, & Smit, 2011; Park, Kee, & Valenzuela, 2009) and Instagram in particular (Alhabash & Ma, 2017). According to Muntinga et al. (2011), social media users consume brand-related messages for fun, to relax and as a pastime. Instagram in particular provides plenty options to create visually appealing and entertaining content. For instance, by using Instagram stories, photos and videos that disappear after 24 hours, luxury brands can provide a behind the scene glimpse of their fashion show or showcase their craftsmanship. Extra creative tools such as boomerang and superzoom or adding stickers, locations and hashtags can make stories even more entertaining.

Customization

The level of customization is based on the extent to which a service is adapted to meet an individual's preference (Schmenner, 1986). Godey and colleagues (2016) state that in the social media world, customization refers to the intended audience of the published message. Following their reasoning, this study conceptualizes customization as the extent to which a profile allows targeted searches and provides a personalized service. However, Instagram provides less options for specific information search and customer service compared to for instance Facebook brand pages, as the platform is mainly used for inspirational purposes by using visual storytelling strategies.

Interaction

Interaction is defined by Godey et al. (2016) as sharing information and exchanging opinions with third parties. Whiting and Williams (2013) identify it as an important motivation of social media use in general. Daugherty, Eastin, and Bright (2008) more specifically find that it is an important motivation for creating user-generated content. Moreover, Muntinga et al. (2011) find it to be an important motivation for contributing to and creating brand-related content on social media. Instagram provides interaction possibilities that differ in level of activeness and public visibility. Consumers, may for instance like the brand's posts, comment to it and reply to other consumers' comments. Moreover, they may send private messages and engage in interactive story features, such as polls or questions. By interacting with their followers, brands may be perceived as more human and approachable. However, this may contrast with the relative inaccessibility, distance and exclusivity luxury brands aim and which at least partly explains their attractiveness (Kapferer, 2015).

Word of mouth

Through social media, consumers are able to engage with brands and fellow consumers and share their possessions and evaluations of brands one-to-many without constraints (Kim et al. 2012; Vollmer & Precourt, 2008). Consumers nowadays are no longer passive recipients of product information, but rather generate and spread it themselves (Stewart & Pavlou, 2002). This word-of-mouth is highly desirable as it appears to be more effective than traditional advertising tactics due to higher credibility, empathy and relevance and consequently lower resistance (de Vries, Gensler & Leeflang 2012; Gruen, Osmonbekov & Czaplewski, 2006). Being aware of its strong impact, brands have been looking for ways to stimulate word-of-mouth and this way increase brand awareness. For instance, by delivering relevant content, brands try to encourage consumers to pass it along and share it on their own social media pages, which is how the word-of-mouth dimension is conceptualized in this study.

Trendiness

To conclude, trendiness refers to the fact that social media include the latest information on products for customers (Godey et al., 2016). This study defines trendiness in terms of the dissemination of the latest information about the luxury brand and whether the brand's Instagram page is considered trendy as such.

2. CONSUMERS' RESPONSES TO LUXURY BRANDS' SOCIAL MEDIA MARKETING ACTIVITIES

Research on how social media marketing activities influence brand equity and consumers' responses toward luxury brands is limited, partly due to the slow adoption of social media by the industry itself. Kim and Ko (2010) were the first to investigate the effectiveness of social media marketing for luxury brands. They explored the effect of five properties of social media marketing (i.e., entertainment, customization, interaction, word of mouth and trend) on customer relationships (involving intimacy and trust) and purchase intention using multiple regression analysis. Entertainment appeared to positively impact all three dependent variables, while customization only leads to higher trust, and interaction enhances purchase intention. Word of mouth increases intimacy and purchase intention and trend only has a positive effect on trust.

In 2012, Kim and Ko elaborated on their initial study (2010) on the use of social media marketing among luxury fashion brands. Using confirmatory factor analysis, they confirmed that brand's social media marketing efforts comprises 5 dimensions, namely entertainment, interaction, trendiness, customization, and word of mouth. These perceived social media activities were found to enhance value equity (i.e., "customers' objective assessment of the utility of a brand, based on perceptions of what is given up for what is received", Vogel, Evanschitzky & Ramaseshan, 2008), relationship equity (i.e., "the tendency of customers to stay in a relationship with a brand, going beyond objective and subjective assessments of it", Kim et al., 2012) and brand equity (i.e., "customer's subjective and intangible assessment of the brand over and above its value", Rust, Lemon & Zeithaml, 2004). Brand equity appeared to have a significant negative effect on customer equity while value equity and relationship equity showing no significant effect. Value equity and brand equity in turn led to higher purchase intention and customer equity (i.e., "the discounted sum of customer lifetime values, which has been considered the most determinant of the long-term values of the firm", Kim, Park, Lee, Knight, Xu & Jeon, 2010), while relationship equity had no significant influence.

Godey et al.'s study (2016) confirmed the finding that for luxury brands, social media marketing activities positively affect brand equity and consumer responses and extended Kim and Ko's (2012) findings by adding extra dependent variables and conducting the study in different countries (China, France, India, and Italy).

Although these studies provide interesting findings, a limitation lies in the fact that they used a general approach and included luxury brands' social media marketing activities as a whole. For instance, Kim and Ko (2010; 2012) created a visual stimulus expressing Louis Vuitton's social media marketing activities on Facebook and Twitter, which were at that time the most popular social media among luxury brands, to question consumers' perceptions. Godey et al. (2016) on the other hand questioned consumers' perceptions of five luxury brands' social media activities in general, using Kim and Ko's (2012) framework. Moreover, research on the effect of visual communication strategies on luxury brands mainly lacks (Lee et al. 2018). In this research, we use Kim and Ko's (2012) proposed framework of five dimensions of perceived social media marketing efforts of luxury fashion brands, including entertainment, customization, interaction, word of mouth (WOM) and trendiness, however, we specifically focus on the image-based medium Instagram, which today is welcomed by most luxury brands. The study develops a structural equation model to explore how each of these dimensions affect consumer responses, including customer brand equity and purchase intention. Moreover, the role of customer brand equity as a mediator of the relationship between the overall assessment of Delvaux's Instagram marketing activities and purchase intention, will be investigated.

3. CASE STUDY: THE DELVAUX INSTAGRAM PAGE

Delvaux, the Belgian luxury leather goods brand known as *"the first luxury leather house in the world"* was founded in 1829 in Brussels by Charles Delvaux and was the first to patent their handbag model in 1908. In 2013, the Belgian leather goods brand embraced Instagram. The brand uses its profile (with the @delvaux username) mainly to promote new collections, models and boutiques. At the time of the data collection (March 2018), their Instagram page counted 163.000 followers, they followed 160 accounts themselves and posted 632 photos. The current study aims to examine how people's evaluation of their Instagram page affect Delvaux's customer brand equity and purchase intent.

More specific, we explore the relationships between Delvaux's perceived Instagram marketing activities on customer brand equity and purchase intention by using a survey study. Further, we investigate which dimensions of the assessment of Delvaux's Instagram page affect customer brand equity and purchase intention. We use Kim and Ko's (2012) conceptual model of social media marketing activities, in which they distinguish five dimensions (entertainment, interaction, trendiness, customization and word of mouth) to predict which of these dimensions impact customer brand equity.

Method, Subjects and Procedure

The study employed an online survey that was conducted among a convenience sample of luxury consumers in Belgium. First, participants were asked if they were familiar with the luxury brand Delvaux and whether they purchased a luxury fashion product in the past five years as this was a criterion for inclusion in the sample. If they did not, they were directed to the end of the survey. There were 199 participants who completed the questionnaire. Four responses were deleted from the data file, as these participants failed to answer one or more control questions correctly. This exclusion leaves 195 participants (142 females, M_{Age} = 34.10 years, SD_{Age} = 11.88). 65.1% of the sample had an Instagram account, of which the majority (68.5%) used it at least one time a day and 24.4% followed Delvaux on Instagram. 21.5% indicated to have bought a Delvaux article in the past.

Participants were exposed to screenshots of Delvaux's Instagram page and Delvaux's latest Instagram post at the time of the data collection (March 2018). After this, participants' completed a questionnaire. First, purchase intention was measured. Next, Delvaux's perceived Instagram marketing activities were questioned, followed by consumer brand equity. The last part of the survey collected demographic information of the participants, including their involvement with luxury fashion brands and their Instagram use. All analyses were performed using Amos graphics 22.

Measures

Delvaux's perceived Instagram marketing activities were questioned with 11 items, adapted from Kim and Ko (2012; α = .88; M = 4.73, SD = 1.00). These items reflect five dimensions of social media marketing activities, namely entertainment, interaction, trendiness, customization and word of mouth. Customer brand equity was measured with three items based on Yoo, Donthu & Lee (2000; α = .94; M = 3.93, SD = 1.69). Purchase intention (α = .96; M = 3.69, SD = 1.97) was measured with three items based on Grewal, Krishnan & Monroe (1998) and Grewal, Krishnan, Baker & Borin (1998). Involvement with luxury fashion brands was measured with three items adapted from Beatty & Talpade (1994, α = .93, M = 4.13, SD = 1.52). All items were measured with 7-point Likert scales. A detailed overview of the used measurement scales can be found in Table 2.

Correlational Analysis

First, we conducted a Pearson correlation analysis to examine correlations among all variables in the conceptual model (see Table 1).

Table 1. Correlational Table.

	1	*2*	*3*	*4*	*5*	*6*	*7*	*Mean*	*SD*
Entertainment	1.00							4.96	1.31
Interaction	.401 **	1.00						5.35	1.03
Trendiness	.721 **	457 **	1.00					4.96	1.13
Customization	.214 **	.469 **	.439 **	1.00				4.67	1.22
Word of mouth	.557 **	.385 **	.657 **	.472 **	1.00			3.73	1.61
Consumer brand equity	.604 **	.266 **	.655 **	.310 **	.573 **	1.00		3.93	1.69
Purchase intention	.596 **	.260 **	.637 **	.382 **	.627 **	.784 **	1.00	3.69	1.67

** = significant at .01 level

Measurement Model

Confirmatory factor analysis (CFA) using Amos Graphics 22 on the whole set of constructs in the structural equation model was conducted to test for convergent factor validity of the conceptual model and Cronbach's α was applied to test the reliability of each construct. The CFA model includes social media marketing activities as proposed by Kim and Ko (2012), customer brand equity and purchase intention. The latent constructs were correlated, whereas the measurement items and their error items were constrained to be uncorrelated. Due to low factor loadings (< .70) and consequently low Chronbach's α (< .70), we decided to drop one of the items that measured trendiness and one of the items that measured customization (see Table 2). As a result, both trendiness and customization were included as measurement items (single items) in the structural model.

Table 2. Confirmatory Factor Analysis.

Construct	Items	Factor loading	Chronbach's α
Entertainment	Using Delvaux's Instagram page is fun.	.915	.897
	Contents shown in Delvaux' Instagram page seem interesting.	.892	
Interaction	Delvaux' Instagram page enables information sharing with others.	.783	.869
	Conversation or opinion exchange with others is	.888	

	possible through Delvaux's Instagram page. It is easy to deliver my opinion through Delvaux's Instagram page.	 .822	
Trendiness	Using Delvaux's Instagram page is very trendy. Contents shown in Delvaux's Instagram page is the newest information.	.763 .480	.488
Customization	Delvaux's Instagram page offers customized information search. Delvaux's Instagram page provides customized service.	.755 .688	.660
Word of mouth	I would like to pass along information on brand, product, or services from Delvaux's Instagram page to my friends. I would like to upload contents from Delvaux's Instagram page on my blog or micro blog.	.915 .862	.882
Consumer brand equity	Even if another brand has same features as Delvaux, I would prefer to buy Delvaux. If another brand is not different from Delvaux in any way, it seems smarter to purchase Delvaux. If there is another brand as good as Delvaux, I prefer to buy Delvaux .	.935 .874 .938	.941
Purchase intention	The likelihood that I would purchase a Delvaux item is… If I were going to buy a luxury fashion item, the probability of purchasing a Delvaux product is… I would purchase a Delvaux item	.940 .961 .928	.959

Model fit: $\chi 2$= 261.13, df= 98, p < .001 AGFI= .80, GFI= .87, NFI= .91, IFI= .94, CFI= .94, RMSEA= .09

Mediation Analysis

First, we study the effect of respondents' overall impression of Delvaux's Instagram marketing activities on purchase intention through customer brand equity, using mediation analysis with structural equation modelling in Amos Graphics 22 (95% confidence level, 2000 bootstrap resamples). The path diagram of Figure 1 of the mediation model includes the unstandardized estimates for the causal paths for the indirect and direct effects. All direct paths were significant, moreover, the estimated indirect path of perceived Instagram marketing activities on purchase intention through customer brand equity appeared to be significant too (β = .40, p < .001). Therefore, potentially, customer brand equity partly mediates the path between perceived Instagram marketing activities and purchase intention.

Figure 1. Mediation Analysis.

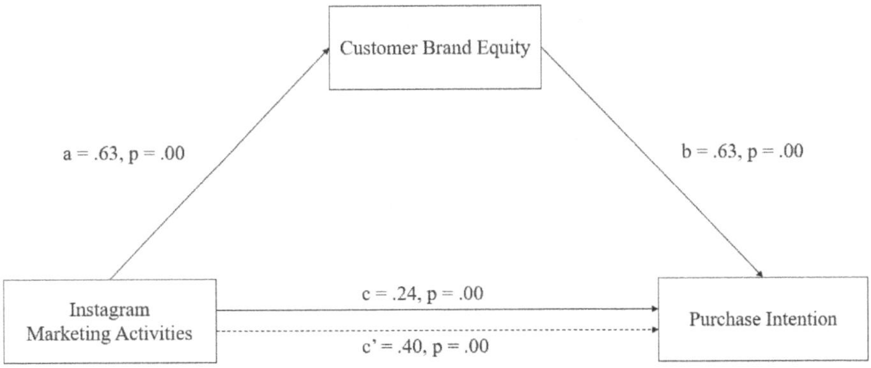

Structural Model

Next, we take a closer look at which specific Instagram marketing activities affect customer brand equity and purchase intention. A structural equation model using Amos Graphics 22 was tested, relating all the independent variables (Instagram marketing activities: entertainment, interaction, trendiness, customization and word of mouth) to the dependent variables (customer brand equity and purchase intention). Overall model fit was satisfactory. The chi-square statistic ($\chi 2$ = 159,76 df = 71) was at a significant level (p <. 001), and the fit indices were within accepted standards (AGFI= .84, GFI= .91, NFI= .94, IFI= .97, CFI= .97, RMSEA= .08).

There is a significant positive effect of trendiness (β = .35, p < .001), entertainment (β = .28, p = .00) and word of mouth (β = .25, p = .01) on customer brand equity. Moreover, entertainment (β = .15, p = .05) and word-of-mouth (β = .27, p < .001) have a significant positive effect on purchase intention. Remarkably, trendiness has a significant negative effect on purchase intention (β = -.16, p = .04). Interaction and customization neither enhance customer brand equity nor purchase intention. As expected, there is a significant positive effect of customer brand equity on purchase intention (β = .84, p < .001). The results are shown in Table 3.

Table 3. Structural Equation Model.

Path			*Standardized effect*	P
Customer brand equity	←	Entertainment	.282	.004
Customer brand equity	←	Interaction	-.045	.581
Customer brand equity	←	Word of mouth	.246	.009
Customer brand equity	←	Trendiness	.347	<.001
Customer brand equity	←	Customization	-.008	.726
Purchase intention	←	Entertainment	.153	.050
Purchase intention	←	Interaction	-.083	.167
Purchase intention	←	Word of mouth	.267	<.001
Purchase intention	←	Trendiness	-.163	.039
Purchase intention	←	Customization	.093	.081
Purchase intention	←	Customer brand equity	.840	<.001

Model fit: $\chi 2$= 159.76, df= 71, p < .001
AGFI= .84, GFI= .91, NFI= .94, IFI= .97, CFI= .97, RMSEA= .08

GENERAL DISCUSSION

Summary of Major Findings

This study adapts Kim et al.'s (2012) conceptual framework of five dimensions of social media marketing activities, namely entertainment, interaction, trendiness, customization, and word of mouth, to understand the antecedents of customer brand equity and purchase intention of luxury brands in the specific context of Instagram. First of all, the current study found that consumers' overall perceptions of Delvaux's Instagram marketing activities determine customer brand equity and consequently purchase intention. These results support Godey et al.'s (2016) finding that customer brand equity partly serves as a mediator of the effect of social media marketing activities on customer responses. This is also in line with previous research which has shown that the attitude towards, and preference for a brand or product plays an important role in purchase intentions (Chen & Chang, 2008; Cobb-Walgren, Ruble & Donthu, 1995; Kim et al., 2010; 2012; Schivinski & Dabrowski, 2013; Yoo et al., 2000).

Then, we conducted an in-depth analysis to see which specific Instagram marketing activities affect customer brand equity and purchase intention. Three dimensions, namely trendiness, entertainment and word of mouth appear to enhance customer brand equity. These results are partly in line with Kim et al. (2012) who found the entertainment, interaction, and word-of-mouth effects of social media marketing activities to work positively in enhancing customer brand equity. Moreover, entertainment and word-of-mouth positively impact purchase intention, while trendiness has a significant negative effect on purchase intention. These findings suggest that positive consumer responses on Instagram are mainly determined by consumers' intention to pass on information available on Delvaux's Instagram page and whether the Instagram page is considered fun. Whether the page feels trendy and fashionable may enhance customer brand equity, but unexpectedly appears to negatively affect purchase intention. This may be explained by naïve theory, in this sense that when a luxury brand's Instagram page is considered to be very trendy, this might trigger thoughts that the brand aims to appeal to a broad audience and thus serve as an indication that the brand's products are commonplace, lack exclusivity, and thus are of low worth (Deval, Mantel, Kardes & Posavac, 2013). Still, further research is necessary to gain more insight into how perceived trendiness of an Instagram page impacts consumers' responses.

Practical Implications

Luxury brands seek to integrate social media into their marketing strategies. This study particularly focused on Instagram as a visual storytelling platform for luxury brands. The findings highlight that positive perceptions of a luxury brand's Instagram page result in positive consumer responses, including higher customer brand equity and consequently purchase intentions. Therefore, a thoughtful Instagram marketing strategy is likely to pay off.

In particular, positive perceptions of the Instagram page's entertaining value and willingness to share the luxury brand's post on one's own social media are of decisive importance. Rather than pushing direct sales messages to their followers, luxury brands using Instagram as a marketing tool could benefit from creating content that is entertaining and appealing to share among consumers' own followers. Instead of merely posting product pictures and official campaign images, Instagram can be used to convey brand stories, provide a look behind the scenes and picture celebrities and influencers they are willing to associate with. This is also supported by previous research which found that subtle promotions on social media create positive attention and increase exposure of the brand (Steinman & Hawkins, 2010) and "humanizing" messages results in greater consumer engagement (Malhotra, Malhotra & See, 2012), which is an important predictor of increased purchases (Goh, Heng, & Lin, 2013).

A concern luxury brands have to deal with, is the fear that the use of social media might diminish perceived exclusivity (Türk, Scholz, & Berresheim, 2012). Indeed, mixed findings for the effect of perceived trendiness on consumers' responses mark the challenge luxury brands experience to appeal to a broad audience on the one hand while striving to create the idea of a limited supply in order to maintain high prices on the other hand (Okonkwo, 2009). Therefore, in-depth insights are needed on which content strategies are most rewarding for luxury brands in particular.

To conclude, Instagram can be a valuable asset for luxury brands to reach consumers and become an important touch point in their customer journey (Lemon & Verhoef, 2016). Content is key, whereby entertaining and engaging content is likely to result in the best outcomes. Moreover, as people are now able to directly purchase from Instagram stories, it has the potential to become a veritable sales channel as well.

REFERENCES

AGICHTEIN, E., CASTILLO, C., DONATO, D., GIONIS, A. & MISHNE, G., 2008, Finding high-quality content in social media. In M. NAJORK, A. Z. BRODER & S. CHAKRABARTI (eds.), *WSDM* (p./pp. 183-194): ACM.

ALHABASH, S., & MA, M., 2017, A tale of four platforms: Motivations and uses of Facebook, Twitter, Instagram, and Snapchat among college students? *Social Media + Society, 3*(1), 1–13.

ATWAL, G. & WILLIAMS, A., 2009, Luxury brand marketing – the experience is everything!, *Journal of Brand Management, 16*(5 & 6), 338–46.

BEATTY, S. E., & TALPADE, S., 1994, Adolescent influence in family decision making: A replication with extension. *Journal of Consumer Research, 21*(2), 332-341.

BERNOFF, J., & LI, C., 2008, Harnessing the power of the oh-sosocial web. *MIT Sloan Management Review, 49*, 36–42.

BLANKS, T., 2014, *Fall 2014 Ready-To-Wear Chanel.* Retrieved from: http://www.vogue.com/fashion-shows/fall-2014-ready-to-wear/chanel

CHEN, C-F. & CHANG, Y-Y., 2008, Airline brand equity, brand preference, and purchase intentions–The moderating effects of switching costs. *Journal of Air Transport Management, 14*, 40-42

CHEVALIER, M. & GUTASZ, M., 2012, Luxury retail management: How the world's top brands provide quality product and service support. Hoboken, NJ: Wiley.

COBB-WALGREN, C.J., RUBLE, C.A. & DONTHU, N., 1995, Brand Equity, Brand Preference, and Purchase Intent. *Journal of Advertising, 24*(3), 25-40.

DAUGHERTY, T., EASTIN, M. & BRIGHT, L., 2008, Exploring Consumer Motivations for Creating User Generated Content. *Journal of Interactive Advertising, 8*(2), 16–25.

DE SOUZA, I. M. & FERRIS, S. P., 2015, Social media marketing in luxury retail, *International Journal of Online Marketing, 5*(2), 18–36.

DEVAL, H., MANTEL, S. P., KARDES, F. R., & POSAVAC, S. S., 2013, How naive theories drive opposing inferences from the same information. *Journal of Consumer Research, 39*(6), 1185-1201.

DE VEIRMAN, M., CAUBERGHE, V., & HUDDERS, L., 2017, Marketing through Instagram influencers: the impact of number of followers and product divergence on brand attitude. *International Journal of Advertising, 36*(5), 798–828.

DE VRIES, L, GENSLER, S. & LEEFLANG, P. S. H., 2012, Popularity of Brand Posts on Brand Fan Pages: An Investigation of the Effects of Social Media Marketing. *Journal of Interactive* Marketing, 26 (2), 83–91.

GOH, K. Y., HENG, C. S., & LIN, Z., 2013, Social media brand community and consumer behavior: Quantifying the relative impact of user- and marketer-generated content. *Information Systems Research, 24*(1), 88–107.

GOLDSMITH, R. E., & HOROWITZ, D., 2006, Measuring motivations for online opinion speaking. *Journal of Interactive Advertising, 6*(2), 1–16.

GODEY, B., MANTHIOU, A., PEDERZOLI, D., ROKKA, J. AIELLO, G. DONVITO, R. & SINGH, R., 2016, Social media marketing efforts of luxury brands: Influence on brand equity and consumer behavior, *Journal of Business Research, 69*(12), 5833-5841.

GREWAL, D., KRISHNAN, R., BAKER, J. and BORIN, N., 1998, The Effect of Store Name, Brand Name and Price Discounts on Consumers' Evaluations and Purchase Intentions. *Journal of Retailing, 74*, 331-352.

GREWAL, D., MONROE, K. B. & KRISHNAN, R., 1998, The Effects of Price-Comparison Advertising on Buyers' Perceptions of Acquisition Value, Transaction Value and Behavioral Intentions. *Journal o fMarketing, 62* (April), 46-59.

GRUEN, T. W., OSMONBEKOV, T. & CZAPLEWSKI, A. J., 2006, eWOM: The Impact of Customer-to-Customer Online Know-How Exchange on Customer Value and Loyalty. *Journal of Business Research, 59*(4), 449–56.

HENNING, N., WIEDMANN, K. P. & KLARMANN, C., 2012, Luxury brands in the digital age – exclusivity versus ubiquity. *Marketing Review St. Gallen, 29*(1), 30-35.
KAPFERER, J.-N., 2015, *Kapferer on luxury: how luxury brands can grow yet remain rare.* London, United Kingdom; Philadelphia: Kogan Page.
KAPFERER, J-N. and BASTIEN, V., 2012, The luxury strategy: break the rules of marketing to build luxury brands (2nd edn). London: Kogan-Page.
KASTANAKIS, M.N. & BALABANIS, G., 2014, Explaining variation in conspicuous luxury consumption: An individual differences' perspective. *Journal of Business Research, 67*(10), 2147–2154.
KAYE, B. K., 2007, *Web site story: An exploratory study of blog use motivations.* In M. TREMAYNE (Ed.), Blogging, citizenship and the future of media (pp. 127-148). New York, NY: Routledge
KELLY, L., KERR, G., & DRENNAN, J., 2010, Avoidance of advertising in social networking sites: The teenage perspective. *Journal of interactive advertising, 10*, 16–27.
KIM, A. J., & KO, E., 2010, Impacts of Luxury Fashion Brand's Social Media Marketing on Customer Relationship and Purchase Intention. *Journal of Global Fashion Marketing, 1*(3), 164–171.
KIM, A. J., & KO, E., 2012, Do social media marketing activities enhance customer equity? An empirical study of luxury fashion brand. *Journal of Business Research, 65*(10), 1480–1486.
KIM, K. H., PARK, S. Y., LEE, S., KNIGHT, D. K., XU, B., JEON, B. J., & MOON, H. I., 2010, Examining the relationships among attitude toward luxury brands, customer equity, and customer lifetime value in a Korean context. *Journal of Global Scholars of Marketing Science, 20*, 27–34.
KO, E., PHAU, I., & AIELLO, G., 2016, Luxury brand strategies and customer experiences: Contributions to theory and practice. *Journal of Business Research, 69*(12), 5749-5752.
LEE, J. E., HUR, S., & WATKINS, B., 2018, *Visual communication of luxury fashion brands on social media: effects of visual complexity and brand familiarity. Journal of Brand Management, 25(5), 449–462.*
LEMON, K. N., & VERHOEF, P. C., 2016, Understanding customer experience and the customer journey. *Journal of Marketing, AMA/MSI Special Issue vol. 80*(November 2016), 1–62.
MALHOTRA, A., MALHOTRA, C. K. & SEE, A., 2013, How to Create Brand Engagement on Facebook. *MIT Sloan Management Review, 54*(2), 18-20.
MCCRACKEN, G., 2005, *Culture and Consumption II: Marketing, Meaning and Brand Management.* Bloomington, IN: Indiana University Press.
MENKES, S., 2017, *#SuzyPFW: Chanel – Ground Control To Major Karl.* Retrieved from: http://www.vogue.co.uk/article/suzymenkes-paris-autumn-winter-2017-chanel

MUNTINGA, D. G., MOORMAN, M., & SMIT, E. G., 2011, Introducing COBRA as exploring motivations for corporate-related social media use. *International Journal of Advertising, 30*(1), 13-46.
OKONKWO, U., 2010, *Luxury online: styles, systems, strategies.* Basingstoke: Palgrave Macmillan.
PARK, N., KEE, K. F., & VALENZUELA, S., 2009, Being immersed in social networking environment: Facebook groups, uses and gratifications, and social outcomes. *CyberPsychology and Behavior, 12*, 729-733.
PHAN, M., THOMAS, R., & HEINE, K., 2011, Social media and luxury brand management: The case of Burberry. *Journal of Global Fashion Marketing, 2*(4), 213–222.
RAMBOURG, E., 2014, *The bling dynasty: Why the reign of Chinese Luxury shoppers has only just begun.* Hoboken, NJ: Wiley.
RUST, R.T., LEMON, K.N. and ZEITHAML, V.A., *2004,* Return *on* Marketing Using Customer-Equity to Focus Marketing Strategy. *Journal of Marketing, 68*, 109-127.
SCHMENNER, R.W., 1986, How can service businesses survive and prosper. *Sloan Management Review. 27*(3). 21-32.
SCHIVINSKI, B. & DABROWSKI, D., 2013, The effect of social media communication on consumer perceptions of brands. *Journal of Marketing Communications, 22*(2), 189-214.
STEINMAN, M., & HAWKINS, M., 2010, When marketing though social media, legal risks can go viral. *Intellectual Property & Technology Law Journal, 22*(8), 1-9.
STEWART, D. W. & PAVLOU, P. A., 2009, From consumer response to active consumer: Measuring the effectiveness of interactive media. *Journal of the Academy of Marketing Science, 30*(4), 376-396.
TURK, B., SCHOLZ, M., & BERRESHEIM, P., 2012, Measuring service quality in online luxury goods retailing. *Journal of Electronic Commerce Research, 13*(1), 88-103.
VOGEL, V., EVANSCHITZKY, H. & RAMASESHAN, B., 2008, Customer Equity Drivers and Future Sales. *Journal of Marketing, 72*(6), 98-108.
VOLLMER, C. & PRECOURT, G., 2008, Always on: Advertising, marketing, and media in an era of consumer control. New York: McGraw-Hill.
WHITING, A., & WILLIAMS, D., 2013, Why people use social media: a uses and gratifications approach. *Qualitative Market Research: An International Journal, 16*(4), 362-369.
YOO, B., DONTHU, N. & LEE, S., 2000, An Examination of Selected Marketing Mix Elements and Brand Equity. Journal of the Academy of Marketing Science, 28(2), 195–211.

LUXURY CONNOISSEURS AND TWITTER: AN EMPIRICAL STUDY OF RELATIONSHIP BETWEEN VOLUME OF TWEETS FROM LUXURY BRANDS AND THEIR STOCK PRICE RETURNS IN THE US

Nabanita TALUKDAR, *DBA*
Hult International Business School
Golden Gate University, San Francisco
email-ntalukdar@ggu.edu

ABSTRACT

The world's financial communities take a huge interest in luxury brands, and financial markets are attracted to them. In today's Web 2.0 climate, characterized by user-generated content (UGC) and social networking sites (SNS) such as Twitter, luxury brands are utilizing Twitter to attract loyal as well as aspirational consumers. This study investigates the effect of marketers' use of Twitter on the stock prices of luxury brands. Using stock return response modeling, this study fits three regression models that use tweet volume from luxury brands, retweet volume of brands' tweets, and their ratio to predict the variability in their stock price returns, after accounting for market returns. The results show that there are negative correlations among Twitter variables and stock returns of luxury brands, after accounting for market returns. The research findings have implications for advancing the understanding of the link between social media marketing and financial interface.

Keywords: Twitter, tweet, retweet, electronic word of mouth (eWOM), luxury brands, stock return response modeling.
JEL codes: M30, M31

Acknowledgement: The paper is based out of author's doctoral dissertation at Golden Gate University, San Francisco. The author is also thankful to the reviews received at the following conferences -Twitter for Research, LVMH-SMU, and The Mystique of Luxury brands.

INTRODUCTION

Luxury brands want to maintain their exclusivity in order to protect their intrinsic aspirational qualities. The democratizing power of the web 2.0 can be at odds with the image of a luxury brand, since the brand could potentially lose its luxury character if it becomes too available (Dubois & Paternault, 1995). However, due to the wide reach of the web, luxury brands have started participating in social media. This participation is crucial to maintain luxury brands' relevance and to attract loyal as well as aspirational consumers.

Luxury brands have high gross margins and strong cash flows. Luxury brands' stocks are often highly valued, and the world's financial communities take a huge interest in luxury brands, (Kapferer & Tabatoni, 2011). According to the Efficient Market Hypothesis (EMH), stock market prices are mainly affected by news rather than their present and past prices (Fama, 1965). Since news influences stock market prices, it is reasonable to expect that social media as a news medium may play a significant role in informing the stock market (Depken II, 2001). Social networking sites (SNS) such as Twitter generate large volumes of news that contain vital information about companies as well as the views and opinions of SNS users. This high volume of news could potentially have influence on the stock market. Luxury brands tweet brand content and use Twitter as a marketing channel. This is done to facilitate consumer engagement which may create electronic word of mouth communication (eWOM), and, consequently, may affect shareholder value. Previous research (Asur & Huberman, 2010; Bollen, Mao, & Zeng, 2010; Evangelopoulos, Magro, & Sidorova, 2012) suggests that the information contained in Twitter data is predictive of stock performances. Despite the potential of Twitter, very little attention has been devoted to studying how luxury brands' Twitter usage may affect their stock prices. The main objective of my study is to address this gap. Specifically, the purpose of my study, the first in the context of luxury brands, is to examine possible correlations between the volume of luxury brands' Twitter feeds, retweets of luxury brands' tweets, ratio of retweets to tweets, and their respective stock prices. I used stock return response modeling to fit three regression models that use these variables and their respective lags across 6-trading days to predict the variability in stock price returns, after accounting for market returns. My empirical study is based on these variables from 6 luxury brands across six diverse sectors, and their stock price returns, after accounting for market returns for 252 trading days. The results show that tweet volume from luxury brands' can predict their stock price returns, after accounting for market returns. I find that tweet volume from luxury brands with a lag of 4 trading days is negatively correlated with their stock price returns, after accounting for market returns.

In the sections below, I discuss the following: theoretical foundations and literature review, conceptual model and hypotheses, research methodology, results, discussion and future research directions, and conclusions and implications.

1. THEORETICAL FOUNDATIONS AND LITERATURE REVIEW

1.1. Luxury brands

Vickers and Renand (2003) suggest that "luxury goods can be differentiated from 'non' luxury goods based on the dimensions of functionality, experience and symbolic interaction" (p. 459). The purchase of luxury brands is associated with emotional and hedonic benefits, while the purchase of value brands is associated with functional and utilitarian satisfaction (Hagtvedt & Patrick, 2009). Multiple motivations such as sociability, self-expression, a desire of differentiation drive conspicuous consumption of luxury brands (Belk, 1988). However, the perceived level of luxury associated with a brand is determined by the consumers and the context. Alleres (1990) developed a hierarchy consisting of three levels of luxury accessibility based on the dimensions of socio-economic status and marketing of the brands. Accessible luxury is located at the bottom of the hierarchy. This level describes luxury products attainable by the "middle" socio-economic class who use their purchase behavior to raise their status. Accessories from Coach and Michael Kors are marketed as accessible luxury. Intermediate luxury is the next level in the hierarchy, and this level describes luxury products attainable by the "professional" socio-economic class. Tumi luggage and Mont Blanc pens are marketed as intermediate luxury. Inaccessible luxury is at the top of the hierarchy. This level is associated with the "elite" socio-economic class. Consumers derive exceptional social stature from the consumption of the extremely high-priced products at this level. Rolex watches and Rolls Royce cars are marketed as inaccessible luxury.

In sum, the consumption of luxury brands can be attributed to the following dimensions: achieving social status, purchasing a dream, and experiencing emotions (e.g. Vickers & Renand, 2003; Dubois & Paternault, 1995; Holbrook & Hirschman, 1982). Consequently, luxury brands require a distinctive approach to brand management, and consumers should be able to connect with the brands in an extraordinary way (Kapferer & Bastein, 2009). Using brand-related experiences to connect with consumers is the key to luxury brands' long-term success (Atwal & Williams, 2009). Such brand-related experiences must be multi-sensory and experiential (e.g. Kapferer & Bastein, 2009; Atwal & Williams, 2009). Louis Vuitton' s 2018 Cruise collections is an example of brand-related experience. One of their globe-trotting shows was staged at

Kyoto's Miho museum, designed by renowned architect I. M. Pei, where models walked on a suspension bridge overlooking the Shigaraki mountains. This brand-related real- world experience can be translated into the world of Web 2.0 using brand content. "Brand content gives content, depth and emotion to a luxury brand by emphasizing the cultural dimensions of a brand and its intangibles. Brand content engages consumers to relate to the brand because it does not talk about its products, but a domain of mutual interest between the brand and its public" (Kapferer, 2012, p. 142).

1.2. Luxury brands and social media

Because the ubiquity of digital communication is at odds with the image of rarity and exclusivity associated with luxury brands, such brands may be apprehensive towards using the internet as a marketing tool. However, with the growth of internet media, it has become necessary to include digital platforms in luxury brand communication strategies. Okonkwo (2009) noted that the consumer is in total control of luxury brands on social media platforms. Consumers not only receive and interpret messages from luxury brands but also decide whether to endorse these messages. It is ultimately the consumer's choice to spread such endorsements or to criticize the brands. Such actions generate discussions about the brand within the consumer's online network and can result in influencing millions of people around the world (Okonkwo, 2009). In order to mitigate the loss of control on social media, luxury brands focus on engaging their clients in a strong dialogue. Such dialogues are double-sided communication, which allows luxury brands to know more about their clients and more accurately predict their desires (Kim & Ko, 2012). This kind of communication is done with an aim of motivating clients to endorse the respective luxury brand and spread that endorsement in their online communities.

1.3. Twitter and electronic word of mouth (eWOM)

On Twitter, companies broadcast tweets as marketing materials in order to attract consumers. Companies strive to form a brand community on Twitter; they want consumers to become their followers, and they also follow consumers. Companies can increase their brand awareness and number of followers by tweeting more frequently and by following more consumers. The higher a company's tweet volume, the greater the impact it has on the Twitter community. From a company's tweets, followers learn more about the brand, and therefore have more things to share about the brand. The marketing potential of Twitter is thus tremendous, as the platform not only allows companies to reach a wide audience, but also lets them promote messages to their self-chosen followers. These consumers can further influence other consumers who are connected with them but not with the brand. Marketers can enhance brand value via eWOM through Twitter's "retweeting" function, which forwards "others' messages to one's own network of followers, [which is] implicit, and often explicit, endorsement" (See, Malhotra, & Malhotra (2012), p. 61). The researchers point out that by retweeting about their favorite brands, brand followers become brand advocates within their own social network. Boyd, Golder, and Lotan (2010) examined the exchange features of retweeting on Twitter. Retweeting not only allow users to share information with others but also encourages them to exchange their opinions about the information. Consequently, this feature results in a large volume of user-generated tweets and influences eWOM. One of the most important advantages of retweets is their wide reach. When a follower retweets a company's tweet, it is likely to be read by more recipients due to the familiarity and the credibility of the source. Some of these new recipients may decide to follow the brand after reading the content of the retweet, thereby increasing the brand's network. Each Twitter user who retweets the original tweet acts as an influencer. For this reason, it is important for companies to publish tweets that will win the attention of their followers and motivate them to retweet.

However, on Twitter marketers face the constant struggle of developing a true luxury brand without compromising its image through excessive distribution. This is because luxury brands' attributes of rarity and exclusivity are instrumental in increasing their desirability. Using Twitter, luxury brands can tweet selective brand content, thereby spreading the brand's dream and attracting new consumers. Such brand content must be "informative/discovery (e.g. invitations to meet JC Elena, the 'nose' of Hermes fragrances), entertaining (e.g. fashion show from LVMH shared on their Twitter handle), practical/useful (e.g. make-up tutorials posted by Chanel on Twitter)" (Kapferer, 2012, p. 142-143). Clearly for luxury brands, all the followers on their Twitter handle are not their potential consumers, but they may be potential advocates. This is because in the digital world, consumers can boast about brand affinities without owning them and this concept is called conspicuous virtual consumption (Belk, 2013). Most consumers consider an association with a luxury brand on Twitter as status symbol, and for personal branding efforts consumers broadcast the association within their social circles (Hennigs, Wiedmann, & Klarmann, 2012). Thus, in order to draw attention such consumers retweet tweets from luxury brands and thereby promoting the luxury brands.

1.4. Twitter as predictor of stock market price

Company--generated tweets are marketing materials that primarily offer brand-related information to consumers. Retweets, on the other hand, are eWOM, which promotes information diffusion, generates immediate sentiment, and provokes emotional reactions towards brands. Most prior research has focused on studying whether Twitter can be a predictor of stock market price. The studies have found that the information generated from Twitter has an impact on stock market price. For example, Feldman (2013) found that sentiments (i.e. opinions of authors about specific entities) generated on Twitter can affect a brand' s reputation, and utilization of such sentiments in selecting stocks can lead to higher portfolio returns. Bollen et al. (2010) found that public mood (i.e. calm and happy moods) as measured by a large collection of tweets is predictive of Dow Jones Industrial Average (DJIA) values. Evangelopoulos et. al (2012) suggested that the information carried by Twitter data can be used to predict the performance of individual stocks. The researchers found that high volume of tweets (i.e. informative and entertaining brand-related information) has a positive effect on company's stock performance. Overall, previous studies have focused mostly on tweet content, but very little attention has been devoted to studying the relationship between the volume of company-generated content on Twitter from luxury brands and its impact on respective stock prices.

1.5. Marketing's impact on financial performance of firms

The link between marketing and financial performance has received much research attention. Mizik and Jacobson (2003) showed a link between a company's marketing strategy and its stock performance. In the study, while the focus of a company's marketing strategy was either value creation or value appropriation, the focus of the company's long-term financial performance was the stock return. The analysis of the stock return was built on the premise of the efficient market hypothesis (EMH) using stock return response modeling. Stock return response modeling is used to establish whether investors perceive information related to continuous marketing actions (such as advertising spending) as contributing to future cash flows (Srinivasan & Hanssens, 2009). According to the EMH, an efficient market is one in which security prices "fully reflect" all available information at any time (Fama, Fisher, Jensen, & Roll, 1969; Fama, 1970). So, the current price of a security represents market expectations of the discounted value of a firm's future cash flow. The market reacts to unanticipated factors such as a change in marketing strategy, and this is reflected in the new stock price. Abnormal returns provide an estimate of the difference in market value before and after such unanticipated factor. Introduced by Sharpe (1964), Capital Asset Pricing Model (CAPM) also known as the as the market model, is the most extensively applied method for modeling the effects of risk on stock returns. On the social media platform, few studies (e.g., Plangger 2012;

O' Connor, 2012) have focused on examining the effect that firms' social media marketing actions have on their respective stock price performance.

2. CONCEPTUAL FRAMEWORK AND HYPOTHESES

The conceptual model (see figure 1) for this research is based on the understanding of Twitter's potential to influence eWOM. Companies need to broadcast tweets as marketing materials in order to attract consumers (See et al., 2012). The higher the volume of tweets from a company (i.e. brand content), the positive effect on its stock price with lag (e.g. with lag 1) (e.g. Evangelopolous et al. (2012). However, luxury brands must tweet selective brand content in order to mitigate the challenges posed by digital communication. Consequently, I believe that a high volume of tweets from luxury brands would affect the brand by lowering the brand's dream value among consumers. Hence, I propose that the volume of tweets from luxury brands would correlate negatively with the brand's stock price. Specifically, I hypothesize,

H_1: The volume of tweets by luxury brand companies correlates negatively with their respective brand company stock price returns, after accounting for market returns.

The brand content from luxury brands engage their followers in a strong dialogue on Twitter (e.g. Kim & Ko, 2012). The followers connected to such brands on Twitter are not only passionate about the brands but are much more than fans (Kapferer, 2015). They want to maintain an exclusive relationship with the brand and want to interact with other passionate followers. I refer to them as 'connoisseurs' who tend to retweet the tweets from the luxury brands. Their retweets further disseminate the luxury dream and create eWOM. Previous research (Zhang, Jansen, & Chowdhury, 2011; Katz & Lazarsfeld, 1955; Barton, 2006) has shown that eWOM affects purchase intent. Since luxury companies tweet brand content and since previous research has shown that there is a significant positive relationship between branding and stock prices, the marketing action of luxury companies' tweeting brand content would lead to high volume of retweets (i.e. eWOM) (Barth, Clement, Foster, & Kasznik, 1998). The high volume of retweets would translate into shareholder value (i.e. stock performance) which is one of the most important benchmarks for measuring marketing performance. Specifically, I hypothesize,

H_2: The volume of retweets of tweets by luxury brand companies correlates positively to respective brand company stock price returns, after accounting for market returns.

H_3: The ratio of the volume of retweets to the volume of luxury brand companies' tweets correlates positively with their respective brand company stock price returns, after accounting for market returns.

Figure 1. Conceptual model

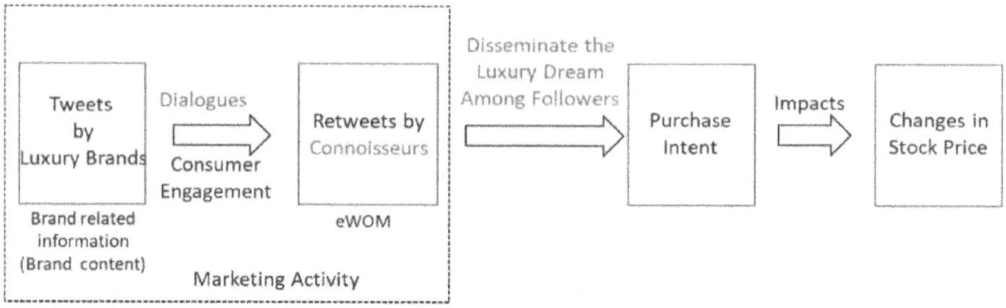

3. RESEARCH METHODOLOGY

3.1. Data

The study used a sample of 6 luxury brand companies in six sectors: apparel, retail, jewelry, automobiles, footwear, and beauty products (see Table 1). The selected companies were publicly listed and had an active official Twitter account for the 12 months under study. The time frame for the study was January 1, 2014 through December 31, 2014 (i.e. 252 trading days). The luxury brands were selected from the accessible and intermediate levels of luxury; most of the luxury brands in the inaccessible level of luxury are privately owned and have no publicly available stock prices. The six luxury brands were selected after consulting articles and reports on luxury goods such as "Global Powers of Luxury Goods 2014" (Deloitte Touche Tohmatsu Limited, 2014), "Top 15 Best Selling Luxury Car Brands in the US" (The Richest, 2015), "North America's High-End Department Stores & Shops" (The International Man, n.d.), and "The Top 10 Luxury Shoe Brands" (The Richest, 2013). To measure the volume of tweets and retweets, this study collected the tweets from the official Twitter accounts (i.e. US) of the chosen companies over a period of 12 months. Data of the variables—volume of tweets, volume of retweets, and stock prices—were collected daily in order to normalize the data across the different companies. The Twitter data was gathered using the tool Twitonomy Premium, which is a web-based Twitter analytics and monitoring tool (http://www.twitonomy.com). Archives of the tweets as well as detailed analytics were downloaded and saved for the designated study period. Each tweet contains a date and time stamp from Twitter marking when it was posted, which made it possible to reference the tweet to a stock-trading day. The daily closing stock prices of the companies and the market index (S&P 500) were extracted from Yahoo! Finance for the 12-month period over which the counts of tweets and retweets were collected. To test the hypotheses, the initial statistical tool used was correlation. The correlation was calculated using the Pearson correlation coefficient between the Twitter variables (volume of tweets, volume of retweets, and the ratio of retweets to tweets) and the stock prices for the respective companies. The predictive relationship was tested using multiple regression models. Since multiple regression can rule out certain alternative explanations for an association such as spuriousness or epiphenomenality, it was used to test the predictive relationship (Hayes, 2018). The daily stock price was the dependent variable, and the daily Twitter variables were the predictor variables. Stock return response model was used to capture the exogenous effects of stock market volatility. Statistical software SAS was used to perform the analyses. In accordance with the conventional guidelines, the alpha levels of 0.05 was accepted as significant results for this research.

Table 1: Sample of Luxury Brands Selected for Research

Serial Number	Brands	Stock Symbol	Brand Category	Sector	Official Twitter Handle
1	Ralph Lauren	RL	luxury	Apparel	@RalphLauren
2	Dillard's	DDS	luxury	Specialty Retail	@Dillards
3	Tiffany & Co.	TIF	luxury	Jewelry	@TiffanyAndCo
4	Tesla Motors	TSLA	luxury	Automobiles	@TeslaMotors
5	Steve Madden[1]	SHOO	luxury	Footwear	@SteveMadden
6	Coty	COTY	luxury	Beauty products	@COTYInc

[1] Steve Madden enters luxury market with Brian Atwood acquisition

3.2. Pre-test

In order to provide empirical evidence that luxury brands' share brand content and engage their followers in dialogues, I conducted a pre-test on one of the luxury brands. I visited the Twitter handle of Ralph Lauren (RL) and downloaded RL 's tweets for the year 2014. Following that I extracted the textual content from RL's collection of tweets using latent semantic analysis (LSA), a topic extraction methodology. LSA is a method that extracts the semantic and conceptual content in textual data. I found that the most frequent keyword in RL's archives of tweets was Pinkponypromise. On further research, I found that Pinkponypromise is a cause related to cancer research and treatment which RL supports. During October 2014 RL ran a specific cause-related campaign on their social media. On Twitter every time someone shared their personal message on wellness, encouragement or prevention with a picture and hashtag #Pinkponypromise for every photo posted, RL would donate $10 to help fight breast cancer. RL had also made an announcement that they would be following and tracking posts daily and would donate an extra dollar for each friend (up to 5 friends) tagged in a photo on Twitter. Thus, Ralph Lauren's tweets were informative and entertaining brand content.

3.3. Method

This study investigates the influence of company-generated tweets on stock return anomalies. The model for this research is based on a study done by Evangelopoulos et al. (2012). The researchers fitted a regression model that used tweet volumes and tweet topic strength to predict the variability in stock prices. In this research I used tweet volume and its lags as predictors in the regression model, thereby extending the research of Evangelopoulos et al. (2012). Additionally, I included additional information in the predictive model: the effects of retweet volumes of company-generated tweets, as well as the ratio of retweet to tweet volumes and their lags on stock prices. Consequently, tweet volume/retweet volume/ratio $(TV_{ij})/(RTV_{ij})/(\frac{RTV_{ij}}{TV_{ij}})$ and up to six-day lags for tweet volume/retweet volume/ratio $(TV_{ij,t-k})/(RTV_{ij,t-k})/(\frac{RTV_{ij}}{TV_{ij}})_{t-k}$ over 252 trading days and across 6 companies are used as predictors for stock return anomaly (RA_{ij}) obtained from company j on trading day i:

$$RA_{ij} = \beta_o + \theta TV_{ij} + \sum_{k=0}^{6} \beta_k TV_{ij,t-k} + \varepsilon_{ij,} 1 \leq i \leq 252, 1 \leq j \leq 6 \quad (1)$$

$$RA_{ij} = \beta'_o + \theta' RTV_{ij} + \sum_{k=0}^{6} \beta_k' RTV_{ij,t-k} + \varepsilon'_{ij,} 1 \leq i \leq 252, 1 \leq j \leq 6 \quad (2)$$

$$RA_{ij} = \beta''_o + \theta''\frac{RTV_{ij}}{TV_{ij}} + \sum_{k=0}^{6} \beta_k''(\frac{RTV_{ij,t-k}}{TV_{ij,t-k}}) + \varepsilon''_{ij,} 1 \leq i \leq 252, 1 \leq j \leq 6 \ (3)$$

I used stock return response modeling to study the impact of the volume of Twitter data on stock price, after considering market fluctuations (Evangelopoulos et al., 2012). This method is similar to an event study; the only major difference between the two is the characteristics of the inputs. While the inputs of an event study are discrete, in the stock return model, the inputs are continuous (Srinivasan & Hanssens, 2009). This method is built on the premise of the efficient market hypothesis (EMH). The current price of a security represents market expectations of the discounted value of the firm's future cash flow. That is,

$$P_t = \sum_{\tau=t}^{\infty} \left(\frac{1}{1+r}\right)^{\tau-t} E(X_{\tau}))$$

where P_t is the dividend stock price at the time period t, X_τ is the net cash flow at period τ, and r is the appropriate discount rate for the market expectation of the firm's future cash flows. When an event occurs, the market rapidly adjusts its financial effects into the price of a security. Positive (or negative) developments affecting cash flows result in increases (or decreases) in stock prices. This adjustment provides a way to evaluate the financial effects related to a variation in a marketing measure. The percentage change in stock price surrounding an event (after controlling for expected movement in the stock price) reflects market expectations of the long-term financial impact of the event. Thus, performing a regression analysis on stock returns based on changes in a marketing measure—for example, consumer engagement in social media, brand perceptions—provides insights into market expectations of the long-term effects of the change.

According to the EMH, only unexpected variables should demonstrate an association with the stock return. Excess stock return (also known as abnormal stock return) is a measure of the difference between the actual return and the expected return if the event had not occurred. Because of market efficiency, the estimate of excess stock return provides an unbiased estimate of the future earnings (change in market value) generated by the event (Fama, 1970, 1991). Bollen et al. (2010) and Evangelopoulos et al. (2012) employed this theory and found that Twitter data related to firms affects public sentiment regarding those firms and leads to stock price fluctuation. Thus, changes in stock price following the sharing and assimilation of Twitter data do provide an unbiased estimate of the future long-term earnings from those actions.

The next section discusses how EMH along with stock return response modeling is implemented in the study of the empirical relationship between tweet volume and stock price of luxury brands. In order to test the predictive relationship between Twitter variables and stock returns, it is important to control the dependent variable. In the stock return response modeling approach, the dependent variable is controlled through market model estimates. Stock return anomaly used as the dependent variable in this model represents that component in a stock return that cannot be explained by movements of the market. The estimate of stock return anomaly provides an unbiased estimate of future earnings (changes in market value) generated by the marketing action. In order to depict the time series properties of tweet and retweet volume, time series model estimates are used as proxy for the independent variables (which is the measure of the unanticipated component). The flowchart of the regression model is outlined in figure 2.

Figure 2. Flowchart of the Regression Model.

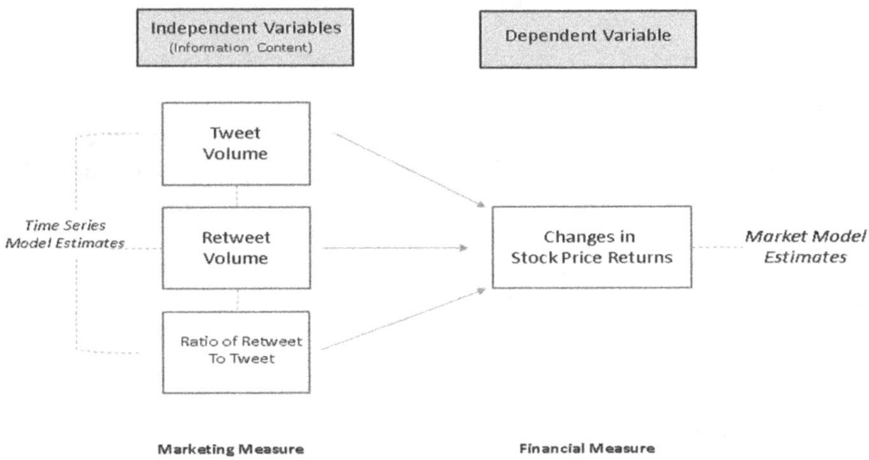

3.4. Modeling expected returns

My study follows the methodology used in the research on Twitter macro messages and stock price by Evangelopoulos et al. (2012). The market model is used to estimate the expected stock returns in this research (e.g. Brown & Warner, 1985) and the next section explains how the market model is used in their work.

The market model was first introduced by Sharpe (1964). Also known as the Capital Asset Pricing Model (CAPM), it is the most extensively applied method for modeling the effects of risk on stock returns. Evangelopoulos et al. (2012) explain Sharpe's idea as follows,

According to CAPM, the return r_i on security i for some given period is associated with a fixed component, a_{iI} and a variable component $\beta_{iI}r_I$, where r_I is the return of the market index I over that period. β_{iI} is known as the beta coefficient of security i with respect to market index I over that period. Beta coefficient is the measure of volatility or systematic risk of a security or portfolio in comparison to the market as a whole. The market model parameters a_i and β_{iI} are estimated by regression analysis. The regression model used is,

$$\widehat{r_i} = \alpha_{iI} + \beta_{iI}r_I + \varepsilon_{iI} \qquad (4)$$

Beta and alpha coefficients are estimated by fitting the regression model (4). Using the data from 300 trading days (October 19, 2012 through December 31, 2013) immediately preceding the main research study period (Jan 1, 2014 through December 31, 2014), and using Standard & Poor's'- (S&P) 500 index, adjusted for splits and dividends as the market index, the market model (4) is fitted for each of the 6 companies in the study's sample. Following this method, 6 pairs of alpha and beta coefficient estimates were obtained.

The stock return anomalies (RA_i) are derived using the following method,

$$RA_i = r_i - \widehat{r_i} = r_i - \left(\hat{\alpha}_{iI} + \hat{\beta}_{iI}r_I\right) \quad (5)$$

Equation (5) shows the return that is expected from an association of the stock return with the market return. Stock return anomalies thus represent that component in a stock return that cannot be explained by the movements of the market. Using the 6 pairs of estimated alpha and beta coefficients, the S&P 500, and individual stock returns from the main research study period (the 252 trading days between January 1, 2014, and December 31, 2014), values are obtained in (5) for 12 companies. The values in (5) are obtained for 252 trading days for a total of 1512 data points. (pp. 254-255)

3.5. Assessing estimates of unanticipated components

The unanticipated components of a series (the independent variables in a stock return response model) are measured utilizing forecasts from the time series model[2] as a substitute for market expectations. The difference between the actual and predicted values (that is, the regression residual) serves as the unanticipated component.

Time series models are econometric models, which utilize time series forecasts as a proxy of market expectations (Cornell, 1983). Time series models provide the most reasonable approximation for market expectations and reduce the measurement error of the regression coefficients of the independent variables. In this study I used a first order

[2] For example, a first order autoregressive model has been widely used to depict the time series properties of advertising expenditures (Aaker & Jacobson, 1994).

autoregressive model[3] to depict the time series properties of tweet and retweet volumes, i.e.

$$TV_{ij} = A_0 + A_1 TV_{ij-1} + \delta_{ij} \quad (6)$$

$$RTV_{ij} = A_0{}' + A_1{}' RTV_{ij-1} + \delta_{ij}{}' \quad (7)$$

where, tweet volume (TV_{ij}) and retweet volume (RTV_{ij}) are from company j on trading day i.

The residuals obtained from these models provide the estimate of the unanticipated components of the series. These unanticipated components are used as the explanatory variables in the estimation of the stock return response models (Equations (1), (2), and (3)).

3.6. Model assessing information content

The question that arises now is whether the information contained in company tweets and retweets (the time series residuals generated from the autoregressive models in equations (6) and (7)) affect stock returns (the return anomaly components obtained in equation (5)). Several recent studies in finance have questioned the assumptions of EMH and show that stock prices do not follow a random walk and can be predicted to some extent. Several studies (Brennan & Xia, 2001; Brav & Heaton, 2002) show that because of the effects of rational learning, stock prices move not only when new information becomes available but also when investors improve their understanding of the numerous economic relationships that influence the market equilibrium. A number of event studies in marketing have also found evidence for long-term effects on stock prices (also known as lag effect), suggesting market inefficiency. For this reason, it is important to study the lag effect of an event. Pauwels, Silva-Risso, Srinivasan and Hanssens (2004) investigated the lag effect of marketing actions such as new product introductions and promotional incentives on stock market performance. One of the findings of their study was that investor reaction to new product introduction occurs over time, indicating that financially useful information unfolds in the first two months after product launch. Company-generated tweets contain brand-related information such as new product announcements (See et al., 2012), and it is unlikely that the effect of such a marketing action would be limited to the day when the tweet is sent out because investors might not react immediately. The marketing action would continue to have an effect on investors for some time, though the effect would eventually significantly dissolve. Since the lag effect of the marketing action does diminish over a certain period of time, it is important to specify the length of time for the lags. This study posits that tweet volume, retweet volume, and their six-

[3] The appropriate autoregressive model will depend on the specific dynamic properties of the measure. Higher order autoregressive models are also used to characterize the dynamic behavior of a series (Mizik & Jacobson, 2003).

day lags will have effects on stock returns similar to those observed by Pauwels et al. (2004).

4. RESULTS

4.1. Empirical analysis, model validation and results

The Twitter posts and stock prices for 6 companies over a period over a period of 12 months (January to December 2014) were analyzed. In order to test the hypotheses, first I derived alpha and beta estimates for the 6 companies. The market model as described in (4) was used to derive six pairs of alpha and beta estimates (see table 2). Then, stock return anomalies were calculated using the formula described in (5). The correlations between stock return anomalies and tweet volume, retweet volume, ratio of retweet to tweet volume, and the respective lags of each of the variables over 6 trading days respectively were calculated for the luxury brands.

The next step was to examine whether company tweet volume, retweet volume of company tweets, the ratio of retweets to company tweets, and the respective lag of each of the variables over 6 trading days can be significant predictors of a company stock price. Regression models described in (1), (2), and (3) were used to test the predictive relationships. Stock return anomalies calculated using (5) were used as dependent variables in each of the regression models (1), (2), and (3). Initially, I tested the regression models in a pilot sample of two luxury brands from the Apparel and the Specialty retail sector. This test was undertaken to assess the validity of the model, to test its predictive accuracy, and to investigate the generalizability of the results. The regression models were then fitted for the entire set of luxury brands. I found that the result was consistent with the result obtained from the initial model tested in the pilot sample.

Table 2. Estimated Alpha and Beta Coefficients

Serial No.	Brands	Stock Symbol	Brand Category	Sector	Estimated alpha	Estimated beta
1	Ralph Lauren	RL	luxury	Apparel	-0.001020271	0.905834069
2	Dillard's	DDS	luxury	Specialty Retail	0.000165392	0.94877309
3	Tesla Motors	TSLA	luxury	Automobiles	0.004717346	1.113494239
4	Coty[4]	COTY	luxury	Beauty Products	-0.001141662	0.342659566
5	Tiffany & Co.	TIF	luxury	Jewelry	0.00039528	1.101757285
6	Steve Madden	SHOO	luxury	Footwear	-0.000066	0.945217196

[4]The alpha and beta of Coty was calculated using 140 trading days instead of 300 trading days because Coty became public on 6/13/2013

Tweet volume (with a lag of 4 trading days) is negatively correlated to the stock return anomalies of luxury brands (see Table 3). I found that retweet volume (with a lag of 1 trading day), ratio of retweets to company's tweets (with a lag of 3 and 6 trading days) are negatively correlated to the stock return anomalies of the luxury brands at higher levels of significance (i.e. $p<0.15$).

The luxury brands' result show that only tweet volume (with a lag of 4 trading days) with a negative coefficient is a significant predictor of stock price returns, after accounting for market returns (see Table 4). The regression model (1) explains that 0.39% variability in stock return anomalies of luxury brands is due to tweet volume (based on R^2 coefficient of the regression model), beyond what is explained by the fluctuations of the stock market. We found that retweet volume and their respective lags, ratio of retweets to tweets and their respective lags are not significant predictors of stock price returns, after accounting for market returns at $p<0.05$ (i.e. significant at $p<0.15$, which is a higher level of significance).

Table 3. Correlation Matrix of the entire set of luxury brands (Pearson Correlation Coefficients Prob >|r|under H_0:Rho=0)

Variables	Ranomaly	Level of Significance
TR4(Tweets_lag_4)	-0.06282	0.0146*
RTR1 (Retweets_lag_1)	-0.03991	0.1209 ***
TL3 (Ratio_lag_3)	-0.03828	0.1368***
TL6 (Ratio _lag_6)	-0.0381	0.1387***

*Significant at p<.05, *** p<0.15

Table 4. Multiple Regression results for the conceptual model (Luxury brands). Dependent Variable: Stock Return Anomalies (Ranomaly)[a]

Variable	Notation	Equation 1	Equation 2	Equation 3
Intercept		-0.00029145*	0.00029895***	-0.00024669**
		(0.00044109)	(0.00044161)	(0.00044209)
Tweets_lag_4_days	TR4	**-0.00137***		
		(0.00056148)		
Retweets_lag_1_day	RTR1		-0.00006582***	
			(0.00004241)	
Ratio_lag_3_days	TL3			-0.000000435869***
				(0.0000002917229)
Ratio_lag_6_days	TL6			-0.000000433797***
				(0.0000002917222)
R^2		**0.39%**	0.16%	0.29%
N		1512	1512	1512

[a]Coefficient estimates are presented on top line; standard errors are in parentheses.
*Significant (p<0.05), *** (p<0.15).

5. DISCUSSION AND FUTURE RESEARCH DIRECTIONS

Hypothesis 1 (The volume of tweets by luxury brand companies correlates negatively with their respective brand company stock price returns, after accounting for market returns) is supported for luxury brands. The Twitter variable, company tweet volume, which is a marketing action, carries information, as tweet volume (with a lag of 4 trading days) is a significant predictor of stock price returns for the luxury brands, after accounting for market returns (see Table 4). The companies' tweet volume (with a lag of 4 trading days) has a negative coefficient, suggesting that an increase in this variable has a negative impact on the stock price returns of luxury brands, after accounting for market returns. As mentioned in the literature review, it is important to consider the lag effect of an event because investors may not react to an event immediately. Investors' reactions may occur in the days following the event, so their reaction is not always evident on the day the event occurs. My results indicate the significance of the lag effect because the marketing action of luxury brands sending out a high volume of tweets does not have an immediate effect on stock price returns but does have an effect after a lag of 4 trading days. In particular, my results indicate that over time investors react negatively to the high volume of tweets from luxury brands.

Hypothesis 2 and hypothesis 3 are not supported for the entire set of luxury brands at 0.05 level of significance. Interestingly, these results are contradictory to the findings from previous research (i.e. more people talk about brands on digital media, the greater is the impact on the brand's stock price) (Awad & Zhang, 2006; Chevalier & Mayzlin, 2006; Duan, Gub, & Whinston, 2008; Liu, 2006; Zhu & Zhang, 2006). I find that for luxury brands, the more people talk about the brands on Twitter the reverse is the impact on the brand's stock price. One possible explanation for this could be that the volume of retweets of company-generated tweets simply isn't as influential for luxury brands. Prior research has shown that consumers trust individuals more than they trust companies, so it is possible that when Twitter users simply forward company-generated tweets from luxury brands, the value of their endorsement is relatively weak: The user is only repeating the company's content, not sharing anything original. A potential area of future research could be content analysis of the retweets of company-generated tweets; this could add value by differentiating retweets with meaningful additional information, such as a user's opinion of or personal experience with a brand, from retweets that simply "forward" the company's tweets without adding any information. Another possible area of future research could be content analysis of the company-generated tweets and study the impact of interaction between the content and volume of a luxury brand company's tweets on company's stock price.

CONCLUSION AND IMPLICATIONS

The objective of my research is to link the impact of social media marketing to the stock performance of luxury brands. Specifically, the purpose of my research is to examine the possible impact of the volume of luxury brands' Twitter feeds and their respective stock prices. In order to investigate this unexplored area, I extended the seminal research of Evangelopoulos et al. (2012) on using Twitter macro messages to help predict stock prices. I included tweet volume, retweet volume, ratio of retweet volume to company tweets, and their respective lags (over 6 trading days) in the predictive models. I examined the effects of the Twitter variables on stock price returns, after accounting for market returns for luxury brands. In order to examine these effects, a database of tweets, retweets, and stock prices of the respective brands was created. I also calculated the detailed analytics of the retweets for the study period. The methodology used in my research can serve as a useful managerial tool: managers can implement the tool to evaluate whether a company's marketing actions on SNS have an impact on shareholder value. As also mentioned in the discussion of the results section, my analyses clearly demonstrate that the Twitter variables carry information, and so it is crucial for managers to measure the distribution of eWOM. For luxury brands, I found that there is a negative correlation among Twitter variable (i.e. tweet volume) and stock returns, after accounting for market returns.

The research makes important academic and managerial contributions about digital communications of luxury brands, contributing to the literature across marketing, information science, and finance disciplines. The results of my research indicate that volume of tweets alone does not positively affect stock prices for luxury brands. While previous research argues that the higher the volume of company-generated tweets, the greater the impact on the company's Twitter community (Zhang et al., 2011), the results of my research indicate the opposite for luxury brands. Counterintuitive to previous research, my results indicate that simply publishing a high volume of tweets may not be a useful strategy for luxury brands. Although, a 2013 Simply Measured Network study suggests that top brands must tweet at least an average of 12 times a day, from a managerial perspective it is important to understand that sending out high volume of tweets may be counterproductive for a luxury brand. The research findings from the empirical analysis of Twitter data will help advance our understanding of the impact of eWOM communication on stock prices for luxury brands.

REFERENCES

AAKER, D. A., & JACOBSON, R., 1994, The financial information content of perceived quality. *Journal of Marketing Research*, 31(2), 191-201.

ALLERES, D., 1990, *Luxe-strategies marketing.* Paris: Editions Economica.
ASUR, S. & HUBERMAN, B. A. (2010). Predicting the future with social media. *Eprint arXiv:1003.5699.* doi:10.1016/j.apenergy.2013.03.027
ATWAL, G., & WILLIAMS, A., 2009, Luxury brand marketing -- The experience is everything! *Journal of Brand Management, 16*(5/6), 338–346.
AWAD, N.F., & ZHANG, J., 2006, *A framework for evaluating organizational involvement in online ratings communities.* Paper delivered at the 1st Midwest United States Association for Information Systems Conference (MWAIS-01), Grand Rapids, MI.
BARTH, M. E., CLEMENT, M. B., FOSTER, G., & KASZNIK, R., 1998, Brand values and capital market valuation. *Review of Accounting Studies, 3*(1/2), 41-68.
BARTON, B., 2006, Ratings, reviews & ROI: How leading retailers use customer word of mouth in marketing and merchandising. *Journal of Advertising Research, 30*(1), 7-27.
BELK, R. W., 1988, Possessions and extended self. *Journal of Consumer Research, 15*(2), 139 -168.
BELK, R. W., 2013, Extended Self in a Digital World. *Journal of Consumer Research, 40*(3), 477–500. https://doi.org/10.1086/671052
BOLLEN, J., MAO, H., & ZENG, X., 2010, Twitter mood predicts the stock market. *Journal of Computational Science, 2*(1), 1-8.
BOYD, D., GOLDER, S., & LOTAN, G., 2010, *Tweet, tweet, retweet: Conversational aspects of retweeting on Twitter.* Paper delivered at the 2010 43RD Hawaii International Conference on System Sciences, Honolulu, HI.
BRACKETT, E., 2015, Ralph Lauren shares soar as founder steps aside. *USA Today.* Retrieved from http://www.usatoday.com/story/money/2015/09/30/ralph-lauren-shares soar-founder-steps-aside/73079776/
BRAV, A., & HEATON, J. B., 2002, Competing theories of financial anomalies. *Review of Financial Studies, 15*(2), 575-606.
BROWN, S. J., & WARNER J. B., 1985, Using daily stock returns: The case of event studies. *Journal of Financial Economics, 14,* 3-31.
BRENNAN, M., J., & XIA, Y., 2001, Assessing asset pricing anomalies. *Review of Financial Studies, 14*(4), 905-942.
CHEVALIER, J. A., & MAYZLIN, D., 2006, The effect of word of mouth on sales: Online book reviews. *Journal of Marketing Research, 43*(3), 345-354.
CORNELL, B., 1983, Money supply announcements and interest rates: Another view. *Journal of Business, 56,* 1-24.
DELOITTE TOUCHE TOHMATSU LIMITED, 2014, *Global powers of luxury goods 2014: In the hands of the consumers.* Retrieved from http://www2.deloitte.com/content/dam/Deloitte/global/Documents/Consumer-Business/gx-cb-luxury-2014.pdf
DEPKEN II, A. C., 2001, Good news, bad news and GARCH effect in stock return data. *Journal of Applied Economics, 4*(2), 313-327.

DUAN, W., GUB, B., & WHINSTON, A. B., 2008, Do online reviews matter? An empirical investigation of panel data. *Decision Support Systems, 45*(3), 1007-1016.
DUBOIS, B. & PATERNAULT, C., 1995, Understanding the world of international luxury brands: The dream formula. *Journal of Advertising Research, 35*(4), 69-76.
EVANGELOPOULOS, N., MARGO, J. M., SIDOROVA, A., 2012, The dual micro/macro informing role of social network sites: Can Twitter macro messages help predict stock prices? *Informing Science, 15*, 247-268.
FAMA, E. F. (1965). The behavior of stock-market prices. *The Journal of Business, 38*(1), 34-105.
FAMA, E. F., FISHER, L., JENSEN, M. C., & ROLL, R., 1969, The adjustment of stock prices to new information. *International Economic Review, 10*(1), 1-21.
FAMA, E. F., 1970, Efficient capital markets: A review of theory and empirical work. *Journal of Finance, 25*(2), 383-417.
FAMA, E. F., 1991, Efficient capital markets: II. *Journal of Finance, 46*(5), 1575-1617.
FELDMAN, R., 2013, Techniques and applications for sentiment analysis. *Communications of the ACM, 56*(4), 82-89.
HAGTVEDT, H., & PATRICK, V. (2009). The broad embrace of luxury: Hedonic potential as a driver of brand extendibility. *Journal of Consumer Psychology, 19*(4), 608-619.
HAYES, A. F., 2018, *Introduction to mediation, moderation, and conditional process analysis: A regression-based approach.* 2nd ed. New York: The Guilford Press.
HENNIGS, N., WIEDMANN, K., & KLARMANN, C. (2012). Luxury brands in the digital age exclusivity versus ubiquity. *Marketing Review St. Gallen, 29*(1), 30-35.
HOLBROOK, M. B. & HIRSCHMAN, E.C., 1982, The experiential Aspects of Consumption: consumer fantasies, feelings and fun, *Journal of Consumer Research, 9*(2), 132-140.
KAPFERER, J., 2012, *The new strategic brand management.* London: Kogan
KAPFERER, J., 2015, *Kapferer on luxury: How luxury brands can grow yet remain rare.* London, & Philadelphia: Kogan Page.
KAPFERER, J., & BASTEIN, V., 2012, *The luxury strategy: Break the rules of marketing to build luxury brands.* London & Philadelphia: Kogan Page.
KAPFERER, J., & TABATONI, O., 2011, Are luxury brands really a financial dream? *Journal of Strategic Management Education, 7*(4), 271-286.
KATZ, E., & LAZARSFELD, P. F., 1955, *Personal influence: The part played by people in the flow of mass communications.* Glencoe, IL: Free Press of Glencoe.
KIM, J. A., & KO, E., 2012, Do social media marketing activities enhance customer equity? An empirical study of luxury fashion brand. *Journal of Business Research, 65*(10), 1480 1486.

LIU, Y., 2006, Word of mouth for movies: Its dynamics and impact on box office revenue. *Journal of Marketing, 70*(3), 74-89.
MIZIK, N., & JACOBSON, R., 2003, Trading off between value creation and value appropriation: The financial implications of shifts in strategic emphasis. *Journal Of Marketing, 67*(1), 63-76.
O'CONNOR, J. A., 2012, The power of popularity: An empirical study of the relationship between social media fan counts and brand company stock prices. *Social Science Computer Review, 31*(2), 229-235.
OKONKWO, U., 2009, Sustaining the luxury brand on the Internet. *Journal of Brand Management, 16*(5-6), 302-310.
PAUWELS, K., SILVA-RISSO, J., SRINIVASAN, S. & HANSSENS, D. M., 2004, New products, sales promotions, and firm value: The case of the automobile industry. *Journal of Marketing, 68*(4), 142-156.
PLANGGER, K., 2012, The power of popularity: How the size of a virtual community adds to firm value. *Journal of Public Affairs, 12*(2), 145-153.
SEE, A., MALHOTRA, C. K., & MALHOTRA, A., 2012, How to get your messages retweeted. *MIT Sloan Management Review, 53*(2), 61-66.
SHARPE, W. F., 1964, Capital asset prices: A theory of market equilibrium under conditions of risk. *Journal of Finance, 19*(3), 425-442.
SIMPLY MEASURED NETWORK STUDY, 2013, *How top brand marketers use Twitter/Q42013.* Retrieved from https://www.scribd.com/document/201400145/Simply-Measured-Twitter- Study-Q4-2013
SRINIVASAN, S., PAUWELS, K., SILVA-RISSO, J. & HANSSENS, D. M., 2009, Product innovations, advertising, and stock returns. *Journal of Marketing, 73*(1), 24-43.
SRINIVASAN, S. & HANSSENS, D., 2009, Marketing and firm value: Metrics, methods, findings, and future directions. *Journal of Marketing Research, 46*(3), 293-312.
THE INTERNATIONAL MAN. (n.d.). North America's high-end department stores and shops [Website]. Retrieved from http://www.theinternationalman.com/shopping-north-america.php
THE RICHEST, 2013, The top 10 luxury shoe brands [Web log post]. Retrieved fromhttp://www.therichest.com/rich-list/most-popular/the-top-10-luxury-shoe brands/?view=all
THE RICHEST, 2015, Top 15 best-selling luxury car brands in the US [Web log post]. Retrieved from http://www.therichest.com/rich-list/most-popular/top-15-bestselling-luxury-car-brands-in-the-us/?view=all
VICKERS, J. S. & RENAND, F., 2003, The marketing of luxury goods: An exploratory study three conceptual dimensions. *Marketing Review, 3*(4), 459-478.

ZHANG, M., JANSEN, B. J., SOBEL, K. & CHOWDURY, A., 2009, Twitter power: Tweets as electronic word of mouth. *Journal of the American Society for Information Science & Technology*, *60*(11), 2169-2188.
ZHANG, M., JANSEN, B. J. & CHOWDHURY, A., 2011, Business engagement on Twitter: A path analysis. *Electronic Markets, 21*(3), 161-175.
ZHU, F. & ZHANG, X., 2006, *The influence of online consumer reviews on the demand for experience goods: The case of video games.* Paper delivered at the 27th International Conference on Information Systems (ICIS-27), Milwaukee, WI.

SUSTAINABILITY IN THE LUXURY FASHION SUPPLY CHAIN: MILLENNIALS' PERCEPTION

Alessandro BRUN
Politecnico di Milano, School of Management
alessandro.brun@polimi.it

Hakan KARAOSMAN
Politecnico di Milano, School of Management
hakan.karaosman@polimi.it

ABSTRACT

The research aims at exploring Millennials' opinions about sustainability in luxury fashion and its scope is threefold. First, it evaluates the perceived coherence between luxury fashion and sustainability at a conceptual level, assesses the centrality of sustainable principles, and clarifies the role of luxury fashion brands within the green trend. The second purpose adopts a higher level of detail, testing young adults' awareness and perceived relevance of specific sustainability elements within the luxury fashion industry. Eventually, the study explores the causes of the discrepancy between a pro-environmental attitude and actual sustainable purchasing in luxury fashion, as well as the post-purchase justifications for unsustainability. The topics are explored through focus group discussions involving the Millennials and results include a strong coherence between luxury fashion and sustainability, accompanied by consumers' challenging expectations from companies. The predominance of social sustainability and the attention to basilar unsustainable practices emerge, together with the relevance of supply chain monitoring. The research also provides an overview of the causal relationships between the barriers that contribute to an attitude-behaviour gap, and an indication of the justifications that facilitates it.

Keywords: fashion luxury, millennials consumption attitude, sustainability, focus group.
JEL codes: M30, M31

INTRODUCTION

The current research aims at exploring the field of sustainable luxury fashion from Millennials' perspective while the ultimate scope is to provide useful insights about the relevance and the expected developments of the phenomenon of sustainable consumption in the luxury market. Among the phenomena shaking the high-end fashion market, a particular relevance is attributed to sustainable consumption, which is already shaping the market and may deeply affect luxury fashion supply chains in the future (Lundblad & Davies, 2015) (Ki & Kim, 2016) (Yeoman, 2011).

The focus on sustainability, beyond the undeniable relevance of this phenomenon, is also motivated by its ambiguous relationship with the industry under analysis: notwithstanding it is clearly a market trend, it is still not officially included among luxury fashion critical success factors of the market (Brun & Castelli, 2013). Sustainable fashion is challenging since the environmental footprint of the sector is huge, as an instance due to water consumption, pollution, waste, exploitation of precious and limited resources, as well as societal impact (Nagurney & Yu, 2012) (Kirsi & Lotta, 2011) (Ivan, et al., 2015) (Crowley et al., 2015). This latter aspect is testified by a number of social sustainability scandals, such as Gucci in 2014, Louis Vuitton and the luxury fashion giant Kering in 2017, concerning workers exploitations, cheap labour, and illegitimate use of the Made in Italy label (FashionUnited, 2014) (Conlon, 2017) (Lembke, 2017).

In order to understand the relevance of investigating the presented topic from future consumers' perspective, a clarification about the central role of the downstream end of luxury fashion Supply Chain (SC) is necessary. Since the seminal paper of Brun *et al.* (2008), the concept of luxury SC has been studied by a few authors, highlighting the various SC strategies implemented by luxury firms (Caniato *et al.*, 2011). Further studies argued that the alignement of SC operations with the peculiarities and the positioning of the brand is fundamental to create value in the modern luxury industry, as this allows to leverage on specific critical success factors (Castelli, 2015) (Moore & Birtwistle, 2004). Lately Brun *et al.* (2017) addressed the topic of differentiated strategies (depending on product-channel-brand) within the same company, to help pursue specific performance improvements. Supply chain decisions depend on end consumers' requirements, preferences and needs, which shape CSFs: luxury fashion operations could become more sustainable only providing that this change added value for final customers.

Among all potential end customers, the study target is on Millennials, the young adults born between 1980s and mid-1990s or 2000s, who are likely to reach their consumption peak in 2026-2029 (Danziger, 2016) (Lyons, 2016). Millennials are under the spotlight as they are expected to deeply change the luxury fashion industry in the near future (Danziger,

2016). Millennials are interesting as they could take more into account sustainability in their purchasing choices, compared to previous generations (Pechar, 2014).

It can be concluded that, in order to investigate the future effects of the sustainability trend in luxury fashion, end consumers' perspective is pivotal and the preferred focus to provide original insights for companies is on Millennials.

1. LITERATURE REVIEW

The aim of the literature review is to highlight more specific areas which are still unexplored or not fully investigated, within the broad field of research presented before.

1.1. Sustainability trend in the luxury market

The consumption of luxury in a more socially aware manner is highlighted by Yeoman (2011) as one of the growing trends emerging after the Global Financial Crisis. The phenomenon of *sustainable luxury purchase* is defined as the conscious preference of luxury *timeless style* and *long-lasting quality*, in opposition with fast fashion and excessive quantity (Blendell & Kleanthous, 2007). Looking at the broad sustainable fashion market, this fast growing sector embodies the concepts of green, organic, slow, and eco fashion, and assures that items are always produced adopting fair trade principles and avoiding production in *sweatshops* (Joergens, 2006) (Cervellon, et al., 2010) (Lundblad & Davies, 2015).

The luxury fashion market is subjected to an increasing pressure towards more sustainable sourcing, manufacturing and distribution processes; notwithstanding, on the overall, companies have been criticised for their hesitation in implementing socially and environmentally responsible practices (Carrigan, et al., 2013). Fashion market and supply chain characteristics may explain this incoherency, as they challenge the adoption of sustainable processes (Ivan, et al., 2015). As an instance, green fashion can even be paradoxical as fashion involves short life cycles, materialism and waste (Morgan & Birtwistle, 2009) as well as multinational sourcing and the risk of uncontrolled labour conditions (Perry, et al., 2013) (Karaosman, et al., 2015). Fashion supply chains are long, inherently complex, highly fragmented and globally dispersed, which inevitably complicate the monitoring of sustainability-related characteristics (Joy, et al., 2012) (Karaosman, et al., 2017). In the specific case of high-end fashion, however, companies tend to constitute more long-term partnerships with suppliers and to exercise a stronger control over their supply chain, aimed by the necessity to preserve core competences, premium quality, brand reputation and authenticity (Perry, et al., 2013).

However, supply chain characteristics are pivotal in this regards and they are influenced by the critical success factors of the market, thus they depend on consumers' potential reaction to sustainable practices and this last element is not completely clear. Numerous researchers share the concern that luxury consumers do not consider ethics when purchasing and that the basilar ideals of luxury concept may be incompatible with sustainability principles (Davies, et al., 2012) (Achabou & Dekhili, 2013) (Kapferer, 2014) (Line & Hanks, 2015). Contrarily, some studies show that new luxury consumers require highest quality and unquestionable ethics, artisanal craftsmanship, heritage, authenticity and they assess the entire life-cycle of the goods they purchase (Collins & Weiss, 2015) (Ki & Kim, 2016); therefore they can be defined as *green (or sustainable) consumers* (Young, et al., 2010).

1.2. Luxury - sustainability fit

Sustainability and luxury can be seen as intertwined concepts, considering common ideals like quality, timelessness, respect for rare resources, authenticity and attention to heritage (Cvijanovich, 2011) (Kapferer & Bastien, 2009). A coherence could also be spotted in luxury consumers' increasing attention to the provenance of goods and supply chain (Collins & Weiss, 2015) (Graj, 2013). Additionally, Karaosman, Morales-Alonso and Brun (2017) stress how the traditional luxury principle of product longevity represents a cornerstone of sustainability as more durable products could drastically reduce natural resource consumption, limit waste and decrease pollution. Sustainability could even become a source of competitive advantage and an opportunity to innovate for luxury brands (Cervellon & Shammas, 2013) (Ivan, et al., 2015). However, the perceived coherence may change in accordance with the consumption context or the product under analysis (Line & Hanks, 2015). The influencing role of product characteristics on the perceived fit is supported by Janssen, Vanhamme, Lindgreen and Lefebvre (2014), who highlights the role of product scarcity and ephemerality: scarce luxury products are inconsistent with sustainability in case of high ephemerality (e.g. clothing) while they are perceived as more sustainable if they are enduring (e.g. jewels). A different opinion, promoted by Achabou and Dekhili (2013), is that the fit may depend on the sustainability practices taken into consideration: as an instance, the presence of recycled material raises negative perceptions in luxury consumers seeking prestige while the use of organic materials is widely accepted. Conversely, some studies suggest that the perceived coherence depends on the definition of luxury, as consumers prioritising traditional values such as *expensiveness* and *rarity* feel a contradiction with sustainability, which is irrelevant in the case of new luxury values i.e. *authenticity* and *exceptional quality* (Hartmann, et al., 2016) (Kapferer, 2014).

Given this background, luxury-sustainability fit is a debated yet not completely explored topic and it represents an open research theme especially because consumers' knowledge, characteristics and preferences constantly vary over time (Chamorro, et al., 2009). In this regard, the luxury fashion market could be a challenging environment as it is affected by frequent fashion trends and it comprises products with high ephemerality, such as clothing (Janssen, et al., 2014). In addition, the investigation is complicated by the fact that suitable sustainable characteristics may not be explicitly mentioned by luxury fashion consumers, yet they could still be relevant as implicit conditions (Kapferer, 2014) (Bryson, et al., 2013).

1.3. Relevant sustainability elements in luxury fashion

Given the vastness of the possible environmental and societal concerns, consumers are likely to have a partial awareness of all potential sustainability-related aspects interesting luxury fashion and to conceive a sort of hierarchy among them (Shaw, et al., 2006) (Wheale & Hinton, 2007). The aim of this analysis is to understand which specific elements have the highest degree of relevance in determining consumers' opinion about luxury fashion goods and brands. As research in this context is highly limited, there is the need to enlarge the study focus to the whole luxury and fashion industries, in order to collect useful insights.

In the broad **luxury market**, long product life cycle, conscious material sourcing, low-impact and artisan manufacturing process, and Fair Trade label are sustainability-related characteristics which arguably represent necessary conditions for green consumers (Cvijanovich, 2011) (Janssen, et al., 2014) (Kapferer, 2012) (Blendell & Kleanthous, 2007) (Schmidt, et al., 2016). On the other hand, the unsustainable practices that are most likely to induce the boycott of a luxury brand are underpaid labour, animal cruelty and unsold product destruction, in order of relevance (Kapferer & Michaut, 2014).

Country of origin is another fundamental aspect in the fashion industry: several studies testify that consumers research information about provenance and value local production (Cervellon & Wernerfelt, 2012) (Shaw, et al., 2006). In Western countries, a close provenance may be valued thanks to its potential association with a higher social sustainability (Dickson, 1999) (Beard, 2008). Concerning the environmental sphere, instead, fashion consumers express a growing interest for eco-design, organic fibres and new natural materials such as bamboo and soy textiles (Karaosman, et al., 2015) (Lundblad & Davies, 2015). However, Cervellon and Wernerfelt (2012) highlight a certain degree of scepticism regarding the benefits of organically grown textiles.

1.4. Determinants and constraints of sustainable purchasing behaviour in luxury fashion

This section of the literature review is dedicated to an analysis of consumers' purchasing intention and actual purchase behaviour. In this case, the focus is strictly on the relationship between attitudes and behaviours, at actual or intentional level.

1.4.1. Attitudes as predictors of sustainable behaviours

Two of the most widespread predictive models for investigating behaviours are the Theory of Reasoned Action (Fishbein & Ajzen, 1975) and the Theory of Planned Behaviour (Ajzen, 1985; 1991). Both these models predicts individuals' actions on the basis of *behavioural intentions* (motivation to perform a specific behaviour), which directly depend on the *attitude* (Ajzen & Fishbein, 1980) (Ajzen, 1985). Looking more specifically at the sustainable purchase behaviour, Laroche, Bergeron, and Barbaro-Forleo (2001) confirm that a positive attitude can significantly affect the willingness to pay a premium price for green products, but only if the consumer perceives a high importance of being environmentally friendly. The element of *inconvenience of being environmentally friendly*, referring to the belief that green activities require additional effort or sacrifice, which negatively affect behaviours (Laroche, et al., 2001) (Baker, et al., 2013). A more optimistic result is proposed by Wei and colleagues (2017), who testify the direct link between attitude toward green products and the relative purchase intention, affecting in turns purchase behaviour. Analogous results are represented by the successful application of Ajzen's Theory of Planned Behaviour to sustainable fashion consumption: Maloney and colleagues (2014) affirm TPB usefulness in the context of organic appaerel purchase while Phau, Teah, and Chuah (2015) apply it in relation to the purchase of apparel made in sweatshops. Similarly, Summers, Belleau and Xu (2006) adopt the Theory of Reasoned Action in the intention to purchase a controversial fashion luxury product, and confirm that the strongest influence on it is possessed by the attitude toward the behaviour.

1.4.2. Attitude-behaviour gap

A number of relevant studies conversely propose an incoherency between these two factors in the field of sustainable purchasing: attitudes may not be good predictors of the actual performance or intention to perform sustainable purchases (Wei, et al., 2017). For example, Blake (1999) stresses the presence of a *Value–Action Gap* between individual's attitudes and their pro-environmental behaviour, which is confirmed by Rajecki (1982) and partially by Kollmuss and Agyeman's study (2002). A more recent study on the purchase of sustainable consumables, shows that attitude has not a significant relationship with self-reported behaviour, which in turns does not affect the actual behaviour (Moser, 2016). A clear proof of this discrepancy in the field of sustainable products is proposed by van Rijnsoever, Farla and Dijst (2009), who report that, although nearly 66% of respondents have a positive attitude toward the environment, only 11.5% translate it into behaviours, while a similar gap is not found with reference to other product performances. An analogue discrepancy is recognised by Cowe and Williams (2000) under the name of *30:3 phenomenon*: despite around 30% of UK consumers affirm to be *ethical purchasers*, the market share of ethic products is limited to 1–3%.

In synthesis, the research identifies a discrepancy, generally named the *attitude-behaviour gap*, between an abundant presence of self-reported sustainable consumers and the actual parameters of green products on the market (O'Rourke, 2015). Nonetheless, the proofs of this phenomenon do not necessarily deny a correlation between attitudes and behaviours, yet they suggest that it is likely that a series of factors impede the effective translation of attitudes into purchase behaviour. It is pivotal to understand the nature of these barriers, as they represent an important impediment to a change towards a more sustainable consumption patterns (O'Rourke, 2015).

1.5. Causes of the attitude-behaviour gap in sustainable consumption of luxury fashion

The highly limited studies investigating the field of luxury fashion focus on the prioritisation of aesthetics and extrinsic values (appearance, fashionable style and status) in order to explain why positive attitudes towards sustainability struggle to be translated into purchases (Ki & Kim, 2016) (Joy, et al., 2012). Summers and colleagues (2006), instead, stress luxury fashion consumers' scarce knowledge of sustainability as a relevant limit to a positive purchase intention. Additionally, they report that consumers intentionally avoid to assess all information sources and they tend to adopt approximate criteria for sustainability assessment in the apparel market (Shaw, et al., 2006). Due to the scarcity of specific studies, further insights has to be collected broadening the focus to the literature research.

In the fashion industry, Beard (2008) spot a certain degree of confusion and scepticism about the actual benefits of green fashion, while Karaosman et al. (2015) accuse a low transparency in the communication of sustainability information about products. Another interesting contribution to the research is represented by Perry and Chung's study (2016), which risees the attention about the lower perceived benefits of eco-apparel, in terms of product characteristics, cost, and emotional value. Additionally, Perry and Chung (2016) confirm as barriers the prioritisation of non-environmental characteristics in fashion and a certain scepticism about the benefits of eco-products.

Highly general barriers are purchasing inertia and low perceived consumer efficacy, meaning a scepticism about individual's impact on sustainability issues (Bray, et al., 2011) (Boulstridge & Carrigan, 2000) (Vermeir & Verbeke, 2006). Eventually, the translation of intentions to actual purchase behaviour could be impeded by the *socially desirability bias*: the tendency to over-report desirable behaviours such as purchasing pro-environmental goods and minimising undesirable actions, seeking the approval from other people (Bishop & Barber, 2014).

1.6. Post purchase justifications: the *Neutralization theory*

Empirical tests report that unsustainable purchases, a posteriori, generate a feeling of guilt and consumers attempt to suppress it by adopting excuses like, for example, referring to the irrelevance of an individual action (Young, et al., 2010) (Bray, et al., 2011). An interesting investigation of the justifications diminishing sustainable consumers' guilt in the after-purchase phase is represented by an application of the *Neutralization theory* in the context of fair trade purchases (Chatzidakis, et al., 2007). The *Neutralization Theory* was originally developed by Sykes and Matza (1957) in the context of juvenile delinquency and it is based on five *techniques of neutralization*, which are categories of justifications for committing actions against social norms. Chatzidakis and colleagues (2007) testify that the these justifications could also be used to explain the avoidance of fair trade products purchase, and, in particular, they reported the following relevant neutralization techniques:

- *Appealing to higher loyalties*

Consumers blame financial constraints, as confirmed by Carrigan and Attalla (2001), or the inferior quality and limited choice of fair trade products.

- *Denial of responsibility*

Buyers accuse the inadequate information, distribution, promotion of fair trade products.

- *Denial of injury*, manifested as *Denial of Benefit* in this context

Interviewees express the belief that fair trade labeling is just a marketing tool or that, however, this initiative cannot produce a systemic change in trading systems.

2. RESEARCH QUESTIONS AND METHODOLOGY

This section introduces the research questions designed to address the gaps identified in earlier studies, and helps understand how said research questions are translated into a concrete investigation and how data are analysed in order to obtain final findings.

2.1. Research Questions

Gaps identified in earlier studies led this reseerch to answer the following research questions.

RQ1: *How do Millennials, as potential future end-consumers, perceive the alignment between sustainability and luxury personal goods industry?*

RQ2: *Which are the most known and relevant sustainability characteristics for a product and brand, according to Millennials, in the luxury personal goods market?*

RQ3: *Which are the limits preventing sustainable purchase intention and behaviour in luxury fashion, and what is the justification for unsustainable ones?*

2.2. Research Methodology

Given the exploratory and qualitative nature of the study, the methodological choice concerning the empirical tests fell on the *focus group*. This inductive and exploratory technique allows to collect qualitative data by incentivising and moderating the discussion about specific topics and it is particularly effective in obtaining in-depth knowledge within an unknown field (Onwuegbuzie, et al., 2009) (Elg, et al., 2008). The amount of focus group settings cannot be defined in advance as *saturation* needs to be reached, meaning the situation in which the moderator cannot receive new relevant information from the interviewees. In this case, saturation is considered to be reached after the fourth focus group, which is in line with a diffused best practice (Saunders, et al., 2009).

All interviewees are recruited among University students and interns within the Milanese area, a well-known location for high-end fashion, and the discussion is conducted in Italian to facilitate individuals' participation and comprehension. The stricter criteria adopted during the sample selection is age: respondents have to belong to the youngest portion of the Millennials' generation (22 - 25 years of age). Additionally, all involved individuals have to be aware of the existence of environmental and societal issues: indeed, a general awareness of sustainability and its implications is considered a pre-condition for a fruitful and meaningful conversation in the focus group.

In order to make the discussion more interactive and interesting, instead, some tests are proposed beyond the traditional direct and highly specific questions. In this case, *test* refers to the creation of a realistic situation through the provision of pictures and information, in order to assess repondents' hypothethic behaviours and reactions. Tests can deal with broader topics and they let participants free to decide the direction of the discussion, thus revealing which are the most well-known and relevant aspects in their perspective. Tests could therefore address multiple research questions, and, on the other hand, each RQ is assessed through more than one question and test request.

3. DATA ANALYSIS

The accurate collection of empirical raw data is granted by the focus group recording and their subsequent transcription, in the original language. The transcripts are then analysed using the coding tecnique, based on the identification, name, categorisation and description of the phenomena found in the various segments of text (Borgatti, 1995).

After extracting the most relevant concepts (opinions and behaviours) from the discussion and synthesising them in concise sentences, these elements are classified according to the specific criteria fitting the topic under analysis. Classification criteria involve the nature of the element and its relationship with sustainability, but also its coherence with an hypothesised scenario or theory: deriving inspiration from Miles and Huberman's opinion, the extant literature is considered as an important source of inspiration for codes classification (Gläser & Laudel, 2013). Indeed, while Strauss and Corbin' *open coding* is exclusively based on the text itself, Miles and Huberman stress the importance of linking codes with existing literature and suggest the possibility to create an initial list of codes based on conceptual framework, research questions, past theories and hypothesises (Gläser & Laudel, 2013).

From codes, sub-themes are extracted at single question and focus group level, aggregated on the basis of the RQ they referred to and compared among the four focus group sessions. The resulting findings undergo a critical analysis, eventually including a comparison with the original theoretical propositions, in order to obtain the final contribution of the research, presented in the next chapter.

Note: for sake of paper length, it is impossible to report the full transcripts of the focus group; reader interested in verbatims may contact the corresponding author in private mail.

4. FINDINGS & DISCUSSION

According to the propositions, the interviewed Millennials judge sustainable luxury fashion as a concrete and desirable possibility that would foster some luxury CSFs; whereas, contrarily to previousy claims, no specific elements are thought to be mediators of the luxury-sustainability coherence (Line & Hanks, 2015) (Janssen, et al., 2014) (Achabou & Dekhili, 2013) (Hartmann, et al., 2016). Empirical tests confirm instead, in the fashion context, the past studies claiming that consumers perceive sustainability as an implicit condition of luxury (Kapferer, 2014), and that luxury brands could (and should) become the leaders in sustainability (Joy, et al., 2012), (Ivan, et al., 2015) (Blendell & Kleanthous, 2007). Additionally, the current research highlights that the large majority of respondents are not satisfied with luxury fashion in terms of sustainability achievements.

Another fundamental result is that sustainability in luxury fashion depends on a limited productive volumes and a strict control over the supply chain; local production instead is a mere facilitator of sustainability implementation since it allows companies to better monitor the SC. This last result sheds a light on the unclear relationship between country of origin and sustainability in luxury fashion and contrasts with Shaw and colleagues' study (2006) in the apparel industry, which propose *Made in the EU* as a synonym of sweatshop-free production. Eventually, an innovative contribution to extant literature is the focus on the unavoidable usage of animal materials as a perceived constraint in the implementation of sustainability in the high-end fashion market.

The present research confirms the predominance of the social concern, embodied by sweatshop-free items, over environmental consciousness (Tomolillo & Shaw, 2003) (Ki & Kim, 2016) (Phau, et al., 2015); whereas it contradicts Summers and colleagues' research (2006) on luxury fashion by denying a general significant attention to animal cruelty and biodiversity. In this regard, a discrepancy emerges from current research: consumers conceptually associate sustainability with the avoidance of animal products or at least with ethical farming conditions, yet they often declare not to be keen on purchasing synthetic leather. This can be easily explained with Millennials' prioritisation of aesthetics in luxury fashion purchases, which would be clearly damaged by the renounce to animal materials.

Another confusing result is that, albeit sweatshops production is a severe unsustainability, extremely limited reference to the social justice emerge while evaluating a sustainable product. A possible explanation is that Millennials rely on brands' sustainable reputation as the only assurance of the respect of social norms, since they cannot directly access these informations.

Looking at results from a broad perspective, consumers appear to be more interested in avoiding the most severe unsustainable practices, such as sweatshops and toxic waste, rather than in researching specific sustainability traits and green innovations. They refer more specifically to sustainable traits only when expressly asked, demonstrating that they might possess the awareness but not the sufficient interest to judge an item on this basis. Eventually, the nature of relevant sustainable characteristics (brand sustainability communications, materials, productive processes and certifications) reaffirms the importance of supply chain monitoring in order to build the perception of true sustainability.

All the elements preventing the performance of sustainable purchases in luxury fashion, despite a potentially positive attitude, are organised on the basis of logic cause-effect relationships and represented in Figure 1. A number of independent factors (shaded boxes) directly or indirectly cause the other barriers and few intermediate conditions (in Italic) added to complete the cause-consequences diagram. The aspects emerging as pure post-purchase justifications (yellow boxes) are connected through dotted lines as they only indirectly contribute to the gap by making unsustainable choices acceptable in consumers' mind.

Figure 1: Cause-effect schema synthesising the factors negatively affecting sustainable consumption in luxury fashion

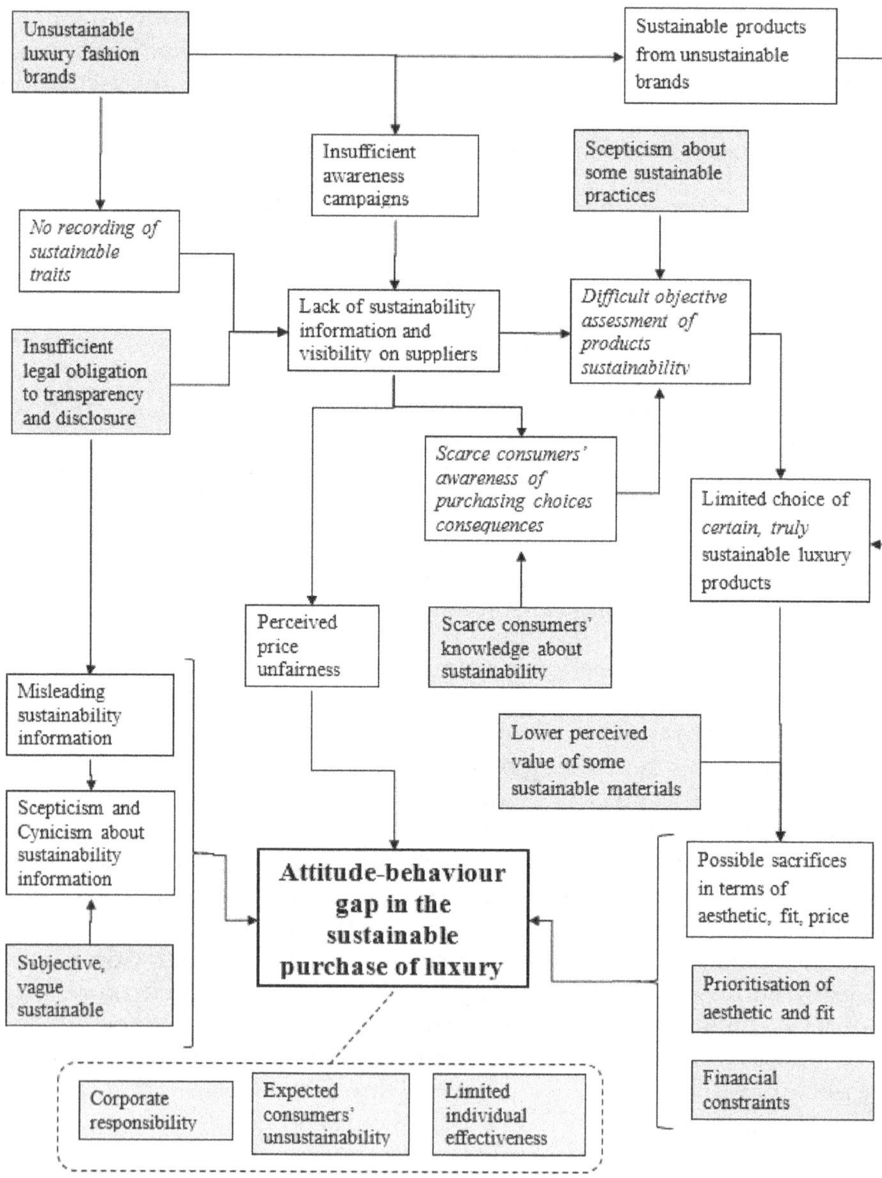

A critical examination of Figure 1 reveals that all the mostly blamed causes can be sinthesised into two main elements: information and aesthetics prioritisation. Concerning the first topic, the insufficient legal obligation to transparency and the consciously misleading information proposed by companies, united with the subjective and vague nature of sustainability traits, generate a widespread scepticism and cynicism among Millennials, which distance them from sustainable purchases. The lack of information also generates the perception of price unfairness, as consumers may not fully understand the motivations behind the extra-price of sustainability. Scepticism also depends by the fact that green products may still be produced by unsustainable brands, which stresses the unexpectedly strong importance of brand sustainability for Millennials.

Regarding the second main aspect, the prioritisation of aesthetics (as well as fit and price) over sustainable traits, together with the lower aesthetic benefits of synthetic materials and the limited choice of sustainable products in luxury fashion, may significantly prevent sustainable purchases. A fundamental element emergin as pure justification is constituted by blaming luxury fashion companies and consumers' unsustainability. This aspect can be considered as an example of the technique of neutralization known as *Condemning the condemners* (Sykes & Matza, 1957), yet its high frequency in focus group discussion represents an original finding. Indeed Chatzidakis and colleagues' study on sustainable consumption (Why People Don t Take their Concerns about Fair Trade to the Supermarket: The Role of Neutralisation, 2007) do not highlight this element as particularly relevant. Another Sykes and Matza's technique of neutralization, *Denial of benefit*, appears as a pure justification in the current study, represented by low perceived consumers' effectiveness in solving sustainable issues; however, its relevance is much weaker than expected (Chatzidakis, Hibbert, & Smith, 2007). Contrarily to what supposed on the basis of Chatzidakis and colleagues' findings (Why People Don t Take their Concerns about Fair Trade to the Supermarket: The Role of Neutralisation, 2007) and luxury fashion characteristics, the interviewees do not mention the limited impact of the luxury fashion industry on sustainability issues, highlighting that its limited volumes do not represent an excuse, but rather a fruitful condition facilitating sustainability implementation.

5. PRACTICAL IMPLICATIONS

The first element that luxury fashion brands should take into account is that the implementation of sustainable practices could potentially strengthen critical success factors like quality and craftsmanship, increase the value of a long life-cycle, reinforce brand reputation and justify the maintenance of a high price range. Millennials may not specifically ask for sustainability-related information when making purchasing decisions, yet sustainability, and especially social justice, could become a market qualifier in the near future. Indeed, results in the luxury fashion industry show challenging beliefs and desires about social responsibility and environmental-friendliness of luxury fashion, contrasting with a general dissatisfaction with current achievements in this regard.

Given the relevance of brand reputation, the primar importance of the social sphere and the focus un unsustainability avoidace, rather than sustainable traits, companies are strongly advised to eliminate the most controversial practices at corporate level. Brands should first assure that adequate working conditions and human rights are always respected, by imposing strict controls all over their supply chain and, ideally, producing locally. In parallel, this commitment should be pro-actively communicated through the official websites and through the involvement of well-informed shop-assistants.

Subsequently, companies should also consider the impact of their productive processes, control materials origin and production and assess suppliers' sustainable certifications. Millennials seem more interested in the respect of the basilar social and environmental norms, which are likely to be already declared on companies' CSR programmes, rather than with additional sustainable traits. This implies the need to impose a strong control over the SC and to guarantee materials traceability, rather investing in innovative green technologies.

Among the various beneficial implementations of sustainability in luxury fashion, only one contradictory element emerges: the avoidance of (rare) animal products, as they are still largely seen as synonym of luxury and value. The path towards a full acceptance of animal welfare in the market is still arduous: high-end fashion brands are invited to avoid, or at least delay, the shift towards synthetic materials, as they minimally affect the perceived sustainability and could indeed damage the product appeal and quality.

Luxury fashion companies willing to undertake the path towards sustainability could particularly benefit from an insight about which product or brand-related factors may prevent sustainable purchasing. A transparent communication through the official channels, fundamental for building a sustainable reputation, would also reduce the perception of limited and misleading information that currently affects sustainable behaviours. Moreover, trustworthy information sources and brands sustainable reputation could considerably reduce the cognitive effort needed for ethical consumption (Shaw, et al., 2006) (Young, et al., 2010).

In addition, given consumers' prioritisation of aesthetics, luxury fashion brands must reassure consumers that a focus on sustainability does not go to the detriment of aesthetic criteria (model, material, colour, details) and fit (Meyer, 2001) (Perry & Chung, 2016). Marketing strategies for sustainable products could even address consumers through aesthetic and hedonism before mentioning sustainability, following the example of

Tesla (Martin & Väistö, 2016). Communication efforts should concentrate on the possibility of a perfect aesthetics and sustainability synthesis, rather than convincing of the importance individuals' contribution to solving social and environmental issues. This last communication strategy may not be fruitful as low consumer effectiveness only emerges as a post-purchase justification, aimed at decreasing consumers' guilt, and not as an actual limit to sustainable choices. The findings concerning post-purchase justifications, testifying that consumers alone perceive to be powerless in changing the market towards higher sustainability and attribute the responsibility on companies, should only be considered as an ulterior incitation to implement sustainable practices, raised by Millennials.

CONCLUSION

Despite the useful contribution that this research provides to extant literature, the study is not without limitations. The main constraints depend on the methodological technique adopted: being obtained from a limited number of respondents, focus group results do not have a strong statistical value (WebFinance Inc., 2017). However, the current study is meant to explore and provide some insights, rather than being representative of the entire population of Millennials or statistically testing specific theories. Indeed, the present research is a first exploratory phase that should desirably be inserted in a broader stream of future research, meant to build new useful theories concerning sustainable luxury fashion.

The structure of the empirical tests, based on self-reported opinions and choices, also implies the risk of the *social desirability bias*, which can generate a discrepancy between the preferences stated during the focus groups discussion and what would be the actual behaviour of respondents in a real situation (Bishop & Barber, 2014). The presence of a restricted groups of peers and the informal atmosphere, allegedly favoure participants' honesty in stating their opinions, yet the possibility of the explained phenomenon cannot totally be excluded. Future studies are invited to test the correctness of self-reported opinions emerged during the presented focus groups discussions by enlarging the repondents base and by assessing the actual market data concerning sustainable luxury fashion.

The only demographic factor expressly considered in sample selection is age, given the importance of new generations in shaping future market trends, and this choice may or may not imply some sort of limitations. Indeed, according to a number of past studies, other demographic characteristics affect individuals' attitude towards sustainability and behavioural patterns (Kollmuss & Agyeman, 2002) (Laroche, et al., 2001) (Achabou & Dekhili, 2013). Contrarily, literature also contains proofs of demographics irrelevance in defining socially responsible consumers and in shaping sustainable behaviours (Summers, et al., 2006)

(Diamantapoulos, et al., 2003) (Pearson, et al., 2010). Given these contradicting results, the effect of demographics in this regard is not certain (Laroche, et al., 2001) (Roberts, 1995).

Eventually, addressing brands owners and retailers, the focus of the research is on the first sale of personal luxury goods. For this reason, the sustainable practices depending almost exclusively on consumers' habits (i.e. extending product life cycle, eco-washing, donating and buying old items) are excluded. This choice neglects, while not denying, the phenomenon of second-hand consumption and the huge impact of the usage phase on sustainability (Cassidy, 2016) (WRAP, 2012). To conclude, the limitations do not mean to decrease the value of the research, they rather aim at suggesting further path of investigation in this interesting field, stimulated by the willigness to fill the gaps of the current study.

BIBLIOGRAPHY

ACHABOU, M. A. & DEKHILI, S., 2013, Luxury and sustainable development: Is there a match?. Journal of Business Research 66, p. 1896–1903.

AJZEN, 1985, From intentions to actions: a theory of planned behavior. In: J. B. J. Khul, a cura di Action-control: From cognition to behavior. s.l.:Springer, pp. 11 - 39.

AJZEN, I., 1991, The theory of planned behavior.. Organizational Behavior and Human Decision Process, 50 (2), pp. 179 - 211.

AJZEN, I. & FISHBEIN, M., 1980, Understanding attitude and predicting social behavior. In: s.l.: Englewood Cliffs, NJ: Prentice-Hall, Inc..

ARRIGUCCI, C. M. & GIANECCHINI, M., 2016, Lusso, il mercato che non conosce crisi. Analisi del settore hotellerie attraverso i casi Marriott e Hilton. Padova : Università degli Studi di Padova Dipartimento di Scienze Economiche e Aziendali.

BAKER, M. A., DAVIS, E. A. & WEAVER, P. A., 2013, Eco-friendly Attitudes, Barriers to Participation, and Differences in Behavior at Green Hotels. Cornell Hospitality Quarterly 2014, Vol. 55(1), pp. 89-99.

BEARD, N. D., 2008, The Branding of Ethical Fashion and the Consumer: A Luxury Niche or Mass-market Reality?. Fashion Theory, 12:4, pp. 447-467.

BISHOP, M. & BARBER, N., 2014, Putting your money where your mouth is: the value of low purchase intention consumers to product pricing. Journal of Product Innovation Management, Vol. 31 No. 5, pp. 908-923.

BLAKE, J., 1999, Overcoming the 'value–action gap' in environmental policy: tensions between national policy and local experience. Local Environment, 4(3), pp. 257-278.

BLENDELL, J. & KLEANTHOUS, A., 2007, Deeper Luxury: Quality and Style When the World Matters, s.l.: Godalming: WWF-UK.
BORGATTI, S., 1995, Introduction to Grounded Theory. [Online] Available at: http://www.analytictech.com/mb870/introtogt.htm[Link verified on May 2017].
BOULSTRIDGE, E. & CARRIGAN, M., 2000, Do consumers really care about corporate responsibility? Highlighting the attitude-behaviour gap. Journal of Communication Management, 4(4), pp. 355-368.
BRAY, J., JOHNS, N. & KILBURN, D., 2011, An Exploratory Study into the Factors Impeding Ethical Consumption. Journal of Business Ethics 98, pp. 597-608.
BRUN et al., 2008, Logistics and supply chain management in luxury fashion retail: Empirical investigation of Italian firms. International Journal of Production Economics, 114(2), 554-570;
BRUN, A. & CASTELLI, C., 2013, The nature of luxury - a consumer perspective. In: 823-847, a cura di International Journal of Retail & Distribution Management Vol. 41 No. 11/12. s.l.:Emerald.
BRUN, A., CASTELLI, C., & KARAOSMAN, H., 2017, A focused supply chain strategy for luxury fashion management, Journal of Fashion Marketing and Management: An International Journal, Vol. 21 Issue: 4, pp.544-56
BRYSON, D., ATWAL, G. & HULTÉN, P., 2013, Towards the conceptualisation of the antecedents of extreme negative affect towards luxury brands. Qualitative Market Research: An International Journal Vol. 16 No. 4, pp. 393-405.
CAMPBELL, C. L., HEINRICH, D. & SCHOENMÜLLER, V., 2014, Consumers' reaction to fair trade motivated price increases. Journal of Retailing and ConsumerServices 24 (2015), pp. 79-84.
CARRIGAN, M. & ATTALLA, A., 2001, The myth of the ethical consumer-do ethics matter in purchase behaviour?. Journal of Consumer Marketing, 18(7), pp. 560 - 578.
CARRIGAN, M., MORAES, C. & MCEACHERN, M., 2013, From Conspicuous to Considered Fashion: A Harm Chain Approach to the Responsibilities of Luxury Fashion Businesses. Journal of Marketing Management 29:11-12, pp. 1277-1307.
CASSIDY, T. D., 2016, Conceptualizing Sustained High Quality Fashion Products in a Devalue Dominated Marketplace. Fashion Practice.
CANIATO et al., 2011, Supply chain management in the luxury industry: A first classification of companies and their strategies. International Journal of Production Economics, 133(2), 622-633
CASTELLI, C. M. S. A., 2015, Supply chain strategy for companies in the luxuryfashion market Aligning the supply chain towards the critical success factors. International Journal of Retail & Distribution Management, Vol. 43 Iss 10/11, p. 940 – 966.

CERVELLON, M.-C. C. & WERNERFELT, A.-S., 2012, Knowledge sharing among green fashion communitiesonline: Lessons for the sustainable supply chain. Journal of Fashion Marketing and Management, Vol. 16 Iss: 2, pp. 176-192.
CERVELLON, M.-C., HJERTH, H., RICARD, S. & CAREY, L., 2010, Green in fashion? An exploratory study of national differences in consumers concern for eco-fashion. Proceedings of 9th International Marketing Trends Conference. Venice, s.n.
CERVELLON, M. & SHAMMAS, L., 2013, The value of sustainable luxury in mature markets a customer-based approach. Journal of Corporate Citizenship 52(12), pp. 90-101.
CHAMORRO, A., RUBIO, S. & MIRANDA, F., 2009, Characteristics of Research on Green Marketing. Business Strategy and the Environment, 18, pp. 223-239.
CHATZIDAKIS, A., HIBBERT, S. & SMITH, A. P., 2007, Why People Don t Take their Concerns about Fair Trade to the Supermarket: The Role of Neutralization. Journal of Business Ethics, pp. 89-100.
COLLINS, M. & WEISS, M., 2015, The role of provenance in luxury textile brands. International Journal of Retail & Distribution Management, Vol. 43 Iss 10/11, pp. 1030-1050.
COWE, R. & WILLIAMS, S., 2000, Who are the Ethical Consumers?, Ethical Consumerism Report, Cooperative Bank. [Online], Available at: http://www.cooperativebank.co.uk/servlet/Satellite?c=Pageandcid=1139903089615andpagename=CoopBank%2FPage%2FtplPageStandard
CPP LUXURY, 2017, The luxury goods market to return to growth in 2017. [Online] Available at: http://www.cpp-luxury.com/the-luxury-goods-market-to-return-to-growth-in-2017/[Link verified on February 2017].
CVIJANOVICH, M., 2011, Sustainable luxury: Oxymoron? In: Lecture in luxury and sustainability. [Online] Available at:http://www.mcmdesignstudio.ch/files/Guest%20professor%20Lucern%20School%20of%20Art%20%20and%20Design.pdf.
[Link verified on February 2017].
DANZIGER, P., 2016, Five luxe trends for 2016 that are shaping the future for marketing to the U.S. affluent luxury consumer market, s.l.: Unity Marketing.
DAVIES, I., LEE, Z. & AHONKHAI, I., 2012, Do consumers care about ethical-luxury?. Journal of Business Ethics, Vol. 106 No. 1, pp. 37-51.
DAVIES, I., LEE, Z. & AHONKHAI, I., 2012, Do Consumers Care About Ethical-Luxury?. Journal of Business Ethics 106, no. 1, pp. 37-51.
DIAMANTAPOULOS, A., SCHLEGELMILCH, B. B., SINKOVICS, R. R. & BOHLEN, G. M., 2003, Can Socio-Demographics Still Play a Role in Profiling Green Consumers? A Review of the Evidence and an Empirical Investigation. Diamantapoulos, A.; Schlegelmilch, B. B.;

Sinkovics, R. R.; Bohlen, G. M. Can Socio-DemograJournal of Business Research 56(4), pp. 465-480.
DICKSON, M. A., 1999, US consumers' knowledge of and concern for apparel sweatshops. Journal of Fashion Marketing and Management. Vol. 3 No. 1, pp. 44-55.
DICKSON, M. A., 2001, Utility of No sweat labels for apparel consumers: Profiling label-users and predicting their purchases. Journal of Consumer Affairs. Vol. 35 No. 1, pp. 96-119.
ELG, U., GHAURI, P. N. & TARNOVSKAYA, V., 2008, The role of networks and matching in market entry to emerging retail markets.. International Marketing Review, 25, 674 - 699.
FIETKAU, H. & KESSEL, H., 1981, Umweltlernen: Veraenderungsmoeglichkeite n des Umweltbewusstseins.. s.l.:Modell-Erfahrungen (Koenigstein, Hain).
FISHBEIN, M. & AJZEN, I., 1975, Belief, attitude, intention and behavior: An introduction to theory and research.. s.l.:s.n.
GLÄSER, J. & LAUDEL, G., 2013, Life With and Without Coding: Two Methods for Early-Stage Data Analysis in Qualitative Research Aiming at Causal Explanations Volume 14, No. 2, Art. 5. [Online] Available at: http://www.qualitative-research.net/index.php/fqs/article/view/1886/3528#g41 [Link verified on May 2017].
GRAJ, S., 2013, After Bangladesh: is apparel provenance the next brand DNA battleground? Forbes Web. [Online] Available at: www.forbes.com/sites/simongraj/2013/05/30/after-bangladesh-is-apparel-provenance-the-next-brand-dna-battleground/ [Link verified on February 2017].
HARTMANN, L. H., NITZKO, S. & SPILLER, A., 2016, Segmentation of German Consumers Based on Perceived Dimensions of Luxury Food. Journal of Food Products Marketing.
IVAN, C.-M., MUKTA, R., SUDEEP, C. & BURAK, C., 2015, Long-term sustainable sustainability in luxury. Where else?. In: M. Gardetti & S. Muthu, a cura di Handbook of Sustainable Luxury Textiles and Fashion 2, pp. 17-34, Environmental Footprints and Eco-design of Product and Processes. s.l.:Springer, pp. 17-34.
JANSSEN, C., VANHAMME, J., LINDGREEN, A. & LEFEBVRE, C., 2014, The Catch-22 of Responsible Luxury: Effects of Luxury Product Characteristics on Consumers' Perception of Fit with Corporate Social Responsibility. Journal of Business Ethics, Vol. 119 No. 1, pp. 45-57.
JOY, A. et al., 2012, Fast Fashion, Sustainability, and the Ethical Appeal of Luxury Brands. Fashion Theory: the Journal of Dress, Body and Culture 16 16:3, pp. 273-295.
JOY, A. et al., 2012, Fast Fashion, Sustainability, and the Ethical Appeal of Luxury Brands. Fashion Theory, 16:3, pp. 273-295.

KAPFERER, J., 2012, What do clients think of the sustainable future of luxury?, Paris: s.n.
KAPFERER, J.-N., 2014, Is luxury compatible with sustainability? Luxury consumers' viewpoint. Journal of Brand Management, January.
KAPFERER, J.-N. & MICHAUT, A., 2014, Is luxury compatible with sustainability: luxury consumers viewpoint. Journal of Brand Management, Vol. 21, No. 1, pp. 1-22.
KAPFERER, J. N. & BASTIEN, V., 2009, The specificity of luxury management: Turning marketing upside down. Journal of Brand Management, 16(5), pp. 311-322.
KARAOSMAN, H., MORALES-ALONSO, G. & BRUN, A., 2017, Strike a Pose: Luxury for Sustainability. In: 145-161, a cura di Sustainable Management of Luxury. Part of the series Environmental Footprints and Eco-design of Products and Processes. s.l.:s.n., p. February.
KARAOSMAN, H., MORALES-ALONSO, G. & GRIJALVO, M., 2015, Consumers' responses to CSR in a cross-cultural setting. Cogent Business & Management: 2.
KARAOSMAN, H., MORALES, G. A., GRIJALVO, M. & BRUN, A., 2015, The impact of ethical fashion on Spanish consumers. Dirección y Organización 57, pp. 63-73.
KI, C.-W. & KIM, Y.-K., 2016, Sustainable Versus Conspicuous Luxury Fashion Purchase: Applying Self-Determination Theory. Family and Consumer Sciences Research Journal, Vol. 44, No. 3, March, p. 309–323.
Kirsi, N. & Lotta, H., 2011, Emerging design strategies in sustainable production and consumption of textiles and clothing. Journal of Cleaner Production 19, pp. 1876-1883.
KOLLMUSS, A. & AGYEMAN, J., 2002, Mind the Gap: why do people act environmentally and what are the barriers to pro-environmental behavior?. Environmental Education Research, Vol. 8, No. 3.
LAROCHE, M., BERGERON, J. & BARBARO-FORLEO, G., 2001, Targeting consumers who are willing to pay more for environmentally friendly products. Journal of Consumer Marketing, Vol. 18 Iss 6, pp. 503-520.
LINE, N. D. & HANKS, L., 2015, The effects of environmental and luxury beliefs on intention to patronize green hotels: the moderating effect of destination image. Journal of Sustainable Tourism, October.
LUNDBLAD, L. & DAVIES, I. A., 2015, The values and motivations behind sustainable fashion consumption. Journal of Consumer Behaviour, 44(3), pp. 309-323.
LYONS, K., 2016, Millennials: the trials of Generation Y.
[Online] Available at:
https://www.theguardian.com/world/2016/mar/08/generation-y-curling-or-maybe-what-the-world-calls-millennials
[Link verified on May 2017].

MALONEY, J., LEE, M.-Y., JACKSON, V. & MILLER-SPILLMAN, K. A., 2014, Consumer Willingness to Purchase Organic Products: Application of the Theory of Planned Behavior. Journal of Global Fashion Marketing.

MARTIN, D. M. & VÄISTÖ, T., 2016, Reducing the Attitude-Behavior Gap in Sustainable Consumption: A Theoretical Proposition and the American Electric Vehicle Market. Diane M. Martin Terhi Väistö. "Reducing the Attitude-Behavior Gap in Sustainable Marketing in and for a Sustainable Society, pp. 193-213.

MEYER, A., 2001, What's in it for the customers? Successfully marketing green clothes. Business Strategy and the Environment Business, Vol. 10 No. 5, pp. 317-330.

MOORE, C. & BIRTWISTLE, G., 2004, The Burberry business model: creating and international luxury business model. International Journal of Retail and Distribution Management, 32, 8, p. 412–422.

MORGAN, L. & BIRTWISTLE, G., 2009, An investigation of young fashion consumers' disposable habits. International Journal of Consumer Studies, Vol. 33 No. 2, pp. 190-198.

MOSER, A. K., 2016, Consumers' purchasing decisions regarding environmentally friendly products: An empirical analysis of German consumers. Journal of Retailing and Consumer Services.

NAGURNEY, A. & YU, M., 2012, Sustainable fashion supply chain management under oligopolistic competition and brand differentiation. International Journal of Production Economics 135, pp. 532-540.

ONWUEGBUZIE, A. J., DICKINSON, W. B., LEECH, N. L. & ZORAN, A. G., 2009, A qualitative framework for collecting and analyzing data in focus group research. International Journal of Qualitative Methods, 8, 1–21.

O'ROURKE, D., 2015, The Impact of Sustainability Information on Consumer Decision Making. Journal of Industrial Ecology, August.

PEARSON, D., HENRYKS, J. & JONES, H., 2010, Organic food: What we know (and do not know) about consumers. Renewable Agriculture and Food Systems: 26(2), pp. 171-177.

PECHAR, E., 2014, Sense & Sustainability: Sustainable Millennials. [Online] Available at:
http://www.senseandsustainability.net/2014/08/08/sustainable-millennials/
[Link verified on May 2017].

PERRY, A. & CHUNG, T., 2016, Understand attitude-behavior gaps and benefit-behavior connections in Eco-Apparel. Journal of Fashion Marketing and Management, Vol. 20 Iss 1, pp. 105-119.

PERRY, P., FERNIE, J. & WOOD, S., 2013, The international fashion supply chain and corporate social responsibility. In: J. F. &. L. S. (Eds.), a cura di Perry, P.; Fernie, J.; Wood, S. The internaLogistics and retail

management: Emerging issues and new challenges. London: Kogan Page, pp. 77-100.
PHAU, I., TEAH, M. & CHUAH, J., 2015, Consumer attitudes towards luxury fashion apparel made in sweatshops. Journal of Fashion Marketing and Management, Vol. 19 Issue: 2, pp. 169-187.
RAJECKI, D., 1982, Attitudes: themes and advances. s.l.:Sunderland, MA, Sinauer.
REIN, G., 2016, Tink Tank: Why Millennials Are the Future of Luxury. [Online] Available at: http://wwd.com/fashion-news/designer-luxury/millennials-luxury-spending-10417737/
[Link verified on May 2017].
REPORTBUYER, 2015, Personal Luxury Goods Market in the US 2015-2019. [Online] Available at: http://www.prnewswire.com/news-releases/personal-luxury-goods-market-in-the-us-2015-2019-300173819.html
[Link verified on January 2017].
ROBERTS, J. A., 1995, Profiling Levels of Socially Responsible Consumer Behavior: A cluster Analytic Approach and its Implications for Marketing. Journal of Marketing Theory and Practice 3(4), pp. 97-118.
ROBINSON, P. & HSIEH, L., 2016, Reshoring: a strategic renewal of luxury clothing supply chains. Operations Management Research, Vol. 9, p. 89–101.
SAUNDERS, M., LEWIS, P. & THORNHILL, A., 2009, Research methods for business students. 5th edition a cura di s.l.:Harlow: Pearson Education.
SCHMIDT, S., HENNIGS, N., BEHRENS, S. & KARAMPOURNIOTI, E., 2016, The Luxury of Sustainability: Examining Value-Based Drivers of Fair Trade Consumption. In: Handbook of Sustainable Luxury Textiles and Fashion, Environmental Footprints and Eco-desig. s.l.:Springer Science & Business Media Singapore.
SHAW, D. et al., 2006, Fashion victim: the impact of fair trade concerns on clothing choice. Journal of StrategicMarketing 14(4), p. 423–436.
SHAW, D. et al., 2007, Intending to Be Ethical: An Examination of Consumer Choice in Sweatshop Avoidance.
SUMMERS, T. A., BELLEAU, B. D. & XU, Y., 2006, Predicting purchase intention of a controversial luxury apparel product. Journal of Fashion Marketing and Management: An International Journal, Vol. 10 Iss 4, pp. 405-419.
SYKES, G. M. & MATZA, D., 1957, Techniques of Neutralization: A Theory of Delinquency. American Sociological Review 22(6), p. 664–670.
TOMOLILLO, D. A. C. & SHAW, D., 2003, Undressing the Ethical Issues in Fashion: A Consumer Perspective. s.l.:s.n.

VAN RIJNSOEVER, F., FARLA, J. & DIJST, M. J., 2009, Consumer car preferences and information search channels. Transportation Research Part D 14, pp. 334-342.
VERMEIR, I. & VERBEKE, W., 2006, Sustainable Food Consumption: Exploring the Consumer "Attitude – Behavioral Intention" Gap. Journal of Agricultural and Environmental Ethics 19, p. 169–194.
VERMEIR, I. & VERBEKE, W., 2006, Sustainable food consumption: Exploring the consumer'attitude – behavioral intention' gap. Vermeir, I. and Verbeke, W. (2006), "Sustainable food consumption: Exploring the consumer'attitude – behavioral intention' gap", Journal of Agricultural and Environmental Ethics,Vol. 19 No. 2, pp. 169-194., pp. 169-194.
WebFinance Inc., 2017. Business Dictionary. [Online] Available at: http://www.businessdictionary.com/definition/focus-group.html[Link verified on May 2017].
WEI, C.-F., CHIANG, C.-T., KOU, T.-C. & LEE, B. C. Y., 2017, Toward Sustainable Livelihoods: Investigating the Drivers of Purchase Behavior for Green Products. Business Strategy and the Environment.
WHEALE, P. & HINTON, D., 2007, Ethical consumers in search of markets. Business Strategy and the Environment 16, pp. 302-315.
WORLD COMMISSION ON ENVIRONMENT AND DEVELOPMENT, 1987, Our common future. Bruntland Report, Oxford: Oxford University Press.
WRAP, 2012, Valuing our clothes. In: The true cost of how we design, use and dispose of clothing in the UK. [Online]
Available at: http://www.wrap.org.uk/sustainable-textiles/valuing-our-clothes%
YEOMAN, I., 2011, The changing behaviours of luxury consumption. Journal of Revenue and Pricing Management 10, pp. 47-50.
YOUNG, W., HWANG, K. M. S. & OATES, C. J., 2010, Sustainable Consumption: Green Consumer Behaviour when Purchasing Products. Sustainable Development 18, pp. 20-31.

A CONCEPTUAL FRAMEWORK ON THE INFLUENCE OF AUTHENTICITY AND RARITY ON LUXURY BRAND VALUE

Jiang ZHIQING
Waseda University
zhiqing-jiang@ruri.waseda.jp

Nagasawa SHIN'YA
Waseda University
nagasawa@waseda.jp

ABSTRACT

The luxury goods market has been expanding globally since the early 1990s. Luxury consumption has witnessed a phenomenon of democratisation with the recent progress of civilisation and technology. It is easier now than 50 years ago to discover a scarce resource or purchase a refined item. Luxury marketers are faced with the challenge of the dilution of rarity and authenticity. This exploratory study is based on existing studies that discuss the definitions and associations of luxury, luxury brand, brand rarity, brand authenticity. The present study proposes a conceptual framework illustrating the internal relations of luxury brand authenticity, rarity and brand behaviour. It emphasises that in post-scarcity world, the nature or technical scarcity will tend to zero. The gap in the quality and functional value between each brand will diminish or even disappear. Intangible value generated by brand authenticity became the brand kernel, thus placing a price tag and attracting consumers, especially for luxury brand. Authenticity becomes the dominant factor distinguishing a luxury brand from others and whether the brand behaviour reflects its authenticity consistently, continuously and individually determines how consumers judge this brand.

Keywords: Authenticity, rarity, luxury brand, individuality, consistency, continuity
JEL codes: M30, M31

INTRODUCTION

Technology has rapidly evolved since the Industrialy Revolution. Its subsequent influence is too impeccable that the world is changing in an unpredictable direction. As the development of civilization and technology evolve, it is easier to discover scarce resource and produce refined goods than ever before. Uniformity in products due to mass production has led to a social identity crisis, which may be the primary reason for the present-day interest in authenticity such as heritage, the past and the original (Laenan 1989). This trend also appears significantly in traditional luxury industry in the past several decades. How can luxury become a social label is long debated, but in ancient eras, because of lack of technology and labour, it was difficult to finding certain scarce material such as precious stones (Berry, 1994). Luxury appeared unnecessary, but only a symbol of status in a society (Baudrillard, 1970; Berg, 2012; Veblen, 1898). Later, as present-day civilisation and technology developed, it was easier to discover a scarce resource or to produce a refined item. It was now easier to possess a luxury item. Kapferer and Bastien (2009) referred to this phenomenon as 'democratisation of luxury', which became obvious since the 1990s. The value of personal luxury goods in the global market witnessed has a sharp increase since 2000s. Recent research reports by Transparency Market Research indicate that this value will reach €260 billion in 2018, which was only €147 euros billion in 2009 (Statista 2019) and the global luxury goods market will cross €322.37 billion by the end of 2020.

Following this trend, as 'brand' assumed an identity independent from the manufacturer, luxury brand and luxury houses started to become distinct at the same time. A brand indicates not only the fame of the luxury house, but also an intangible value generated by branding, especially authenticity and rarity. Since then, the debate on luxury shifts from ancient to modern and from luxury goods to luxury brand is ongoing. The boundary between product and brand appears and then becomes distinct, which also impacts the luxury industry. In modern luxury, brands are critical because the more one sells intangible values beyond the functional ones, then more of these intangible values must be certified: which the fame of the brand alone can guarantee. Thus, scholars and marketeers have been striving to find the new boundary of luxury and luxury brands to explore the brand attributes that increase brand rarity (Catry, 2003; Phau and Prendergast, 2000, etc.) and authenticity (Gundlach and Neville, 2012; Schallehn, 2014; Coary, 2013, etc.). On the other hand, the high growth and penetration of luxury brand goods leads to a problem: rarity is diluted, and the luxury brand becomes less desirable (Kapferer and Valette-Florence, 2016). The constant growth in the number of brands, similar product offerings and fast imitation of product innovation have led to high levels of brand parity (BBDO Consulting GmbH, 2009) and escalating brand competition. The kernel of most luxury definitions is elitism. However, in the present day, elitism is more an image than a reality (Thomas, 2008). Luxury brands have had little choice but to abandon natural rarity as a precondition of luxury and instead adopt 'abundant rarity' strategy (Kapferer, 2012) which creates feelings of exclusivity rather than actual exclusivity and by artificial rarity tactics (Kapferer and Valette-Florence, 2016). Some researchers view brand authenticity as a potential new pillar to create brand rarity and exclusivity (Beverland, 2005a, 2005b; Pine and Gilmore, 2008; Gilmore and Pine, 2007; Blackshaw, 2008, Eggers et al., 2013).

Luxury, luxury brand and brand value

There is ongoing debate on 'luxury' for centuries and 'luxury' is also a swerve positioned with respect to a norm, a rule, a law that changes from society to society and era to era. Thus, luxury is always relative and impossible to define without situating it in time and space (Sicard, 2013:25). In his famous book *Luxury and Capitalism*, Sombart (1913, 1922) introduced two aspects of luxury regarding subjective evaluation of 'the necessary', quantitative and qualitative, which are most often combined. Quantitative luxury is synonymous with prodigality, while qualitative luxury is the use of superior-quality goods. He also characterised 'luxury goods' as 'refined goods' derived from the concept of qualitative luxury which is also defined similarly in marketing research literature. 'Luxury' is usually something related to self-indulgence and unnecessary (Ghosh and Varshney, 2013). Besides, although not all rare things can be considered luxury, luxury is something that must be rare or difficult to access. Rarity is one feature of luxury goods (Bourdieu, 1984; Veblen, 1899; Mauss, 2006; Sombart, 1913/1922; Berry, 1992; Douglasand Isherwood,1979; Hirsch, 1977).

Brands are interfaces: they mediate between production and consumption and symbolise industrial production of differences (Baudrillard, 1970/2003) and a hegemonic vehicle for endless diversity (Askegaard, 2006). Studies on brand value grew since the 1950s. Earlier research concentrated more on the product itself rather than the brand value. The extensive value created by a brand despite of the product has been widely debates since decades, including some well-known theories such as brand equity (Aaker, 2001) and brand identity (Kapferer, 2008). When a product/commodity becomes a brand, its value is supplemented by a number of further associations (Danesi, 2006: 3, 21). Branding generates 'luxury brand' from 'luxury' and makes it a more complex. The divergence lies in the way how a brand creates the value as a luxury and by what brand associations. Luxury is a controversial and sophisticated topic in sociology and anthropology for centuries, while the contents of luxury brand became more complex than luxury itself, for brand attaches several associations with luxury goods. It is composed of not only attributes and functions of luxury but also that of brand, which makes luxury brand a separate facet distinct from other commercial brands.

In the past century, economists or sociologists have defined 'value' variously. In philosophy, 'value' refers to the standards for behaviour or an optative, an expectation, with a view to perfection. However, precise concepts of value are still lacking. Marketers and researchers introduced perceived value, which is a specific inference-making mechanism based on consumers' intuitions of market efficiency (Chernev and Carpenter, 2001). Consequently, studying benefit components is one the main approaches of perceived value. Monroe's (2003) pioneering conceptualisation has finally been transformed into a model of perceived value with four components. A few others have focused on the perceived value and consumer behaviour using the means–end method. Zeithaml (1988) states that the components of perceived value include perceived quality, perceived sacrifice, extrinsic attributes, intrinsic attributes and high-level abstractions; and perceived quality is influenced by extrinsic attributes, intrinsic attributes and perceived monetary price (a part of perceived sacrifice).

Table-1. Review of luxury brand dimensions.

Vigneron and Johnson (2004)	Conspicuousness	Uniqueness	Quality	Hedonism	Extended self	
Berthon et al. (2009)	Functional	Experiential	Symbolic			
Brakus et al. (2009)	Behavioural	Feelings	Cognition			
Vickers and Renand (2003)	Functionalism	Experientialism	Symbolic Interactionism			
Gofman et al. (2010)	Design	Style	Experience	Emotions	Exclusivity	
Heine and Phan (2011)	Price	Quality	Aesthetics	Rarity	Extraordinariness	Symbolic meaning
Reyneke et al. (2011)	Modern	Classic	Post-modern	Wabisabi		
Walley et al. (2013)	Affect	Characteristics	Status	Gifting	Involvement	
Kapferer and Valette-Florence (2016)	Objective rarity	Exclusivity	Prestige	Creative Leadership		

Table-2. Selected luxury brand dimension and attributes

Vigneron and Johnson (2004)'s BLI scale		Kapferer (1998)	Dubois et al., (2001)
Conspicuous	Conspicuous Elitist Extremely expensive For wealthy	Belonging to a minority Its price	Conspicuous Elitist Very high price
Uniqueness	Very exclusive Precious Rare Unique	Exclusiveness Its uniqueness Its great creativity Grown out of a creative genius Knowing that few have one	Scarcity Uniqueness Not mass-produced Differentiate from others Few people own
Quality	Crafted Luxurious Best quality Sophisticated Superior	Craftsman Its quality Beauty of object Excellence of product	Rather like luxury Excellent quality Good taste
Hedonism	Exquisite Glamorous Stunning	Its sensuality Its magic	Pleasure Pleasing Aesthetics and polysensuality Makes life beautiful Make dream
Extended self	Leading Very powerful Rewarding Successful		Refined people Reveal who you are
		Savoir faire and tradition International reputation Long history Never out of fashion Forefront of fashion	Ancestral heritage and personal history Superfluous and non-functional

In research on luxury, researchers defined aspects of luxury products and brands semiotically using means–end method. Table 1 lists an initial review of describing luxury products and brands. These findings have little in common with each other. According to the literature in sociology, a necessary condition of luxury is refined goods (Veblen, 1899; Mauss, 2006; Sombart, 1913/1922; Berry, 1992), which implies that the functional, physical and aesthetic attributes of the goods must reach a basic standard that is higher than mass products. However, majority of the research reaches a consensus that rarity and authenticity are critical parts of a luxury brand and distinguishes a luxury brand from common commercial brands (e.g. Berthon et al., 2009; Brakus et al., 2009; Vickers and Renand, 2003; Vigneron and Johnson, 2004; Gofman et al., 2010; Kapferer, 1997, 1998).

Scarcity, Post-scarcity and rarity

Scarcity is an economic term and basically framed by assuming finite productive resources, infinite and insatiable social needs and a market mechanism as the best means for optimal allocation of resources (Matthaei,1984). It is determined by supply and demand conditions, while the mechanisms of access are often considered as playing an important role as well (O'Connor,1993; Hoeschele, 2010; Panayotakis, 2013). A scarce good is one that has more demand than the quantity supplied (Jeffrey and Stephan, 2010). Infinite and insatiable needs are part of a metaphysically conceived human nature, underlining instead that human needs are socially determined, manipulated and artificially expanded to serve the interests prevailing in the market (Liodakis, 2016). From a neo-Marxist approach, technological development and increasing energy-intensive capitalist production have led to an increasing economic surplus, building this as a basis for transcending scarcity (Baran and Sweezy, 1966). Scarcity falls into three distinctive categories: demand-induced, supply-induced and structural (Homer-Dixon, 2001). Demand-induced scarcity occurs when the demand for the resource increases and the supply remains the same. Supply-induced scarcity occurs when the supply is very low in comparison to the demand. Structural scarcity occurs when part of a population does not have equal access to resources owing to political conflicts or location (Homer-Dixon, 2001). In terms of luxury goods, by the beginning of the 20th century, the scarcity mainly indicated supply-induced and structural scarcity and for a short period of demand-induced scarcity by the 1990s.

Aguilar-Millan et al. (2010) claim that human history has fluctuated through periods of relative scarcity and relative abundance. The period from 1975 to 2005 was one of relative abundance, which ended after 2005 with a recession to mark the transition from a world of abundance to a world of scarcity. Between 2010 and 2050, the world is transforming from scarcity to post-scarcity, which means it will be a world without scarcity. Economic growth and rapid technological development (material substitution, etc.) will drastically reduce scarcity (Gowdy, 1984; Reuveny, 2002). In the post-scarcity world, technological advances will facilitate reduction in costs until conceivably almost everything is free to the consumer, an idea well explored by *Wired* editor Chris Anderson (2009) in *Free*. Scarcity will no longer exist in this world, and, without scarcity, the concept of charging a price to consumers as a means of generating revenue will be unworkable.

Assume that the nature and technical scarcity of luxury goods, such as material, technology and productivity, tends to decrease and vanish in the future.

A distinctive Marxist approach contends that scarcity can be considered on an aggregate societal level in relation to a particular class or social category. Relative scarcity is meaningfully conceived as a class-based relative access to the means to satisfy human needs, while absolute scarcity should be understood as a limiting factor, determined by ecological/material conditions of production and a social configuration of production and social needs (Liodakis, 2016). In field of marketing, ever since perceived value was introduced, 'rarity' involved the perceived scarcity of either product or brand, because 'luxury' is dependent on the subjective interpretation of the consumers. In ancient eras, rarity had a strong association with luxury (Veblen, 1899; Sombart, 1913/1922; Berry, 1992). Rare raw materials, low productivity and the unique mechanism of access dominated by social hierarchy led to high rarity of luxury goods. These days, from the classic viewpoint of scarcity, both marketers and scholars recognise that a luxury brand suffers from losing its rarity. They are facing a dilemma that there is a decrease in scarcity when luxury goods are increasingly produced and there is homogeneity in competition. Uniformity in products, similarity in raw materials and technology, increasing accessibility of traditional luxury brand goods and high-quality counterfeit products are diluting scarcity and making luxury brand goods less rare. This dilemma becomes increasingly obvious during this period of transformation to post-scarcity world. Luxury brands, thus, create artificial rarity rather than actual, which is the scarcity of items that exist even though the technology for production or the sharing capacity exists to create a theoretically limitless abundance or at least a greater quantity of production than that which currently exists. Once luxury loses scarcity and becomes less rare, its social function will also disappear simultaneously and turn into a normal commodity, which is a significant damage to the traditional luxury brands. Dubois and Paternault (1995) describe this dilemma in their dream formula which identifies the luxury brand attraction in a regression equation and adopts accessibility as a dependent variable. In the regression equation, an increase in the ownership of a luxury brand decreases the purchasing intention of the brand. It is logical to assume that awareness of a brand excites consumers to dream of owning it, and eventually stimulates purchase. This crucial factor together with luxury since born, but due to the development in science and technology as well as changes in market, the boundary of rarity became blurred. Scholars intend to find the trail and its tendency (Berry, 1992; Catry, 2003).

DREAM=-8.6+0.58AWARENESS-0.59 PURCHASE

In the studies by Catry (2003), rarity of luxury brand is categorised into four clusters (see Table 2): nature rarity, techno-rarity, limited edition and information-based rarity. Catry (2003) broadens rarity's contents from product scarcity to a brand level and indicates that modern luxury brand differs from traditional luxury goods; it is more diversifying and changeable.

Table-3. The rarity of luxury brand (Catry, 2003)

Natural rarity	Techno- rarity	Limited edition	Information-based rarity
Limited availability of Raw ingredients, Components, Production capacity, Human expertise, etc.	Innovations in product features: New product, New technology, Creation of designers, etc	Virtual supply constraints: A maximum number of special pieces, Together with events Special orders and series of one, etc.	Information communicated to consumers: High price, Distribution, Advertising, Public relations, Stratification of designers, etc.

Hypothese-1: Luxury brand rarity is determined by not only a set attributes of products but also a series of brand behaviour.

Hypotheses 1-1 Luxury brand rarity is related to two dimensions: product and brand.

Hypotheses 1-2 Influence of product-related rarity tends to become less important.

Authenticity

Despite of rarity, authenticity is another key attribute of brand, especially for luxury brand. Ever since the Industrial Revolution increased mass production, there has been conflict between imitation and authenticity (Orvell, 1989). It is this struggle between consuming the mass production while desiring the original that engages and ignites consumers' quest for an authentic consumption or product experience. Over the past century, this tension has increased due to technological advances, facilitating the effective simulation of authenticity (Halliday, 2001). Researchers have demonstrated that authenticity is critical in both product consumption and the role consumers that play within many subcultures and communal consumption experiences (Holt, 1997; Muniz and O'Guinn 2001; Penaloza, 2000). Culture and national identity are explanatory attributes in the consumption of luxury goods (Kapferer and Bastien, 2009; Kapferer, 1998; Dubios et al., 2001; Douglas and Isherwood, 1979) and consumer's purchase intention become higher when no information on country-of-origin (COO) is provided than when an impression of a moderate country exists (Lin, 2012). These attributes such as culture, national identity and COO can be attributed to authenticity (Leigh et al., 2006). Authenticity is central to consumer roles within virtually every subculture and communal consumption, but few consumer researchers have explicitly defined authenticity; this has allowed the term authenticity to be used in several ways and with various meanings (Leigh et al., 2006).

Webster's Dictionary defines authentic as 'not false or copied; genuine; real' and 'having the origin supported by unquestionable evidence'. In reference to objects, the authentic is often considered as the 'original' and is contrasted with the copy (Peterson, 2005). This genuineness can manifest itself in numerous ways, reflecting the key dimensions of brand authenticity. As consumers use genuineness as a broad concept of authenticity, each consumer begins to apply it to the many products or attractions around them, creating an aggregated, socially constructed shared meaning. Consumers begin to realise that they are surrounded by authentic and inauthentic items (Lowenthal 1992). Earlier studies have stressed the concepts of genuineness or reality in definitions of authenticity (Fine, 2003; Costa and Bamossy, 2001; Bruner, 1994; Arnould and Price 2000). Typically, authenticity is used to describe an object that is the real thing and not a fake or an imitation (Bruner, 1994). However, the term can be used in numerous contexts that may stretch this definition, or it can be used to convey a different sentiment by different people or groups. For example, from a socio-psychological perspective, the term authentic is conceptualised as self-fulfilment (Fine, 2003). Authenticity generally centres on a brand or an experience as being original and grounded in tradition and history (Beverland, 2005; Beverland et al, 2008; Ilicic and Webster, 2014). Fritz et al. (2017) found that brand authenticity can be influenced by the identified variables (i.e. brand heritage, nostalgia, commercialisation, clarity, social commitment, legitimacy and actual self-congruence and employee's passion). Moreover, brand authenticity positively influences brand relationship quality, which in turn positively impacts consumers' behavioural intentions. Meanwhile, brand authenticity can increase brand uniqueness and stimulate consumer`s purchase intention (Coary, 2013; Fritz, et al., 2017). Thus, it is critical to understand the drivers and dimensions of authenticity to arrive at a universal definition and understanding of the term. Authenticity is a much more complicated to consumers than simply being genuine or the original. In addition to genuineness and realness, consumers often seek traditional products in their search for authentic experiences. For example, the wine industry commonly advertises traditional methods of wine making, while obscuring the industrial processes that have increased its quality and lowered prices (Beverland 2006). This notion of authenticity highlighting the timeless value demanded by consumers while downplaying commercial motives is key to understanding brand authenticity (Beverland 2006). Furthermore, a few studies also indicate that authentic product is rare and exclusive (Gundlach and Neville, 2011; Catry, 2003). These researches reveal that some contents of authenticity and rarity in a broad definition overlap to some extent (Gundlach and Neville, 2011; Catry, 2003) and these contents distinguish a brand from others, which can be an irreplaceable part of a luxury brand.

Hypothesis-2: Authenticity has a positive influence on luxury brand rarity.

From consumer research perspective, Grayson and Martinec (2004) refine the concept of authenticity as indexical and iconic authenticity. In their research, indexical authenticity distinguishes 'the real thing' from its copies (Benjamin, 1969; Goodman 1976; Kingston 1999) and perceivers must have some confidence that it in fact has the factual and spatio-temporal link that it has claimed. Iconic authenticity refers to something whose physical manifestation resembles something that is indexically authentic. These two dimensions of authenticity are not mutually exclusive. Although perception can sometimes stress iconicity more than indexicality and vice versa, every perceived cue has iconic and indexical authenticity (Grayson and Martinec, 2004). Most scholars who study authenticity concur that authenticity is not an attribute inherent in an object and is better understood as an assessment by an evaluator in a particular context (Bruner, 1994; Cohen, 1988; Delyser, 1999; Haslam, 1985). Indexical authenticity of brand stresses on the original, not an imitation (Huntington, 1988, p. 157; Bruner, 1994, p. 400) and verifies an object being 'the real thing', both legitimate and genuine (Benjamin, 1969; Kingston, 1999; Ilicic and Webster, 2014). In addition, one brand with high iconic authenticity will be assumed to be an object that 'resembles something that is with indexical authenticity' (Grayson and Martinec, 2004, p. 298; Ilicic and Webster, 2014), where an object is an 'authentic reproduction' or an 'authentic recreation' of the original (Bruner, 1994, p.

399; Peterson, 1997, p. 208). For example, when an individual sees a BMW 5 series, he can recognise this car by both indexical authenticity (BMW logo) and iconic authenticity (typical design style of BMW). In marketing, brand indicates the spatio-temporal link between branded goods and its origin and verifies its indexical authenticity.

Hypothese 3 Luxury brand authenticity is composed of brand-related authenticity and product-related authenticity.

Hypothese 3-1 Luxury brand-related authenticity refers to brand indexical authenticity that can be directly associated with this brand (history, origin, promise, service, etc.).

Hypothese 3-2 Luxury product-related authenticity refers to brand iconic authenticity that can be directly associated with this brand (brand name, logo, design style, prints, etc.)

Table-4. Content categories for analysis of authenticity

Content category	Source
Heritage and pedigree Relationship to place Unique method of production Commitments to consistency and quality Genuineness	Beverland (2006)
Ingredients and materials Company/ craftsperson Aesthetics Uniqueness and originality Experience/prioritising craft motives	Littrell et al's (1993)
Exclusivity	Gundlach and Neville (2011)
brand heritage, brand nostalgia, brand commercialisation, brand clarity, brand's social commitment, brand legitimacy, actual self-congruence, employee's passion	Fritz, et al. (2017)
Being the Category Pioneer Maintaining the Original Product Adhering to Principles	Coary (2013)
Celebrity authenticity, Heritage and essence	Ilicic and Webster, (2014)

Figure-1. Conceptual framework of luxury brand authenticity and rarity

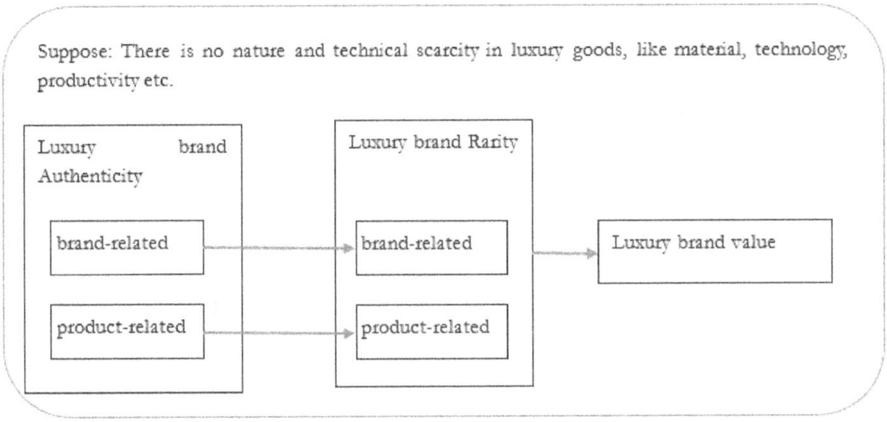

Characteristics of luxury brand authenticity

Key, high-level dimensions that highlight the term authenticity depend on everyone's perspective and quest for authenticity. Schallehn et al. (2014) offer a scientific analysis of the concept of authenticity from a socio-psychological perspective. Their research discusses the characteristics of brand authenticity instead of actual contents or dimension. Schallehn et al. (2014) claim that brand authenticity includes consistency, continuity and individuality. Individuality is defined as the unique way in which the brand fulfils its promise. Consistency measures those attributes which are expressed by its reiterative current brand behaviour. Hence, high consistency is perceived if the brand promise is fulfilled at each brand touch-point. Continuity refers to the core brand attributes remaining stable over a longer period. Hence, the consumer judges continuity to be high if the present brand promise reflects past brand behaviour. Identity-based brand management model comprises two main components: brand identity and brand image (De Chernatony et al., 2011; Kapferer, 1996). An authentic brand has a clear understanding of its position and gels with its identity, and its behaviour reflects its invisible brand identity. Schallehn et al. (2014) argues that a low degree of brand authenticity implies a brand image which does not coordinate with its identity. Therefore, the origin of the brand promise is attributed to external forces rather than to brand identity. Thus, brand attributes should be reflected in its individual, consistent and continuous brand behaviour. However, this work has only discussed the association between brand authenticity (keeping brand promise) and brand trust based on a beer brand and a restaurant.

Hypotheses 4 Luxury brand authenticity is perceived to be individual, consistent and continuous.

Hypotheses 4-1 Perceived brand individuality of brand behaviour has an influence on perceived luxury brand authenticity.

Hypotheses 4-2 Perceived brand consistency of brand behaviour has an influence on perceived luxury brand authenticity.

Hypotheses 4-3 Perceived brand continuity of brand behaviour has an influence on perceived luxury brand authenticity.

Figure-2. Conceptual framework of luxury brand authenticity and rarity

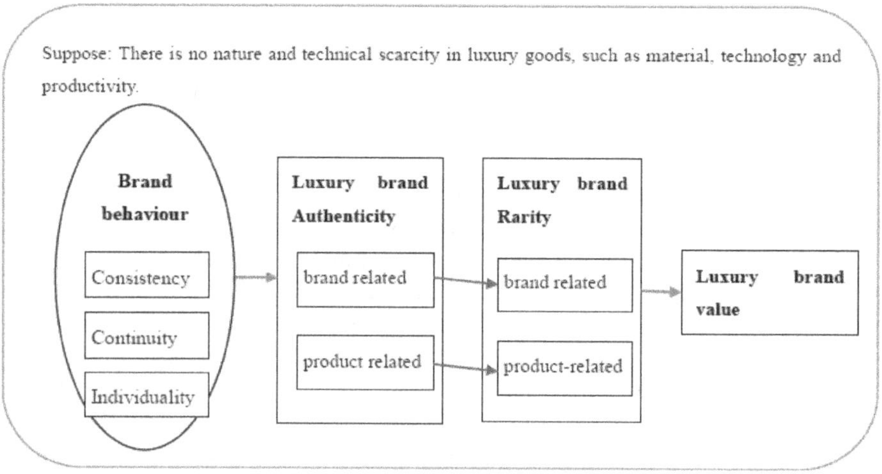

DISCUSSION

This conceptual framework stresses that when it is transforming into post-scarcity world, nature or technical scarcity will tend to no scarcity. It means that the gap of quality and functional value between each brand will become lesser or may even disappear. Intangible value generated by brand authenticity becomes the kernel of a brand placing a price tag and attracting consumers, especially for a luxury brand. Authenticity becomes the dominate factor distinguishing a luxury brand from others and whether brand behaviour reflects its authenticity consistently, continuously and individually determines how consumers judge this brand. Different from commodity, luxury has more cultural, social and aesthetic contents and its universe is full of diversity which contributes to a high intangible value rooted in its authenticity. Although the functional value is the same, luxury brand goods can be charged a higher price than are commodities. For example, a Celine plastic PVC shopping bag is tagged $590, while that of a fashion brand only costs $30. The materials of both the products are transparent PVC, the style is similar and there is almost no difference in function. However, in the market, there is over a $500 gap of value between these two brands' shopping bag.

Photo: Courtesy of céline.com

Photo: http://www.blackgemdrivingschool.ca

Grand Seiko

'Grand Seiko' is a luxury line provided by Seiko Group, one of the reputed Japanese conglomerates. Although the line of Grand Seiko was released in early 1960s when the manufacturing industry in Japan was rising to be a centre of precision manufacturing, Grand Seiko was not a separate brand but had remained a high-end product line of Seiko since 2017. The Grand Seiko line was retired in 1976 as quartz movements dominated. However, the company revived the brand a decade later, introducing a quartz Grand Seiko for the first time in 1986. As mechanical watches regained market share, Seiko responded, then re-launching the Grand Seiko mechanical line in 1998. It turned a halo for the company, with the return of GMT in 2002, the introduction of a Grand Seiko Spring Drive model in 2004 and the return of a Hi-Beat model in 2009. In 2017, Seiko officially split Grand Seiko from the mother company, launching it as a brand and removing 'Seiko' from the dial. It has two ateliers in Shiojiri and Shizukuishi, which has the top Japanese watch craftsmen and technology. Spring drive is Seiko's original hybrid power movement which adopts the quartz and IC chips mechanism to create a quiet, smooth and consistent rotation of the second hand. It achieves highest precision in the existing mechanical movements and is monopolised by Seiko Group. In case of monopoly, a scarcity is created (Lionel, 1932). Typically, Grand Seiko has an extremely high product-related rarity due to its strength in technical development of watch movement. However, in a semi-structured interview with the brand manager and design director, they stated that Grand Seiko is finding it difficult to establish itself as a luxury watch brand, although it is considered as a brand with high technology that can provide refined watches as other giants, such as Rolex, or even has a higher quality than mastige watch brand, such as Omega. However, the brand is perceived to be a high-end manufactured brand instead of a luxury brand. They also stressed that Grand Seiko has enough technique and know-how to manufacture top-level timepieces, but there must be something wrong in branding when adding intangible value into brand.

Based on a conceptual framework of luxury brand behaviour, authenticity and rarity, a summary of brand authenticity and behaviour is listed in Table 5. It shows that Grand Seiko makes great efforts to create product-related authenticity, but few special or unique actions and policies are taken to increase its brand-related authenticity; accordingly, the major value lies in product-related brand authenticity, brand-related authenticity is quite limited. As a comparison, a summary of that of Omega is listed in Table 6. We can clearly find that Grand Seiko and Omega are in the two directions of creating and presenting its brand authenticity. As mentioned earlier, Grand Seiko strives to increase product-related authenticity to create product-related rarity; conversely, Omega endeavours to maintain and elevate its brand-related authenticity in a series of brand actions such as sponsorship.

Table-5. A summary of brand authenticity and brand behaviour of Grand Seiko

Brand authenticity	Brand behaviour
● Product-related Spring drive, movement/ calibre, precise, durable iconic design style	● Consistency Keep its brand promise: high precision and durability Research and develop high precise mechanical movement
	● Continuity Keep its brand promise: high precision and durability Research and develop highly precise mechanical movement
● Brand-related Origin in Japan Traditional watch maker	● Individuality N/A

Table-6. A summary of brand authenticity and brand behaviour of Omega

Brand authenticity	Brand behaviour
● Product-related Movement/ calibre, precise, durable iconic design style	● Consistency Keep its brand promise: provide durable refined watches Have a clear design policy
	● Continuity Keep its brand promise: provide durable refined watches Have a clear design policy
● Brand-related Origin in Switzerland; First watch on the moon Space exploration Traditional watch maker	● Individuality Sponsorship Celebrities PR events

CONCLUSION AND FUTURE DIRECTION

Based on extant literature, this exploratory study discusses the definitions of luxury, luxury brand, brand rarity, brand authenticity and the association among them. This study proposes a comprehensive conceptual framework that illustrates the internal relations of luxury brand authenticity, rarity and brand behaviour. This conceptual framework emphasises that when it is transforming into post-scarcity world, nature or technical scarcity will tend to zero. The gap of quality and functional value between each brand will become less or even disappear. Intangible value generated by brand authenticity becomes the kernel of a brand placing a price tag and attracting consumers, especially for a luxury brand. Authenticity becomes the dominant factor distinguishing a luxury brand from others and whether brand behaviour reflects its authenticity consistently, continuously and individually determines how consumers judge this brand.

However, this research is qualitative and descriptive and mainly based on literature review. Thus, the structure of the conceptual framework should be modified on large brands and consumer database through a quantitative approach. Furthermore, the detailed items on each dimension have not been studied yet. In a future study, it should be done to complete this conceptual model and describe each attribute more accurately.

REFERENCES

AAKER, D.A., 2001, *Strategic Market Management (Sixth ed.).* New York, NY: John Wiley & Sons.

AGUILAR-MILLAN, S., FEENEY, A., OBERG, A. and RUDD, E., 2010, "The post-scarcity world of 2050-2075", *The Futurist*, Vol. 44 No. 1, pp. 34

ANDERSON, C., 2009, *Free: the future of a radical price.* New York, NY: Hyperrion.

ARNOULD, E. and PRICE, L., 2000, "Authenticating acts and authoritative performances", in Ratneshwar, S., Mick, D.G. and Huffman, C. (Eds), *The Why of Consumption: Contemporary Perspectives on Consumer Motives, Goals and Desires,* London: Routledge, pp. 140-163.

BARAN, P. and SWEEZY, P., 1966, *Monopoly Capital.* New York, NY: Monthly Review Press.

BAUDRILLARD, J., 1970, *The Consumer Society: Myths and Structures* (translated by Chris turner). London: Sage.

BENJAMIN, W., [1935] 1969, "The Work of Art in the Age of Mechanical Reproduction",(translated by Harry Zohn), in Hannah Arendt (Eds), *Illuminations,* New York: Schocken Books, pp.217-51.

BERG, M., 2012, “Luxury, the Luxury Trades and the Roots of Industrial Growth”. Chap. 9, in Trentmann, F. (ed.), *The Oxford Handbook on the History of Consumption*, pp.173-212, London: OUP.
BERRY, C.J., 1994, *The Idea of luxury: A Conceptual and historical Investigation*, Cambridge University Press, Cambridge, MA.
BEVERLAND, M., 2005, “Crafting brand authenticity: The case of luxury wines”, *Journal of Management Studies*, Vol. 42, No.5, pp.1003-1029.
BEVERLAND, M., 2006, “The ‘real thing’: Branding authenticity in the luxury wine trade”, *Journal of Business Research*, Vol.59, pp.251-8.
BEVERLAND, M. B., LINDGREEN, A., and VINK, M. W., 2008, “Projecting authenticity through advertising: Consumer judgments of advertisers’ claims”. *Journal of Advertising*, Vol. 37 No.1, pp.5-15.
BERTHON, P.R., PITT, L.F., PARENT, M. and BERTHON, J.-P., 2009, “Aesthetics and ephemerality: observing and preserving the luxury brand”, *California Management Review*, Vol.52 No.1, pp.45-66.
BRAKUS, J.J., SCHMITT, B.H. and ZARANTONELLO, L., 2009, “Brand experience: what is it? How is it measured? Does it affect loyalty?”, *Journal of Marketing*, Vol.73 No. 3, pp.52-68.
BLACKSHAW, P., 2008, " The six drivers of brand credibility ", *Marketing Management,* Vol. 17 No. 3, pp. 51-54.
BOURDIEU, P., 1984, *Distinction: A Social Critique of the Judgment of Taste.* Cambridge, MA: Harvard University Press.
BRUNER, E. M., 1994, "Abraham Lincoln as Authentic Reproduction: A Critique of Postmodemism," *American Anthropologist*, Vol. 96 No. 2, pp. 397-415.
CATRY, B., 2003, “The great pretenders: the magic of luxury goods”, *Business strategy review.* Vol.14 No.3, pp. 10-17.
CHERNEV, A. and CARPENTER, G. S., 2001, “The role of market efficiency institutions in consumer choice: A case of compensatory inferences”, *Journal of Marketing Research*, Vol.38, pp.349–361.
COSTA, J.A. and BAMOSSY, G.J., 2001, " Le parc disney: creating an 'authentic' American experience ", *Advances in Consumer Research*, Vol. 28 No. 1, pp. 398 - 402.
COHEN, E., 1988, "Authenticity and Commoditization in Tourism," *Annals of Tourism Research*, Vol.15 No.3, pp. 371-86.
DUBOIS, B., LAURENT, G. and CZELLAR, S., 2001, “Consumer rapport to luxury: analysing complex and ambivalent attitudes”, *IDEAS Working Paper Series from RePEc*, 736, HEC, St. Louis: Federal Reserve Bank of St Louis.
DANESI, M., 2006, *Brands*, Abingdon: Routledge.
DOUGLAS, M. and ISHERWOOD, B., 1979, *The World of Goods: Towards an Anthropology of Consumption.* New York: Basic Books.
DELYSER, D., 1999, "Authenticity on the Ground: Engaging the Past in a Califomia Town," *Annals of the Association of American Geographers*, Vol.89 No.4. pp. 602-632.

DE CHERNATONY, L., MCDONALD, M. and WALLACE, E., 2011, *Creating Powerful Brands*, Routledge: Kidlington
EGGERS, F., O'DWYER, M., KRAUS, S., VALLASTER, C. and GUELDENBERG, S., 2013, " The impact of brand authenticity on brand trust and SME growth: a CEO perspective ", *Journal of World Business,* Vol. 48 No. 3, pp. 340-348.
FINE, G.A., 2003, " Crafting authenticity: the validation of identity in self-taught art ", *Theory and Society*, Vol. 32 No. 2, pp. 153-180.
FRITZ, K., SCHOENMUELLER, V. and BRUHN, M., 2017, "Authenticity in branding–exploring antecedents and consequences of brand authenticity", *European Journal of Marketing*, Vol. 51 No. 2, pp. 324-348.
GOWDY, J M., 1984, "Marx and Resource Scarcity: An Institutionalist Approach." *Journal of Economic Issues,* Vol.18 No.2, pp. 393–400.
GILMORE, J. H. and PINE, J. B., 2007, *Authenticity: What Consumers Really Want.* Harvard Business School Press.
GHOSH, A. and VARSHNEY, S., 2013, "Luxury goods consumption: a conceptual framework based on literature review ", *South Asian Journal of Management*, Vol. 20 No. 2, pp. 146 - 159.
GOFMAN, A., MOSKOWITZ, H.R., BEVELO, M. and METS, T., 2010, "Decoding consumer perceptions of premium products with rule-developing experimentation", *Journal of Consumer Marketing*, Vol. 27 No. 5, pp. 425-436.
GOODMAN, N., [1968] 1976, "III: Art and Authenticity," in *Languages of Art*, Indianapolis: Hackett, pp. 99-123.
GROTH, J. C. and MCDANIEL, S.W., 1993, "The exclusive value principle: the basis for prestige racing". *Journal of Consumer Marketing*, Vol. 10 No. 1, pp. 10 – 16
GRAYSON, K. and MARTINEC, R., 2004, "Consumer perceptions of iconicity and indexicality and their influence on assessments of authentic market offerings", *Journal of Consumer Research*, Vol. 31 No.2, pp. 296-312.
GUNDLACH, H., and NEVILLE, B., 2012, "Authenticity: Further theoretical and practical development", *Journal of Brand Management*, Vol.19 No.6, pp. 484-499.
HALLIDAY, J., 2001, *Australia and New Zealand Wine Companion*, Sydney: Harper Collins.
HASLAM, G., 1985, "A Question of Authenticity: Who Can Write What?", *Westem American Literature*, Vol.20 No.3, pp.246-250.
HIRSCH, S., 1977, *Rich man's, Poor man's and Every Man's Goods*, Tubingen; J.C.B.Mohr.
HOESCHELE, W., 2010, *The Economics of Abundance: A Political Economy of Freedom, Equity, and Sustainability*. London: Gower
HOMER-DIXON, T. F., 2000, *The Ingenuity Gap: How Can We Solve the Problems of the Future?* New York; Toronto: Knopf.

HOLT, DH., 1997, "A comparative study of values among Chinese and U. S. entrepreneurs: pragmatic convergence between contrasting cultures". *Journal of Business Venturing*, Vol.12 No.6. pp. 483–505.
ILICIC, J. and WEBSTER, C. M., 2014, "Investigating consumer–brand relational authenticity", *Journal of Brand Management*, Vol.21 No.4, pp. 342-363.
KJELDGAARD, D. and ASKEGAARD, S., 2006, "The glocalization of youth culture: the global youth segment as structures of common difference", *Journal of Consumer Research*, Vol. 33 No. 3, pp. 231-47.
KAPFERER, J-N. and BASTIEN, V., 2009, *The Luxury Strategy: Break the Rules of Marketing to Build Luxury Brands*. London: Kogan Page.
KAPFERER, J-N. and BASTIEN, V., 2009, "The specificity of luxury management: turning marketing upside down", *Journal of Brand Management*. Vol.16 No 5/6, pp.311-322.
KAPFERER, J.N. and VALETTE-FLORENCE, P., 2016, "Beyond rarity: the paths of luxury desire. How luxury brands grow yet remain desirable", *Journal of Product and Brand Management*, Vol.25 No.2, pp. 120-133.
KAPFERER, J.N., 2012, "Abundant rarity, the key to luxury growth", *Business Horizons*, Vol. 55 No.5, pp. 453-462.
KAPFERER, J.N., 1997, "Managing luxury brands", *Journal of Brand Management*, Vol.4 No. 4, pp. 251-260.
KAPFERER, J.N., 1998, "Why are we seduced by luxury brands?", *Journal of Brand Management*, No.6 Vol.1, pp. 44-49.
KAPFERER, K., 2008, *New Strategic Brand Management - Creating and Sustaining Brand Equity Long Term* (4th ed.), London: Kogan Page.
KINGSTON, S., 1999, "The Essential Attitude: Authenticity in Primitive Art, Ethnographic Performances and Museums," *Journal of Material Culture*, Vol.4 No.3, pp. 338-51.
LAENEN, M., 1989, "Looking for the future through the past", in Uzzell, D. (Ed), *Heritage Interpretation*, Volume 1, London: Belhaven Press.
LIODAKIS, G., 2016, "An Exploration of Scarcity in Historical Perspective", *Science & Society*. Vol. 80, No. 2, pp. 221-247.
LEIGH, T. W., PETERS, C. and SHELTON, J., 2006, "The Consumer Quest for Authenticity: The Multiplicity of Meanings Within the MG Subculture of Consumption", *Academy of Marketing Science*. Vol.34 No. 4, pp. 481-494
LIN, E.Y., 2012, "A Cross-Cultural Study of Luxury e-Branding: Standardization vs. Adaptation, Product Category, and Country-of-Origin", *Ying Xiao Ping Lun*. No.9 No.1, pp.91-120.
MAUSS, M., 2006, *Techniques, Technology and Civilization* (N. Schlanger, ed). New York: Berghahn.
MATTHAEI, J., 1984, "Rethinking Scarcity: Neoclassicism, Neo-Malthusianism, and Marxism." *Review of Radical Political Economics*, Vol.16 No.2–3, pp. 81–94.

MONROE, K.B., 2003, *Pricing: Making Profitable Decisions (3rd ed.)*, McGraw-Hill/ Irwin, Burr Ridge, IL .
MUÑIZ, A. M. Jr., and. HAMER, L. O., 2001, "Us Versus Them: Oppositional Brand Loyalty and the Cola Wars," in Mary C. Gilly and Joan Meyers-Levy, eds. *Advances in Consumer Research*, vol. 28, Provo, UT: Association for Consumer Research, pp. 355-361.
O'CONNOR, M., 1993, "On the Misadventures of Capitalist Nature." *Capitalism Nature Socialism*, Vol.4 No.3, pp.7–40.
ORVELL, M., 1989, *The real thing, imitation and authenticity in American culture, 1880-1940*. The university of North Carolina Press.
PARKER, R.S., HERMANS, C.M. and SCHAEFER, A.D., 2004, "Fashion consciousness of Chinese, Japanese and American teenagers", *Journal of Fashion Marketing and Management,* Vol.8 No. 2, pp.176-86.
PANAYOTAKIS, C., 2013, "Theorizing Scarcity: Neoclassical Economics and its Critics." *Review of Radical Political Economics*, Vol.45 No.2, pp.183–200.
PENALOZA, L., 2000, "The commodification of the American West: marketers' production of cultural meanings at the trade fair ", *Journal of Marketing*, Vol. 64 No. 4, pp. 82 - 109.
PETERSON, R.A., 2005, "In search of authenticity ", *Journal of Management Studies*, Vol. 42 No. 5, pp. 1083-1098.
PHAU, I. and PRENDERGAST, G., 2000, "Consuming luxury brands: The relevance of the 'rarity principle'". *Journal of Brand Management*, Vol. 8 No.2, pp. 122-138.
PINE, J. and GILMORE, J., 1999, *The Experience Economy,* Boston, MA: Harvard Business School Press.
REUVENY, R., 2002, "Economic Growth, Environmental Scarcity, and Conflict." *Global Environmental Politics*, Vol.2 No.1, pp. 83–110.
SOMBART, W., 1913, 1922, *Luxury and Capitalism*, translated by Dittmar, W.R., 1967, Ann Arbor: The University of Michigan Press.
SICARD, M.C., 2013, *Luxury, lies and marketing: shattering the illusion of the luxury brand.* Translated by Merill, T.C. Chennai: palgrave macmillan.
STATISTA.COM, 2019, Value of the personal luxury goods market worldwide from 2009 to 2018 (in billion euros) available at: https://www.statista.com/ statistics/266503/ value-of-the-personal-luxury-goods-market- worldwide/ (accessed 8th March 2019).
SCHALLEHN, M., BURMANN, C. and RILEY, N., 2014, "Brand authenticity: model development and empirical testing ", Journal of Product and Brand Management, Vol. 23 No. 3, pp. 192-199.
THOMAS, D., 2008, *Delux: How luxury lost its Luster*, Thorndike Press, New York, NY.
VEBLEN, T., 1899, 2004, *Theory of The Leisure Class*, Oxford Classics, Oxford: Oxford University Press.

VIGNERON, F. and JOHNSON, L. W., 1999, "A review and a conceptual framework of prestige-seeking consumer behaviour", *Academy of Marketing Science Review*, Vol.8 No. 2, pp.122-138.
VIGNERON, F. and JOHNSON, L. W., 2004, "Measuring perceptions of brand luxury", *Journal of Brand Management*, Vol.11 No.6, pp.484-506.
VICKERS, J.S. and RENAND, F., 2003, "The marketing of luxury goods: an exploratory study", *The Marketing Review,* Vol.3 No.4, pp. 459-478.
ZEITHAML, V. A., 1988, "Consumer Perceptions of Price, Quality and Value: A Means-End Model and Synthesis of Evidence", *Journal of Marketing*, Vol.52 No.3, pp.2-22.

DIGITAL CHANNELS AND DISTRIBUTION IN LUXURY MARKET

Fabrizio MOSCA
Università degli Studi di Torino
fabrizio.mosca@unito.it

Valentina CHIAUDANO
Università degli Studi di Torino
valentina.chiaudano@unito.it

ABSTRACT

This paper focuses on distribution strategies in the luxury brand market and digital channels. With the evolution of new technologies and new devices such as smartphones and tablets, companies that operate in the high-value market started to embrace digital channels as a part of their distribution strategies.
However, little research has been done regarding luxury brand companies and the new distribution patterns available online. By analysing the distribution strategies implemented online by well-known luxury brand companies, this paper aims to demonstrate that companies operating in the luxury brand market have overcome their scepticism about the use of digital technologies for selling products via online channels.
In fact, thanks to the new digital technologies luxury firms are able to recreate online the same distribution models available offline, thereby responding effectively to new consumption patterns and the needs of luxury brand consumers.

Keywords: luxury brand, distribution strategy, digitalisation, omnichannel experience, e-commerce.
JEL codes: M30, M31

INTRODUCTION

At the beginning of the twenty-first century, the advent of the Internet announced that all companies, operating both in the mass and luxury markets, had to face new challenges. In fact, they had to learn how to exploit the potential of Web 2.0 to respond more effectively to the new needs of consumers in terms of communication, interactions and services. In particular, luxury brand consumers require to be engaged towards an immersive brand experience involving brand attributes such as exclusivity, quality and heritage (Atwal et al., 2017).

According to diverse studies, at first, luxury brand companies embraced digital technologies exclusively as communication tools (Hennigs et al., 2012; Kapferer & Bastien, 2012; Okonkwo, 2009). Subsequently, digital innovations and new luxury consumption patterns arose, allowing luxury brand companies to use digital channels also to deliver luxury goods.

The hesitation of luxury brand companies to implement online sales is strongly dependent on the strategic value of distribution, representing one of the most important variables in managing the marketing mix for goods of high symbolic value (Mosca, 2016).

In fact, the perception of uniqueness and exclusiveness of luxury goods is deeply influenced by the distribution strategy.

Specifically, to be successful, companies that operate in the luxury market must promote selective and controlled retail distribution, thereby guaranteeing low availability of luxury products, which increases the prestige and therefore the value perceived by consumers.

For the above reasons, a digital channel is considered to be an unsuitable tool for selling luxury goods. In fact, it is fair to ask, how could the Internet, a mass medium available to everyone, practically sustain luxury brand attributes such as prestige, uniqueness and scarcity?

This paper aims to demonstrate that after an initial hesitation, luxury brand companies not only started to sell their products online, but they also have recreated online the same distribution patterns available in physical distribution. In fact, analysing distribution strategies managed via online channels by well-known luxury brand companies, we identify the different distribution models implemented via direct digital channels and the one created via indirect digital channels.

Moreover, we analyse the main features of each distribution model providing some successful examples of distribution strategies created by luxury brand companies.

1. DIGITAL CHANNELS AND LUXURY

When luxury companies started to embrace digital technologies, academics as well managers wondered whether luxury brands should use the Internet purely as a communication tool or whether a digital channel could also represent a sales channel (Hennigs et al., 2012; Kapferer & Bastien, 2012; Okonkwo, 2009).

After a first phase characterised by the exploitation of a digital channel only to create showcase sites for the dissemination of information about the company and the products, the use of a digital channel as a sales channel has become inevitable (Okonkwo, 2010).

However, the process of adapting digital innovations to distribution channels was not immediate. From 2005 up to recently, the integration between digital and physical channels was gradual and consisted of four main phases.

Figure 1. Levels of use of the digital channel's potentials

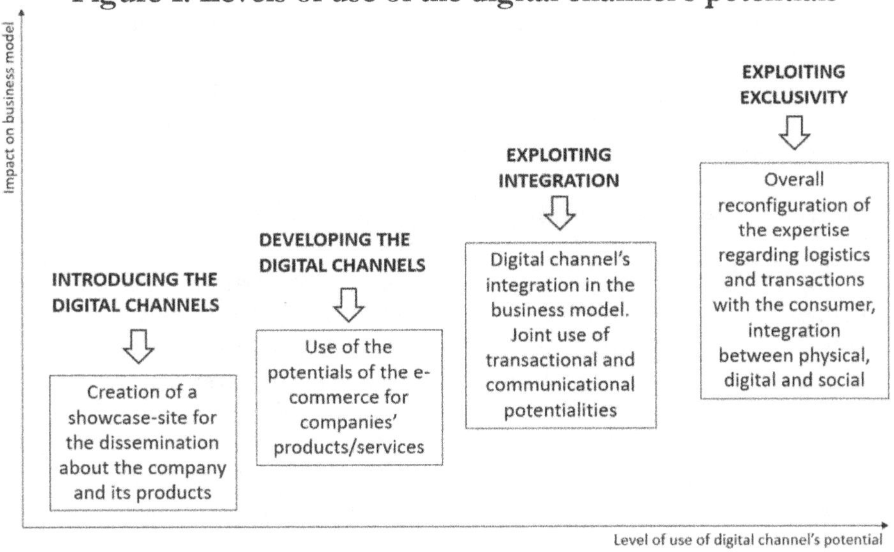

1.1. First phase: Introducing the digital channels

Initially, luxury brand consumers expected that luxury companies guaranteed an active online presence, even if they preferred to get in contact with luxury brand products in the physical stores. In fact, at that time, luxury brand consumers were intrigued by digital innovations, but, while they were navigating on a website, they perceived a loss of quality. Moreover, consumers had no intention of buying luxury products online because touching and testing products (especially clothing items) was impossible on the website and, in addition, the risk of buying counterfeit goods was higher online than offline.

Kapferer (2000) affirmed that Web 2.0 represented both an opportunity and a threat for luxury brand companies.

The opportunity consisted of the ability of the Internet to reach consumers who couldn't access a distribution channel due to their geographical location or their unease to visit the luxury store. The threat, instead, concerned the impact of digital technologies on luxury brand perception: a presence on the Web seemed to be incompatible with the finest quality, prestige, exclusiveness and hedonism of luxury brands (Kapferer et al., 2012; Batat, 2017).

In particular, Web 2.0 was characterised by its worldwide accessibility rather than targeting an exclusive niche of consumers (Liu, Burns, & Hou, 2013).

As Dall'Olmo and Riley (2003) theorised, at the beginning, luxury brand companies didn't use all the innovations made available by the Internet. In fact, luxury companies exploited digital channels only to create showcase sites for the dissemination of information about the company and the products.

An advanced use of digital channels, including functions such as sales and dual-way communication, can be identified from the following stages of the exploitation of digital channels.

1.2. Second phase: Developing the digital channels

In the second phase, managers of luxury companies had come to understand that increasing the use of digital technology was necessary to effectively satisfy the new needs of consumers whose interest in the possibilities for browsing and buying online was extremely high (Geerts, 2011).

All luxury brand companies were aware of digital technologies' potential and, first of all, the biggest conglomerates started moving towards e-commerce, implementing the purchase function on their websites.

However, diverse issues concerning digital adoption still remained.

First of all, some academics argued that being able to maintain the attribute of exclusivity remained difficult, due to the nature of Web 2.0, which was perceived as a platform for mass-market tools. Moreover, the security of transactions was an issue that luxury brand companies had to solve, as well as addressing the concerns of luxury brand consumers about the online experience. How could luxury brand companies recreate on the website the same experiences offered offline in the physical stores? The improvement of digital technologies and the spread of digital devices such as smartphones and tablets allowed luxury companies to offer an engaging brand experience in the online store.

1.3. Third phase: Exploiting integration

In this phase, the digital channel is considered by luxury brand companies as an important tool not only in terms of communication but also for distribution.

Thanks to the improvement of Web 2.0 technology, luxury brand companies were able to recreate online the brand's atmosphere (Kim et al. 2015), respecting all luxury codes (Larraufie et al., 2013).

Furthermore, websites of luxury companies not only provided consumers with some information about the brand, such as history and news, events, but most of them integrated an e-commerce platform that offered different categories of products (Geerts, 2017).

In the third phase, the digital channel was no longer considered to be an additional or complementary tool to the physical one.

On the contrary, luxury brand companies completely integrated the digital and physical channels, giving luxury brand consumers the chance to buy online or offline and a real 360-degree experience called the 'customer journey'. In fact, this term refers to a new type of purchasing experience, which is no longer the linear sum of several phases, but a process that includes diverse touch points that straddle the digital and traditional environments (Lemon & Verhoef, 2016).

1.4. Fourth phase: Exploiting exclusivity

Digital has profoundly changed the logic of managing and organising luxury brand companies, which have to evolve to remain in line with consumers' expectations.

In fact, the most successful luxury companies demonstrate their ability to change as quickly as possible: 'Run faster than a bullet', is the new leitmotif of luxury companies (Altagamma, 2017).

Today, digital technology plays a leading role in the luxury goods market, and luxury brands' strategies promote a total integration between digital and physical channels, both in distribution and communication.

In 2025, it is expected that online channels will represent 25% of the market value for luxury brand companies, and 100% of luxury brand purchases will be influenced by online communication (Altagamma, 2018).

2. DIGITAL CHANNELS AND DISTRIBUTION

Distribution is considered to be one of the strategic variables in managing the marketing mix for a luxury brand (Mosca, 2017).

In fact, distribution strategies implemented by luxury brand companies represent a source of competitive advantage.

This fact explains the initial hesitation of luxury brand companies when they considered using the Internet as a distribution channel.

However, the evolution of new technologies, the development of broadband, the spread of new devices such as smartphones and tablets and the changing of consumer culture encouraged companies that operate in the high-value market to include digital channels in their distribution strategies (Corbellini & Saviolo, 2015).

Analysing the luxury brand strategies implemented online by well-known luxury brand companies makes it possible to identify diverse distribution patterns that can be classified, as well as the distribution via physical stores, in two main groups:

- distribution via direct digital channels;
- distribution via indirect digital channels.

In the following sections, we analyse each model of distribution.

Figure 2. Distribution strategies of luxury brand companies

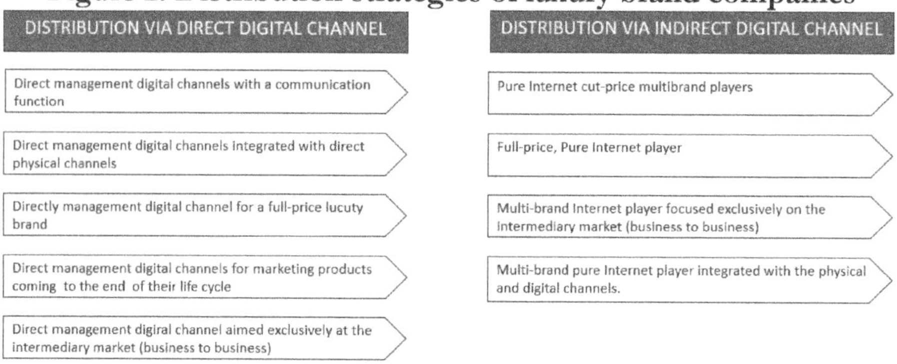

2.1. Distribution via direct digital channels

Generally speaking, direct distribution involves contact between the company and the final consumers without the presence of intermediaries.

In other words, the company monitors and manages distribution and/or communication directly.

In a digital channel, this distribution model includes diverse approaches that can be classified according to the exploitation of the digital channels and the diverse objectives that the company aims to achieve (Mosca et al., 2016).

2.1.1. Direct management digital channels with a communication function

In this case, the digital channel represents a virtual showcase, which allows consumers to find general information about the company, such as mission, heritage, history and corporate social responsibility (CSR) activities (Seringhaus, 2005).

In other words, the website acts as a communication tool because it interacts with consumers and provides them with information about the brand's universe. Between 2000 and 2005, most luxury brand companies configured the website as a showcase, fostering one-way communication with their consumers.

For example, Louis Vuitton Moët Hennessey created a website that contained all information about the Group, also acting as an access point for numerous sites arranged by the brands and products marketed.

The same strategy was adopted by Trussardi with its site that promoted some information about the company and its products.

Bulgari is another company that created a website to illustrate its products and new collections of watches and jewellery but with no option to buy them.

Even if today some luxury companies maintain the website as a showcase to promote their products, they also tend to integrate this option with an e-commerce site to give consumers the possibility to buy the promoted products.

LVMH *is an example of a luxury brand that created a showcase site. In fact, LVMH's site provides consumers with information about the brand, but no option to purchase online is available.*

The information collected in the website is about the Group, the various brands and products, product categories and the latest news.

Consumers can choose to navigate using three different languages. To view the products consumers have to choose the desired category and then the brand.

BOFFI *created a purely informative site. This choice depends on two main reasons: the technical characteristics of the product and the fact that consumers require personalised products. The site, available both in Italian and English, shows the available kitchens, bathrooms, outdoor items furnishings and different collections. Moreover, consumers can navigate on some sections about the history of Boffi and its CSR activities.*

2.1.2. Direct management digital channels integrated with direct physical channels

This distribution model is configured as an integration between the digital channel directly managed by luxury brand companies and the direct physical channel.

In some cases, this model may involve the integration of a digital channel directly managed with indirect physical channels, even if this option is less frequent.

In general, this model of distribution aims to identify and invite consumers to visit the physical sales' outlets of a luxury brand, where they can personalise the product. When the consumer decides to personalise the product, payment can be made at a physical store or online.

This solution supports two main advantages: the absence of logistical expenses and the reduction of any conflict with physical intermediaries that can consider the digital channel as a valuable tool to develop sales.

In recent times, some companies have decided to integrate digital channels with the physical one. For example, Swarovski promotes integration between the physical channel and its presence on the digital channel with a website dedicated to communication and an e-commerce site.

CHANEL *integrated its direct digital channel with its direct physical channel. In fact, it created a showcase section that allows consumers to collect information about some kinds of products such as bags and apparel items, which can be purchased offline.*

Only certain kinds of products such as perfume, makeup and cosmetics can be purchased on Chanel's website.

2.1.3. Directly managed digital channel for a full-price luxury brand

Some luxury brand companies entered e-commerce and managed online stores to sell their full-price products directly online. This model of distribution demonstrated that all concerns about the negative effects of the Internet on the prestige and exclusivity of the luxury brand have been overcome. In fact, thanks to digital innovations, luxury brand companies can create a genuine online store that preserves the luxury brand image in the digital context. Cartier, on its website, does not immediately declare the price of its products, but first requires the customers to subscribe to the site or even make a phone call to the sales manager.

BELL & ROSS *is one of the first luxury brand companies to have made its products available online. In fact, on its website consumers can buy different watches, with the exception of limited series.*

The bellross.com site opens with an initial video showing its latest collection and heightens brand awareness. On the homepage, you can access all the collections and see the latest news about the brand's products. It is also possible to search for your nearest sales outlet. A site map is also available, which directs the customer to an e-boutique, the products and a summary of the company's history.

2.1.4. Direct management digital channels for marketing products coming to the end of their life cycle

This model of directly managed distribution is adopted to sell products that are coming to the end of their life cycle. In this case, the previous season's luxury items that are no longer stocked at a physical store are offered for sale on the online sales' platform directly managed by dedicated business units or third parties.

The time span between the launch phase and the decline is reduced to just a few months, especially for apparel items. This kind of distribution model allows luxury brand companies to sell the previous collection's items in less time, inducing consumers to buy with the lure of price reductions.

Linked to this model, three main advantages can be identified.

The first one is reducing the risk of the uncontrolled spread of unsold items. In fact, the channelling of products in a digital system reduces the possibility that they are disposed of on parallel markets with serious damage to the brand image.

The second advantage concerns the chance to cover different segments of the market. The consumer who buys on digital channels belongs to a different market segment than the traditional or occasional consumer who buys through physical intermediaries. For the consumer buying luxury goods on digital channels, the elasticity of the demand price ratio is very high, and the emotional component of the brand is perceived with less intensity.

Finally, price discrimination is another advantage. This refers to the fact that price differences applied to the product can be justified by keeping separate the channels and times when the product is sold.

With this approach the consumer who purchases through the physical channel perceives the product available on the digital channel in a bidding system that is not comparable and therefore does not notice the injustice of a reduction, although significant, in the sales price.

2.1.5. Direct management digital channel exclusively dedicated to the intermediary market (business to business)

In this case, the digital channel is dedicated to wholesalers and retailers, which can place online orders to establish or extend their assortment of products. This digital channel is exclusively dedicated to an intermediary, so final consumers can't access it.

Such a digital channel exclusively dedicated to the intermediary market can be adopted by companies that supply both direct sales outlets and independent outlets.

2.2. Distribution via an indirect digital channel

Indirect distribution means that one or more intermediaries operate between the producer company and the final consumers. The complexity of the indirect distribution channel depends on the number of intermediaries, which can vary from a few intermediaries in a short channel or numerous intermediaries in a long one (Kotler, 2016).

Even if companies that operate in the high-value goods market tend to prefer selective or exclusive direct distribution, they also use the indirect channel to improve the distribution coverage.

In recent years, the development of digital channels and the increase of online sales have favoured the spread of numerous models of distribution via indirect channels, also online.

The indirect distribution models available online consist of pure internet players, a kind of company that, operating as an independent intermediary, sells luxury products online.

2.2.1. Pure internet cut-price multibrand players

This indirect distribution model consists of an independent agent who sells luxury brand products using a price reduction.

The products are disposed of on digital channels by using the factory outlet centre logic.

At the early stage of its development, Yoox.com promoted this type of distribution, selling cut-price products, previous season and top-of-the-range goods on the digital channel.

However, after the merger with the Net-a-Porter Group, it modified its business model because today the Yoox Net-a-Porter Group sells special products exclusively online, sometimes at very high prices.

2.2.2. Full-price, pure internet player

This model consists of the presence on digital channels of an independent agent, operating as an intermediary, who sells luxury products at full price. This implies that it competes directly with luxury brand e-commerce sites, as well as the physical sales outlets.

Neimanmarcus.com, myteresa.com and Net-a-Porter in its first phase, represent some examples of pure internet players that adopted this model.

NET-A-PORTER.COM *was a website for the sale of current season clothing, footwear and fashion accessories at full prices.*

In March of 2015, it merged with Yoox.com becoming the biggest pure internet player within the luxury brand market.

Net-a-porter.com was created by Natalie Massenet and launched with $1.3 million in 2000.

In 2004 the site had already made a $400,000 profit with a total sales of over $21 million. In the same year, it was voted the best shop of the year by the British Fashion Council.

After only eight years in development, net-a-porter.com has become the leading e-commerce site, representing the pure internet player with the highest growth rate in the UK.

During its growth, net-a-porter.com acquired some sites such as girl.shop.com, which allowed the access to a database of more than thousands of contacts and fashion.com.

All the acquisitions enabled net-a-porter.com to rapidly increase the number of clients in the site's database. Moreover, the growth was supported by the opening of a new distribution centre in New York, which optimised the distribution costs and market share in the US.

Net-a-porter.com structured its website both as a magazine and a catalogue. In fact, it provides the visual impact of a traditional magazine, while at the same time it can be consulted as a catalogue.

The homepage is streamlined, and it allows users to reach the different sections effectively, without complicated steps.

'Magazine' is the first section where the consumer has the option to make purchases. Instead of finding a list of products broken down by categories, the consumer consults the table of contents of fashion magazine of a fashion magazine, where diverse trends are presented.

Another section is called 'Special'. It contains diverse items of clothing or designers and information related to the products' style.

Moreover, the consumer can access different resources such as photographic services, which represent the central point of the new purchasing process: passing the mouse over the different garments worn by models, consumers can read some information about items of clothing and then decide whether to buy the product.

Some areas of the website are developed in collaboration with journalists and stylists from Elle, Vogue *and* Marie Claire, *in order to inform the consumers about events concerning fashion shows, new trends and products.*

Figure 3. Net-a-porter.com: lines of business

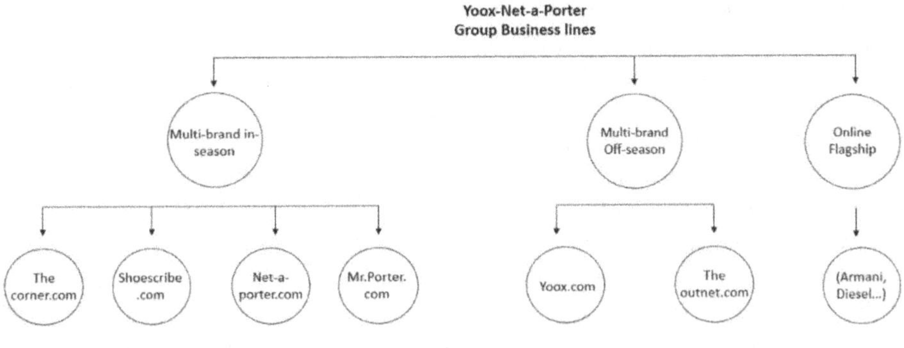

2.2.3. Multi-brand internet player focused exclusively on the intermediary market

This model refers to an independent intermediary who sells online luxury products to other physical or virtual intermediaries such as other outlets or websites.

In other words, this intermediary does not refer to the final consumers, but it operates as a real intermediary within the distribution channel.

BRANDSDISTRIBUTION.COM *is an Italian start-up that has experienced notable development in the field of B2B marketing in the high-end fashion and accessories sector. Brandsitribution.com focuses its attention on small retail stores, helping to increase sales and profits with quantitatively small product orders, through continuous modernisation of the collections without warehouse and operating costs thanks to drop-shipping. Recently the company has developed a website dedicated to the Chinese market – xiu.com – and has developed synergies in the e-commerce arena for the North American market.*

2.2.4. Multibrand pure internet player integrated with the physical and digital channels

This option consists of an intermediary who sells luxury goods both online and offline, integrating its e-commerce website with a presence on the physical channel of distribution. In this case, luxury products can be searched for and selected online and picked up at the physical store or, on the contrary, the purchase can be made in the store, and the products can be shipped to the consumer's home. An example of this formula of distribution is Sugar.it.

SUGAR.IT *represents an effective example of the online platform that was integrated with a physical store already existing. In fact, the e-commerce was founded in 2016 by Beppe Angiolini, a famous buyer and stylist who was already the owner of a famous boutique called Sugar in Arezzo. Mr. Angiolini, supported by a group of web designers, in addition to a pre-existing physical store created this unique website characterised by an exclusive design.*

The website was characterised by three main sections: "men", "women", and "no sugar please" section. While the first two sections are dedicated to selling the "new season" products at full price for men and women, the third one evokes the innovative traits of sugar.it platform. In fact the "no sugar please" section is divided into different product rooms whose name, consisting of hastag (#sugarbaby), is strongly linked language used by social media like Instagram and Twitter.

Navigating the sugar.it website offers customers a really positive experience: it is user friendly with an effective menus that allows consumers to access all the sections. Moreover, the exclusivity of this website depends not only on the design of the site that looks like a magazine, but also on the products offered. In fact, Sugar.it is a sort of boutique that sell selected and unique products different from other multibrand websites like Yoox Net-a- Porter that offers a wider range of luxury products. Finally, it is interesting to analyse the integration between this e-commerce and the physical store located in Arezzo. We can perceive that they are totally integrated: the website acts as communication channel to promote the visibility of the physical store as well as in the physical store is possible to pick up the products bought online.

3. EMERGING TRENDS AND MODELS OF DISTRIBUTION

The scenario of digital technologies is rapidly changing. This fact implies that the digital channels are also evolving to be in line with new trends and features.

3.1. New digital channel functions

With the technological evolution, the digital channels are progressively developing a special ability to guarantee the consumer of luxury goods an extraordinary virtual experience, updated in real time, thus positively influencing the buying process (Villanueva et al., 2008).

The increase in online transactions for luxury goods and the increase in their average value demonstrates the facts mentioned above.

At this time, digital channels are also being used by luxury brand players to distribute innovative collections and dedicated products. A digital channel's original function of selling an unsold product is now integrated with the new marketing function of supply system characterised by uniqueness and exclusivity at a high price (Curty & Zang, 2011).

3.2. Digital channels and personalisation

In recent years, another use of digital channels includes personalisation. In other words, a digital channel allows the luxury brand company to enhance the level of product and service personalisation, improving customers' perception of the brand.

While the sales are made in the store, the personalisation is offered mainly on the website.

Mia Bag is a clear example of a luxury brand company that has promoted personalisation on its website. In fact, on Mia Bag's website, consumers can personalise diverse models of a bag by adding their initials, and then the bags are delivered to the customer's home.

3.3. Digital channels and product life cycle

Traditionally, the function of a digital channel as a distribution channel is selling products coming to the end of their life cycle.

In recent times, some luxury brand companies have started to use digital channels to sell luxury goods that are being introduced onto the market.

In fact, numerous campaigns for launching new products consist of an online presale of a limited number of copies, sometimes personalised and numbered.

The use of digital channels in this approach aims to transfer the idea of the luxury product's uniqueness and limited availability at the moment of introduction onto the market.

3.4. Digital channels and virtual communities

Another instrument introduced by digital technologies is the virtual community, which consists of a group of consumers who share an interest in a product, brand or style and visit an e-commerce system, subscribe to a specific list and are regularly informed of events, latest news, producers and special offers (Brodie, 2013).

The latest trend that involves the virtual communities of luxury brand consumers is transferring to them the idea of exclusive access to the community and immediate offers to the potential customer (Schau, 2009).

In this case, for example, the new community member is presented and accepted via a selection process.

VENTE-PRIVEE.COM *is the marketing leader in offering unsold collection items at a low price. It works as a club where products are available for limited periods of time and exclusively to people who are members of the club.*

BAGBORROWANDSTYLE.COM *is the first site that in 2004 created the online rental concept for luxury goods. It built a network of more than 250,000 customers and more than 3,000 different items that can be selected from among 100 different designers including Chanel, Gucci, Prada, Louis Vuitton and others. The rented product can be kept as long as consumers want and then consumers have the option to purchase or exchange the rented product with a new product.*

3.5. Integration between the communication function and the digital channel

Another development path in digital channels is that of informative sites and those communicating the latest news and fashion, style and design trends. In their initial development stage, these sites assume the form of online media for communicating information, trends, fashion phenomena, style and design; they are often linked to a founder of a group of charismatic people who proclaims the site as a reference point (Brogi et al., 2013). The next step towards legitimising the sites as a provider of information can be starting to develop e-commerce and luxury services.

4. MANAGERIAL IMPLICATIONS

The scenario previously described showed the growth of the digital channel as an important vehicle for the distribution of luxury goods, not just for the liquidation of unsold products.

The digital channel is assuming the similar characteristics of the physical one with direct distribution patterns, achieved through active management of e-commerce sites by luxury brands, and indirectly with the presence of specialised products or multibrand intermediaries that are often highly innovative.

Two variables can be considered to classify how luxury brand companies use a digital channel as a distribution channel:

- the main function of the distribution channel, which may be disposing of lower-priced collections and disposal of unsold products (online outlets) or selling full price
- the quality of interaction with the customer, understood as the user's level of the sensory elements available, in order to ensure a positive customer experience

In fact, certain companies adopt a digital channel just to dispose of unsold collections, others give the Internet a primary position in competition with other channels. The majority of the examined companies use all the best techniques to ensure a positive digital experience for their referent customers. Finally, companies that own a huge brand portfolio employ a digital channel for a certain brand and in the determined market.

5. LIMITATIONS AND FUTURE RESEARCH

The current study is focused on distribution strategies implemented online by luxury brand companies. While this group comprises a representative portion of luxury brand companies, it may not represent all luxury brand organisations. Therefore, future research needs to include more luxury brand companies to provide a more accurate overview of distribution strategies in the luxury market.

Only distribution via an online channel is analysed in our work. A logical next step would be to analyse consumers' understanding of both physical and digital channels of distribution, in addition to the consumer's perception towards each of them. In fact, in this way, luxury brand companies could be made aware of the best solutions for selling luxury goods to consumers. In particular, future research needs to look at how these factors influence consumers' online and offline experiences.

BIBLIOGRAPHY

ATWAL G., WILLIAMS, A., 2017, Luxury Brand Marketing – The Experience Is Everything!. In: Kapferer JN., Kernstock J., Brexendorf T., Powell S. (eds) Advances in Luxury Brand Management. *Journal of Brand Management*: Advanced Collections. Palgrave Macmillan, Cham

BATAT, W., 2017, Luxe et expérience client. Dunod.

BRODIE, R. J. et al., 2013, 'Consumer engagement in a virtual brand community: An exploratory analysis', *Journal of Business Research*, 66, pp. 105–114. doi: 10.1016/j.jbusres.2011.07.029.

BROGI, S., CALABRESE, A., CAMPISI, D., CAPECE, G., COSTA, R., DI PILLO, F., 2013, The Effects of Online Brand Communities on Brand Equity in the Luxury Fashion Industry. *International Journal of Engineering Business Management.*

CORBELLINI, E. & SAVIOLO, S., 2009, Managing Fashion and Luxury Companies. ETAS.

CUTY, R.G., ZHANG, P., 2011, Social Commerce: Looking Back and Forward, Proceedings ASIST, New Orleans, October 9-13.

DALL'OLMO RILEY, F. and LACROIX, C., 2003, Luxury branding on the Internet: lost opportunity or impossibility? Marketing Intelligence & Planning, 21 (2): 96-104.

FONDAZIONE ALTAGAMMA, 2017, Il lusso digitale. Da omnichannel a "reverse omnichannel".

FONDAZIONE ALTAGAMMA, 2018, The future of luxury: a look into tomorrow to understand today.

GEERTS, A. and VEG-SALA, N., 2017, Luxury brand on Internet: an analysis of website dimensions and websites tipology's. 33ème Congrès International de l'Association Française du Marketing", Tours, France.

GEERTS, A., 2013, Cluster Analysis of Luxury Brands on the Internet. *International Journal of Management and Marketing Research*, 6 (2): 79-82

HENNIGS, N., WIEDMANN, K.-P. and KLARMANN, C., 2012, "Luxury brands in the digital age – exclusivity versus ubiquity", Marketing Review St. Gallen, Vol. 29 No. 1, pp. 30-35.

KIM, H., CHOI, Y.J., LEE, Y., 2015, "Web atmospheric qualities in luxury fashion brand web sites", *Journal of Fashion Marketing and Management*, Vol. 19 Issue: 4, pp.384-401, https://doi.org/10.1108/JFMM-09- 2013-0103.

KAPFERER, J.N., BASTIEN, V., 2012, The Luxury Strategy: Break The Rules of Marketing to Build Luxury Brands, Kogan Page Ltd (2nd ed.)

KAPFERER, J.N., 2000, How the Internet impacts on brand management, *Journal of Brand Management*, Vol. 7 No. 6, pp. 389-91.

KIM, A. KO, E., 2010, Impacts of Luxury Fashion Brand's Social Media Marketing on Customer Relationship and Purchase Intention. *Journal of Global Fashion Marketing*. 164 – 171.

KLUGE, P. N., KÖNIGSFELD, J. A., MITSCHKE, F., FASSNACHT, M., 2013, "Luxury web atmospherics: an examination of homepage design", *International Journal of Retail & Distribution Management*, Vol. 41 Issue: 11/12, pp.901-916, https://doi.org/10.1108/IJRDM-01-2013-0013
KOTLER, P. et al., 2016, Marketing management. [electronic resource], Harlow, England: Pearson.
LARRAUFIE, A. & KOURDOUGHLI, A., 2014, The e-semiotics of luxury, *Journal of Global Fashion Marketing*, 5:3, 197-208.
LEMON, K. N., & VERHOEF, P. C., 2016, Understanding customer experience throughout the customer journey. *Journal of Marketing*, 80(6), 69–96. https://doi.org/10.1509/jm.15.0420
MOSCA, F., GIACOSA, E., 2016, Old and New Distribution Channels in the Luxury Sector. Italy, Europe: IGI Global Publisher.
MOSCA, F., 2017, Strategie nei mercati del lusso. Marketing, digitalizzazione, sostenibilità. Egea.
OKONKWO, U., 2009, Sustaining Luxury Brands on the Internet. *Journal of Brand Management*, 16 (5/6): 302-310.
OKONKWO, U., 2010, Luxury Online: Styles, Systems, Strategies, Palgrave Macmillan, Hampshire.
SCHAU, H. J., MUÑIZ, A. M. and ARNOULD, E. J., 2009, 'How Brand Community Practices Create Value', *Journal of Marketing*, 73(5), pp. 30–51. doi: 10.1509/jmkg.73.5.30.
SERINGHAUS, F. H. R., 2005, 'Selling Luxury Brands Online', *Journal of Internet Commerce*, 4(1), p. 1.
VILLANUEVA, J., YOO, S. and HANSSENS, D. M., 2008, 'The Impact of Marketing-Induced Versus Word-of-Mouth Customer Acquisition on Customer Equity Growth', *Journal of Marketing Research (JMR)*, 45(1), pp. 48–59. doi: 10.1509/jmkr.45.1.4

INNOVATIVE IN-STORE ICT MARKETING SOLUTIONS FOR AN ENHANCED LUXURY SHOPPING-EXPERIENCE

Adele MAGNELLI
ETT s.p.a
adele.magnelli@ettsolutions.com

Valeria PIZZIOL
ETT s.p.a
valeria.pizziol@ettsolutions.com

Mario MANZO
Torino Wireless Executive
mario.manzo@torinowireless.it

ABSTRACT

Over the last few years, the luxury retail sector has undergone a profound change. This can largely be linked to the relationship between new technologies and purchasing behaviour. The sector has moved from its elitist and aristocratic perception to the creation of innovative and digital experiences.

The new challenge facing the luxury sector is how to reconcile the potential offered by technology while preserving the sense of exclusivity in brand names. In the meantime, however, it has a unique opportunity of forming new and lasting relationships with clients by focusing not only on the product but also on an in-store shopping experience making client participation ever more dynamic.

This outlook makes it fundamentally important to create an immersive and satisfying in-store shopping experience. Digital innovations redefine interaction models between clients and brands. Buying a product is not enough; clients wish to engage in unique and immersive experiences that are authentic, exclusive - and easily shared online.

This conceptual upheaval has seen the development of new solutions blending design, technology and storytelling into a revolutionary experience. It has become a combination of

exclusivity and playful sharing, both in-store and at temporary installations.
Some relevant case studies about digital experiences are described, related to brands Bulgari (multimedia fittings at New Curiosity Shop in Rome, Mirror Cube Experience at 2018 Design Week in Milan) and Acqua di Parma (interactive mirror in Milan and Rome stores).

Keywords: Customer satisfaction, innovative technologies, retail experience.
JEL codes: M30, M31

INTRODUCTION

Over the last few years, the luxury retail sector has undergone a profound change. This can largely be linked to the relationship between new technologies and purchasing behaviour. The sector has moved from its elitist and aristocratic perception, an area fixed in its ways and impervious to technological innovation, to looking at things in new ways that increasingly aspire to the creation of innovative and digital experiences. It is true to say that the present-day digital revolution is a direct result of decisive changes in society, culture and in parts of the economy. So we find that even the luxury sector, which has always justified premium prices through a blend of exclusivity and limited accessibility, has come up against a new digital world embracing, by its very nature, principles of democracy and social sharing.

The new challenge facing the luxury sector is how to reconcile the potential offered by technology while preserving the sense of exclusivity in brand names and their accompanying heritage. In the meantime, however, there is a unique opportunity to form new and lasting relationships with clients by focusing not only on the product but also on an in-store shopping experience making the "customer journey" ever more dynamic through conceptual changes that have distinguished experience design in recent years.

Indeed, the theory of self-indulgent consumerism puts multisensory-engagement fantasy and product-linked emotional aspects at the centre of the buying process. This outlook makes it fundamentally important to create an immersive and satisfying in-store shopping experience. Digital innovations redefine interaction models between clients and brands. Buying a product is not enough; clients wish to engage in unique and immersive experiences that are authentic, exclusive - and easily shared online. A store is no longer a place where you merely buy something. It has become a repository of satisfying experiences where traditional retail boundaries are overcome.

In the first part of the paper the concept of luxury is analyzed from a historical, social and anthropological point of view. The model and the evolution of the concept of experience and co-creation of value in retail are then analyzed, and how it has gained ever greater importance, even for the luxury market. A specific analysis was then made on the use of ICT tools for enhancing and enriching the consumer experience in the luxury sector, with the description of some relevant case studies, related to projects realized by the brands Bulgari and Acqua di Parma.

1.THE LUXURY CONCEPT

The human race has always sought out luxury. This has been demonstrated by anthropologists and ethnologists (Lipovetsky and Roux 2003) and, throughout history, the concept of luxury has always been the subject of social and cultural appraisals. In ancient Greece and Rome, indulging in luxury was a sign of powerful social and political influence. In the Middle Ages, gold and precious stones, symbols of luxury, were reserved for royalty and theologians. In later times, they first became the prerogative of the aristocracy, followed by the rich bourgeoisie. The modern luxury goods industry originated in Europe during the nineteenth century. In the wake of the industrial revolution, outstanding products were intentionally manufactured to serve the new lifestyle of that period's social elite. Before then, luxury goods had usually been handmade by local craftsmen and mainly sold in the vicinity. Modern industries, however, needed relatively high volumes and, as local growth potential was limited, they began to extend their sales areas abroad. In this way, reaching a larger customer base set the stage for today's global luxury market (Antoni et al., 2004). Even today, the ownership of particular luxury goods is still an indicator of social class or of belonging to an elite group. Psychologically, the possession of luxury products is linked to the concept of admiration by various parts of society. The luxury goods market, with its high symbolic and social value, can ideally be epitomised as a series of markets retailing goods and services that inherently represent and visibly communicate an elegant and refined way of life. What is more difficult is the actual definition of the complex concept of goods with high symbolic value. A certain possession may be associated with luxury and exclusivity in a particular country and at a specific time. At other times, however, it may not be identified as being luxurious at all. How the intangible attributes of a luxury product are perceived takes on great importance, since it is appreciated for its ability to generate positive experiences and emotions. But the physical dimension must also be carefully assessed in order to establish why and how something can be considered to be a luxury commodity. Although this may seem unimportant, an in-depth analysis is needed of what people actually think the luxury concept is. Some people could define luxury by referring to products made from precious materials, while others might associate the concept of luxury with the lifestyle of a privileged elite. Some might consider luxury to refer to any expensive item, while others might consider luxury as referring to any product that costs at least two or three times more than a basic version of the same product. Some may focus on luxury goods; others may believe that the only real luxury is related to the availability of time. Some might associate the concept of luxury with positive feelings, while those who consider luxury to be unnecessary might link the concept with negative implications. We can, therefore, say that the perceived utility and cost of a product are not the only features used to classify a luxury product. A luxury product is often intended both to show wealth and as a vehicle for self-expression. The impulse to buy luxury products, such as self-indulgence or status seeking, can also vary. In order to create a shared conceptualization, the literature on the subject defines luxury goods as those with six specific and coded attributes (Dubois, Laurent and Czellar, 2001). The first distinguishing requirement is excellent quality, deriving from various factors such as the quality and exclusivity of the raw materials used and the precision of the manufacturing process. These features guarantee reliability and durability, giving a psychological sense of eternity to the user of the purchased luxury product. Many people identify the quality requirement itself as a concept of luxury. The second specific characteristic is linked to aesthetic importance, in that luxury goods are often likened to real works of art. The act of purchasing – and using – luxury goods guarantees the prospect of a multifaceted experience involving all the senses. The guarantee of exclusivity not only refers to the product but also to the whole context in which it is chosen and purchased. The third aspect is the high, or premium, price, defined in this category as the comparative price relative to other products performing the same function. The price is justified by the perceived high quality and longevity that the product transmits, instilling in the final user a sense of investment security. The fourth feature is exclusivity, a fundamental attribute in the luxury industry affecting both supply and demand. Luxury goods have particular distinctiveness, so the concept of its consistency and the desire to purchase are directly proportional. The rarity concept is closely related to the idea of exclusivity and is central to the creation of a luxury product identity. Specific literature (Catry, 2006) identifies five drivers: strictly high-quality ingredients; techniques that search for perfection; production, linked to limited quantity and aimed at triggering desire for emulation; distribution, aimed at reinforcing the perception of rarity by strict selection of marketing channels; information, based on direct and indirect communications through opinion leaders and élites. The fifth characteristic is the "superfluous aspect" of goods which do not naturally satisfy primary needs. This can be traced back to the concept of abundance, meaning that the number of products purchased may exceed the number required to satisfy functional needs. The final aspect that exemplifies luxury goods is the link with tradition. The heritage concept is the link to past craftsmanship and cultural heritage that writes the history of the product and, consequently, the history of the brand. The origin of a product must be far in the past and not be affected by fleeting fashions. This link with the past is a guarantee of quality and added-value. Recently, however, the concept of luxury has moved from a fundamentally elitist and aristocratic outlook, which considered it as a class divider and as a driving force for imitative processes (Veblen, 1981; Mason, 1981), to forms that regard it in evolved and multidimensional perspectives (Berry, 1994; Evrard and Roux 2005). Of the main theories to emerge over the years, two interpretations of luxury consumption can be traced back to ostentatious consumer behaviour and hedonistic forms of consumption. The ostentatious forms can be classified into three basic types (Liebenstein, 1950). The first type conforms to the Veblen effect whereby individuals give great importance to price as an indicator of prestige. The second type conforms to the Snob effect, according to which consumers link the value of a luxury product to the exclusivity of the product itself, considering it a luxury simply because it is not widely available. The third refers to the Bandwagon effect, in which consumers perceive the product to be a luxury only if it is used by so-called "important others". The first theory refers to social orientation (Fionda and Moore, 2009; Truong et al., 2008) where luxury is identified as a status symbol, while the second refers to personal orientation (Dubois and Duquesne, 1993; Vickers and Renand, 2003) where luxury is identified as an individual style. Alongside ostentatious forms of luxury spending, we find forms of self-indulgence which can be traced back to theories on recreational shopping and hedonistic consumption (Holbrook and Hirschman, 1982), according to which multisensory fantasies and emotional aspects are linked to product use. Literature produces a contradiction when explaining the motivations that lead to buying luxury goods. Social and interpersonal external motivations on the one hand, and subjective and confidential internal motivations on the other. External motivations essentially involve the objective of showing off a luxury item in public, in order to establish that one is of a certain status (O'Cass and Frost, 2002) while internal motivations involve emotions, mental state and subjective sensations relating to a person's self-perception (Vigneron and Johnson, 1999, 2004). In the first case, luxury spending is typically related to ostentation, social positioning and accumulation of status symbols (Fionda and Moore, 2009; Truong et al., 2008). In the second case, it involves more personal or cultural objectives, linked to the pursuit of pleasure, originality and perfection (Dubois and Duquesne, 1993; Vickers and Renand, 2003). Consumers can choose luxury items according to agreed conventions and display them in order to show others how much they have paid, to emulate people they admire or because they are driven by a competitive spirit. But consumers can also purchase luxury goods when motivated by aesthetic, cultural or personal sensitivity to certain values. They choose products based on individual taste and style, going beyond criteria imposed by others. These two apparently conflicting rationales can potentially coexist in a single person. Given that the purchaser is important, but in the knowledge that not all luxury consumers agree on the same values but have various driving forces, companies have to catch the attention of clients in different ways in order to induce them to buy. Although the luxury market was a niche market before the second half of the twentieth century, with extremely limited access channels, recent years have seen a trend towards what is known as market "massification", accompanied by a growth in demand, expansion from traditional European and US markets towards emerging markets and an extension of the range of products to mass-accessible luxury or more accessible luxury items (Lallement, 1999; Catry, 2003; Silverstein and Fiske, 2003; Dalton, 2005). Specialist literature (Letzelter, 1996, Nueno and Quelch 1998) describes the emergence of new categories of consumers and new concept elaborations of luxury products. They are linked, for example, to the distinction between luxury as a means for personal satisfaction or as a way to achieve social status and the democratisation of luxury.

2.EXPERIENCE AND CO-CREATION

Over the last few decades, the experience concept has received increasingly more recognition and attention from world academia, gaining many definitions and meanings. In the luxury sector too, the desire to live exciting and immersive experiences is growing. The experience economy concept (Pine and Gilmore, 1999) states that the creation of experiences is necessary and fundamental for every type of business and economic sector, as the mere fact of offering products and services is seen as something repeatable and interchangeable (Morgan, 2010). Although the importance of the experience is currently undisputed, we need to analyse the changes that have upset the theoretical and practical study of how the experiences, and their associated value, are created. Companies operating in the luxury sector have spent the last few decades developing retail networks that reflect a monolithic global identity. In light of this new experience concept, it is clear that the model needs to be updated as consumers now look for experiences related to emotional relationships, together with the sense of discovery of unique products linked to a specific brand. Studies have shown that while consumers can see if a commodity refers to them, the likelihood that they will make a purchase increases the longer they spend in the store. Although client attraction elements are different from one market to another, emotional leverage is effective in most economic sectors. Understanding these nuances is fundamental in order to get the most out of retail networks. Luxury consumers are usually attracted to shops that project a sense of authenticity and originality.

Companies create new stores or renovate existing stores using differing concepts, layouts or collections. The original concept of the experience economy has been redefined as stated consumer desire versus the desire to play an active role in the co-creation of experiences (Prahalad and Ramaswamy, 2004). Rather than take part in ready-made experiences, consumers are looking for greater authenticity and expect a better balance between creators of planned and unplanned purchasing experiences and their role as co-creators of the experience and the added value that comes from it. The process of creating very artificial experiences is certainly perceived as unidirectional, business-oriented and superficial. It consequently no longer satisfies the needs of contemporary consumers (Boswijk et al., 2007) who are increasingly active in the assessment of products on the market. The concept of added-value is inextricably linked to competitive advantage. Creating memorable experiences is the essence and *raison d'être* of industries operating in all economic sectors (Pizam, 2010) and new models show that this concept can also be applied to the design of luxury digital experiences. Traditional marketing has long focussed on the concept of exchange value, where something of value is proposed by companies and the passive client can either accept or refuse it (Vargo and Lusch, 2004). Recent studies, however, point out that the co-creation of value between a brand and a "connected, enabled and active" client (Prahalad and Ramaswamy, 2004) determines perceived value "in a unique and phenomenological way" (Vargo and Lusch, 2008). This concept of perceived value thus replaces the exchange value, and this, in turn, suggests the use of marketing approaches that are experiential, interactive, progressive, flexible and in continuous evolution (Tynan and McKechnie, 2009). The marketing of luxury goods comprises complex practises, meaning that "classic marketing is the surest way to fail in the luxury business" (Bastien and Kapferer, 2009). The success of luxury goods requires the client to perceive a value that is high enough to match the high price asked, particularly in times of recession. It is therefore essential to understand the types of value sought and the value creation processes. A value experience should be personally significant for the client. It should be innovative and offer aspects that are associated with surprise and wonder, involving the user in every way – physical and emotional (Poulusson and Kale, 2004). As technologically feasible in-store solutions become more available, the possibilities of co-creating experiences multiply, making them richer and reaching an increasingly higher level of added-value and brand recognition. Technology is an experience-mediator but, at the same time, its use is in itself an experience (Gretzel and Jamal, 2009). Global competition is increasing and with it the ease with which experiences can be emulated. So the luxury sector must also systematically explore new opportunities linked to co-creation and use of ICT, so that it may create dynamic "augmented" experiences. In the continuing digital evolution, we can identify several trends (Mazzù and

Perrey, 2011) that apply to the luxury sector relative to "two-way marketing" processes. In the digital world, the relationship between consumers and companies changes, putting them on an equal footing. When compared to traditional channels, a critical mass forms much faster in this context. Consumers frequently and spontaneously divulge negative or positive impressions, without the brand being able to control what is being communicated and on which channels. The other factor to consider, in digital evolution, is consumer control. The digital generation exercises active and selective control over the use of social media, taking on the role of editor and generating content directly. Information diffusion mechanisms triggered in this way escape normal brand control on communications. This is why the brand manager needs to monitor bad feedback from the market and act quickly, credibly and reliably. Brands are able, however, to take back control of the communications process by providing consumers with specially developed multimedia content, linked to the in-store experience and sharable on social media. In this way, the brand reaches the fundamental objectives of the new retail model. Even luxury retail outlets are changing strategy, moving from a one-to-many approach to as personalised as possible one-to-one solutions. The luxury sector already naturally identifies with highly personalised choice and purchase processes, so the use of in-store technological solutions creates emotional involvement linked to wonder and awe.

3. IN-STORE TECHNOLOGIES

3.1. Multi-channel and omni-channel strategies

Communications channels are constantly evolving, as are the touch-points used by potential clients. The omnichannel contact concept is defined as the evolution of the multichannel contact concept. The multi-channel strategy concept refers to the use of many interactions and transaction channels between brands and clients on their "customer journey", previously seen as a one-way process with a division between the physical and the online store. But in the omnichannel strategy configuration, various channels and touch-points are orchestrated to cooperate, and users move freely between the online world, mobile devices and the physical store, sometimes during a single transaction. Mobile channels and social media are added to traditional online and physical channels. Luxury brands must strive to impeccably meet client expectations both in the store and via all online touch-points. Luxury companies must be creative and understanding in their approach to the online world, just as they are in the real world. In general, the luxury goods industry has been slower than other economic sectors to recognise the potential of going online, but in recent years it has been catching up with the global impact trend. With more and more luxury consumers being attracted by online retailers, who aggregate brands and often give substantial discounts, the industry cannot afford to underestimate the meaning of this channel, be it an opportunity or a threat. At the same time, it is worth mentioning the strategic choice made by some luxury goods brands that continue to prefer sales in their physical stores only, so as to offer a unique and complete shopping experience that cannot be repeated online. These brands use their online channels for information services only, regarding products and brands, shops and customer services. Keeping up with this rapid digital revolution is fundamental for success and ignoring this evolution could lead to serious economic and positioning repercussions (Rigby, 2011). Digitisation is, therefore, a matter that luxury retailers cannot afford to ignore. The continuous evolution of technologies aimed at consumers in the context of retail sales is undeniable (Pantano, 2015). This evolution requires a deep understanding of how the expectations of consumers of luxury goods are growing and evolving.

3.2. From the traditional store to an "experiential hub": digital tools for retail

The concept of a customer journey has evolved and becomes dynamic, fluid and is aimed at presenting an exciting experience to the client. Since the channels work together, the perceived interaction is not with the channel, but directly with the brand, adding value to the concepts of heritage and exclusivity that are associated with luxury goods. Despite using various channels, clients still need to see, hear, touch and try the product, as well as feel the store atmosphere. However, the role of a traditional store is changing as it moves toward the concept of an "experiential hub", the point of integration of all communications channels. A store is now a place that delivers a personal experience, attracting and amazing clients. Digital Signage techniques are used to achieve these new objectives. This innovative form of nearby communication, used in points of sale or in public spaces, shows ad hoc content on electronic devices. The term Digital Signage denotes an audio-visual information system in network form, permitting remote control of content, either automatic or manual, on a centralised system. It consists of several peripheral digital displays connected to a centralised content management system. The effectiveness of Digital Signage is also highlighted by academic literature that explains how digital communications are gaining popularity and becoming increasingly common. Trend observation shows that the replacement of conventional signage is increasing (Harrison and Andrusiewicz, 2004). Digital Signage offers new opportunities and advantages over traditional "static" signage. To give an example, it can manage the showing of communications such as news or advertisements in the form of dynamic multimedia products. The distinctive feature of Digital Signage is that content may be continuously modified. With no need for structural changes in the point of sale, dynamic layout innovation can direct specific time and space messages to clients. In essence, it is possible to distinguish three types of position where Digital Signage can be successfully installed: point of sale (POS), point of wait (POW) and point of transit (POT). The point of sale (POS) area is currently the largest user of Digital Signage, and the luxury sector is adapting to this trend. Considering that, on average, 75% of purchase decisions are made at the point of sale, it follows that multimedia content in stores is the key to marketing success. Showing calibrated ad hoc multimedia in-store content, relative to brand communication needs, can directly result in an increase in sales levels, as well as an improvement in the general shopping experience. To be successful, the in-store experience must match customer needs, which are mostly linked to previous personal experience. This dimension is undeniably connected to the growing role of in-store technologies. These include personalised technologies such as interactive screens, augmented reality and "magic mirrors", as well as technologies for staff management and training. In order to add value to the shopping experience, technologies must fully assimilate to previous client experiences. They must not be isolated or perceivable as separate from the rest of the store layout. The physical store layout must, therefore, be optimised and, if necessary, redesigned in order to fit in the new technologies that ensure fluid use of multimedia products. If the assimilation of technological solutions is carried out in tune with changing consumer desires and expectations, a physical store becomes not only an embodiment of the place where a sales transaction takes place, but it becomes an "experience place" and goes from being identified as a have-to-go-place to being a want-to-go-place (Kotler and Stigliano, 2018). The signs of change are already there and may be seen in the increasing use of augmented reality (AR) and virtual reality (VR). These technologies have the enormous potential to really shake up the customer experience. By 2020, 100 million consumers will be making online and in-store purchases using AR and, according to Gartner Inc., by 2020, 46% of retailers worldwide have planned to implement AR or VR solutions to meet new customer experience requirements. Generally speaking, and as a result of their considerable investment in digital technology, the goals of enhanced technology stores can be summed up as follows: integrated communications and the dependable promotion of brand values for consumers; the increase of sales and the creation of memorable purchase experiences.

3.3. Methodology: case study approach

Luxury as a concept, as we have seen, is defined in the sphere of sociology as a result of its connection with a culture, a state of being and a lifestyle, either personal or collective. When it is linked to brands, it is characterized by a recognizable style, a strong identity, a high awareness and a greater emotional and symbolic association. It evokes uniqueness and exclusivity, and is interpreted in products through high quality, controlled distribution and premium prices. These elements have also led to the synthesis of luxury as a dream (Okonkwo, 2008), which leads to justifiable curiosity and interest. The luxury retail, on the other hand, is inspired by the principles of art and magic to assemble the creator's charismatic personality and spread his aesthetic ideology to the brand.

Recent researches (Pantano et al., 2018) show that the luxury sector is well aware of the advantages of using smart technologies as marketing tools, while the effective use of these innovative systems is still limited.

In the last part of this paper we will analyze the main ICT tools supporting consumer experience in digital environment, and we will describe in detail the most relevant case studies in terms of engagement and creation of an innovative link between brand, product and customer.

The selected case studies concern two companies: Bulgari jewels, with the exhibits New Curiosity Shop and Mirror Cube, and the historical brand of perfumes Acqua di Parma. The main feature of these exhibits is the orientation to the customer and not to the product, to the experience and not to the good: renewing the art of wonder, the public (no longer the consumer) experiences a playful and exciting interaction with the luxury brands, becoming the protagonist of an experience that has a lot to do with art and entertainment. The result is the intimacy with the values of the brand, its culture and its history. To obtain these results, a thorough and conscious use of the possibilities offered by digital tools is necessary, to enhance the emotional and magical experience of the user.

The illustrated exhibits spring from a joint design between ETT and the two brands referents, with the participation of heterogeneous professionals: the Bulgari New Curiosity Shop project was developed in cooperation with the Visual Merchandising and Interior design areas, the 360 Selfie Cube Project with the Visual Merchandising and Marketing areas. The Acqua di Parma project was developed with the Trade Marketing and Visual Merchandising area.

3.4. Bulgari and Acqua di Parma: relevant case studies description

Digital technology is now part of the buying process and most consumers are so used to it they wouldn't go without it (VanScoyoc et al., 2015). One poorly defined value, however, is the financial advantage of investing in such technology as retailers in the luxury sector generally prefer not to release return on investment (ROI) information on their investment in digital in-store solutions. As a result of this conceptual revolution, new solutions have been designed that combine design, technology and storytelling to revolutionise the experience; all serving to match exclusivity with good-humoured sharing in in-store settings and temporary installations. In this sense, three interesting case studies are described below, developed by the Italian company ETT s.p.a., specialized in experience design and digital solutions for corporate communication, marketing and retail.

For the Bulgari New Curiosity Shop, multimedia furnishing elements were developed, such as touch-counters and monitors fitted behind shelves, in which, after careful designing, multimedia devices were fitted. With the New Curiosity Shop, Bulgari acclaims the art of wonder. Not far from this historic boutique in the famous Via Condotti in Rome, this innovative space – inspired by curiosity rooms – exemplifies the creativity of the Maison and offers a unique experience to visitors, linking Bulgari's future to its past. It is a renewed version of the Old Curiosity Shop, inaugurated in 1905 by Sotirio Bulgari, founder of the Maison. The New Curiosity Shop engages visitors in the brand's universe and pays tribute to the passion of this Roman jeweller for the extraordinary objects and his continuous search for wonders and curiosity. The store has a double soul, evocatively linked to both day and night, where the colours of the flooring and the shelving are coordinated with the selected conceptual dualism passed on to clients. The new display space is perfectly in line with the previously examined concepts of a revolutionary in-store experience. The layout is based on dual elements, denoted by a play of contrasts among materials, colours, selected objects and interior design. An imaginary line divides the space into two areas: on one side, warm colours and vintage finished materials like woods and velvet; on the other, essential lines and marbles with luminous hues. Every detail is designed to engage visitors, offering them a unique and memorable experience.

At the boutique entrance, the central counter turns into an interactive screen on which clients may browse through the collections, while new creations are on the shelves. In detail, the innovative touch-counter was tailor-made for this type of use by applying a layer of film to a regular monitor and turning it into a touch-surface. The user-experience starts when a tagged token is placed on the touch-counter and dedicated software recognises it, activating previously associated multi-media content.

Tag-recognition technology is potentially usable with any type of object and accessory, recognised by the purpose-made digital surface. When the tag is recognised, the monitor displays video content organised according to that area of interest, with bites describing the brand, linking its identity to the concept of heritage and added value, and various collections of jewellery and accessories. This mechanism creates an experience that combines physical client interaction and the use of the multimedia content, breaking down barriers between the real and digital worlds, and revolutionising the traditional concept of an inanimate counter; traditionally used in jewellery shops as an ordinary means of display. Shelving provides further innovation and is transformed from a flat characterless furnishing into an animated state. There are 4K monitors fitted in the shelves which, through the use of players, transmit specially created loop animations and graphics that are programmed to interact with each other. Animations visible in the shelves positioned on one side of the store are programmed to create a lively connection – based on the dualism of day and night – with the shelves located on the other side, creating a real "multimedia dialogue" that captures attention as soon as clients enter the shop. These solutions help in the discovery of the brand and its collections, in a captivating and dynamic way. For this brand, at the Milan Design Week 2018, a Mirror Cube was positioned in the garden of the Bulgari Hotel Milano, an installation with an eye-catching mirror-covered profile inside which 36 Reflex cameras took pictures in sequence to make GIFs, sharable on social profiles. Using the experience is designed to be intuitive and enjoyable in order to give the user a moment of leisure. The feelings of psychological satisfaction that remain derive from the interaction of the individual with the luxury sector, through playful interaction. The experience begins with a short accreditation procedure, completing a default form with an e-mail address. After this, the cube closes, creating an environment with graphic patterns in black and white, and a red neon with the words, "Reinventing Design Rules". A countdown ends with the sequential shooting of the 36 cameras. Software processes the shots in a very short time and the user can see the GIF when exiting the cube. At this point, the user can decide if the GIF is acceptable or whether a new one would be preferable. When the GIF is selected, it is emailed and is ready to be shared on the main social channels and through dedicated hashtags.

A different project was developed for Acqua di Parma, a famous Italian perfumery and cosmetics brand with over 100 years of history. Its strong connections with the emotional world of up-market fragrances made it possible to create a multimedia infrastructure for the windows of their Rome and Milan stores. Maintaining a strong bond with the elegant and refined style of the original shop-window displays, Digital Signage solutions were developed to emphasise the skills linked to the creation of the product, and the precious quality of the raw materials that are the basis of their world-famous fragrances. When creating the multimedia solutions, the basic concept was linked to Mother's Day, which in Italy is celebrated in May, a time of the year associated with spring and the rediscovery of natural fragrances. For this occasion, the brand had planned a market launch of five new female fragrances, inspired by the enchanting flowers of italian gardens, *Le Nobili*. The project investigation for the best-personalised solution began with a technical evaluation of the lighting and windows in the two stores. The use of projectors was excluded, because of the constant presence of direct sunlight on the windows. A different solution was devised for each location, in compliance with the philosophy of creating ad hoc multimedia solutions to match the specific needs of a particular store. For the Milan store shop window, the solution included the installation of a large-format 85-inch monitor, rented for the month of May, positioned at the back of the display as a digital background. Five plexiglass cylinders of differing heights were placed in the window, on the top of which the original bottles of the five new fragrances were placed. At the highest point of each bottle, starting from a white background, digital animations representing the five flowers at the base of the fragrances were shown: peony, iris, jasmine, magnolia and rose. The animations, elegant and sinuous, captured the attention of passers-by with vivid reproductions of the flowers that seem to sprout directly from the elegant bottles of fragrance. In a setting often characterised by the indifference or distraction of passers-by, this explosion of colours drew attention not only to the final product but to the raw materials from which it is made, creating a moment of emotional engagement that will be remembered.

The Rome store shop window followed the same concept but the Digital Signage had a different technological composition. Instead of a large screen, the artistic arrangement comprised three 10-inch monitors suspended in the window in the form of an inverted V. The five smaller bottles were replaced with a single large bottle, from the top of which appeared, in succession, captivating reproductions of the flowers that make up the collection's fragrances. In both displays, the multimedia content was continuously looped day and night, presenting a digital solution with complete and constant synergy between a classical physical window display and a digital set-up, with its selected project hardware.

The three diverse multi-media solutions described here, show only part of the Digital Signage potential linked to communications strategies and in-store experiences.

CONCLUSIONS AND CONTRIBUTIONS

As we have seen, emotions and emotional conditioning are the key differentiators in the decision-making process for the luxury sector. The three cases presented highlight some fundamental factors for customer experience strategies. In summary, the craftsmanship and heritage linked to the brand, the emotions and involvement created by in-store experiences, the presence of the consumer in the creation of the product or a customization based on the authentic knowledge (now possible) of real thoughts and needs and personal requirements (Bowen & Bowen, 2018).

Following recent developments linked to concepts regarding the experience economy and added value, the new needs and desires of in-store luxury-goods consumers are emerging. Trends in luxury products and services, as well as marketing and distribution, indicate a growing need to connect with consumers.

Companies need to recognise new growth opportunities resulting from demographic changes, market dynamics and motivations for buying. Two aspects coexist in the motives of the most affluent and sophisticated consumers. One is the demand for products that exemplify the quality of raw materials, craftsmanship and heritage linked to the brand. The other is related to the emotions and involvement created by in-store experiences.

The gulf between the tangible content of the product and the intangible appeal of the experience is lessening, mostly thanks to new omnichannel dynamics that are the future of retail. The market is moving towards a newer, more complete and advanced classification of luxury consumers. The creation of personalised Digital Signage solutions, meeting the converging needs of brands and clients, is the best way to develop the value co-creation processes associated with a purchase experience.

The main objective of brands operating in the luxury sector is hereby summarised. It is in response to the demand of clients who are increasingly used to information technology, particularly in-store solutions, capable of influencing luxury-brand strategic communications choices. This implies a clear impact on business models and the new role that stores have in creating a customer journey. This may now be outlined as a dynamic and changing process in which the coordination of both the online world and brick-and-mortar activities is driven by the digital revolution. This description appears essentially to benefit all market players.

Janan Ganesh, editor of the Financial Times, wrote: *"Money spent in restaurants, travel and celebrations can give you goods that are more protected from inflation: memories"*. As a matter of facts, purchasing habits are becoming increasingly "experience-oriented". As scholars very well highlighted in the last years, the postmodern digital consumption society is looking for intangibles: experiences beyond physical goods. The luxury sector, which was reluctant to go "online", is today reshaping its strategy to be able to fit the new generations, Millenials and post-millenials, and the new Emerging Markets (BRICS), that are "always-connected", "always online". The introduction of the new customer journey dimension, physical and digital at the same time (phygital), has been one of the answers. The clients are engaged digitally, but still need to visit the physical store to complete the experiential journey. The cases mentioned in this paper confirmed that in some markets it is very important to be able to leverage between tradition, consumers still want to have physical "touchable" relationship, and digital, from web to virtual-reality-touch-points, in the "phy-gital" customer journey dimension. The same kind of experiential approach is advisable and used by other important economic sectors. For instance, consumers are looking for experience before than products in the research of the best vines DOC, where the Vineries are engaging customer in a multi-dimensional experiential journey. The client can enjoy the "experience", beyond testing the wine, both online and physically visiting the multi-media-digital Vineries. The same applies for many other sectors such as gourmet restaurants, experiential hotels and touristic offers.

Saviolo, in the very recent essay "Managing fashion and luxury companies" (2019), dedicated to what she defines the eco-system of luxury, identifies in the transition from the approach to the product to the creativity and consumer oriented approach, the real challenge that these companies must face and, from this point of view, she defines the conceptual structure to the "emotional" concept of experiences, trips, points of contact and commitment, to then build a unique, stimulating and memorable experience that we call "signature".

The brand, in short, would consist in designing and managing the customer experience both as art and as science: brands should "design" the customer's journey as they do with products, injecting creativity and their special "touch" in all points of contact with the customer.

Whether it's the aesthetics or functionality of the product, a delicious in-store service, a personalized commitment to brand activities or sharing feedback online, it's the experience that matters most, making the brand something memorable and meaningful. Consumers have always known this, rewarding with their loyalty to companies and brands able to offer product experiences. What is certain is that it is the value of experiences with respect to the mere "possession" of the object that has profoundly changed the way companies create their products, whatever they are.

If the customer is more satisfied when he spends money to experiment, to live than in possessing, in the near future experiential goods will take the place of the product. Experiences are defining our social identities through social media so that a trip to an exotic destination or participation in an exclusive fashion show appears much more valuable than wearing a pair of designer shoes, concludes Saviolo. The product itself is only the starting point of the value proposition which must be enriched by layers of experiences through physical, digital and human interactions between the consumer and the brand.

Consequently, the process of value creation and value extraction is shifting from a product and company-centric vision to a consumer-centered experience and vision, in which the breadth and depth of the relationship between brand and consumer are fundamental. And this applies to every sector in which the customer is offered an experience.

BIBLIOGRAPHY

ANTONI, F., BURGELMAN, R. A., MEZA, P., 2004, *LVMH in 2004: the challenges of strategic integration*, Harvard Business School Case

BASTIEN, V., KAPFERER, J., 2009, Luxury marketing plays by a different set of rules, *Financial Times* June, Vol.2

BERRY, C.J., 1994, *The Idea of Luxury – A Conceptual e Historical Investigation,* Cambridge University Press, Cambridge.

BINKHORST, E., DEN DEKKER, T., 2009, Agenda for co-creation tourism experience research, *Journal of Hospitality Marketing & Management*, Vol. 18

BOSWIJK, A., THIJSSEN, T., PEELEN, E., 2007, *The experience economy: A new perspective,* Amsterdam: Pearson Education

BOWEN, G. & BOWEN, D., 2018, Luxury Product Decision-Making Strategy: Leveraging Social Media to Create the Emotional Component of the Strategy. In Digital Marketing Strategies for Fashion and Luxury Brands (pp. 289-308).

CATRY, B., 2003, The great pretenders, *Business Strategy Review*, Vol. 14

DUBOIS, B., CZELLAR, S. and LAURENT, G., 2001, Consumer Rapport to Luxury: Analyzing Complex and Ambivalent Attitudes, *Les Cahiers de Recherche*, Vol. 33

DUBOIS, B. and DUQUESNE, P., 1993, The Market for Luxury Goods: Income versus Culture, *European Journal of Marketing*, Vol. 27

EVRARD, Y., ROUX, E., 2005, *Culture vs. luxury: the paradoxes of democratization*, Centre d'études et de recherche sur les organisations et la gestion, Puyricard : CEROG

FIONDA, A.M., MOORE, C.M., 2009, The anatomy of the luxury fashion brand, *Journal of Brand Management*, Vol. 16

GRETZEL, U., JAMAL, T., 2009, Conceptualizing the creative tourist class: Technology, mobility, and tourism experiences, *Tourism Analysis*, Vol. 14

HARRISON, J.V., ANDRUSIEWICZ, A., 2004, A virtual marketplace for advertising narrowcast over digital signage networks, *Electronic Commerce Research and Applications*, Vol. 3

HOLBROOK, M.B., HIRSCHMAN, E.C., 1982, The experiential aspects of consumption: consumer fantasies, feelings, and fun, *Journal of Consumer Research*, Vol. 9

KOTLER, P., STIGLIANO, G., 2018, *Retail 4.0. 10 regole per l'era digitale*, Mondadori

LEIBENSTEIN, H., 1950, Bandwagon, Snob and Veblen Effects in the Theory of Consumers' Demand, *The Quarterly Journal of Economics*, No. 64

LIPOVETSKY, G., ROUX, E., 2003, *Le Luxe éternel: De l'âge du sacré au temps des marques (Le Débat)*, Gallimard

MASON, R.S., 1981, *Conspicuous Consumption*, St. Martin's Press, New York.

MCCARTHY, J. C., WRIGHT, P. C., 2004, *Technology as experience.* Cambridge, MA: MIT Press

MORGAN, M., LUGOSI, P., RITCHIE, J.R.B., 2010, *The tourism and leisure experience: Consumer and managerial perspectives*, Bristol: Channel View

O'CASS, A. and FROST, H., 2002, Status brands: examining the effects of non-product-related brand associations on status and conspicuous consumption, Journal of Product and Brand Management, Vol. 11

OKONKWO, U., BRAND MANAG, J., 2009, 16: 287. https://doi.org/10.1057/bm.2008.

PANTANO, E., 2015, *Successful technological integration for competitive advantage in retail settings*. IGI Global. doi:10.4018/978-1-4666-8297-9

PANTANO, E., PASSAVANTI, R., PRIPORAS, C. V. & VERTERAMO, S., 2018, To what extent luxury retailing can be smart? Journal of Retailing and Consumer Services, 43, 94-100

PINE, J. B., GILMORE, J. H., 1999, The experience economy: Work is a theatre and every business a stage, Cambridge: Harvard Business School

PIZAM, A., 2010, Creating memorable experiences, *International Journal of Hospitality Management*, Vol. 29

POULSSON, S., KALE, S., 2004, The experience economy and commercial experiences, The Marketing Review, Vol.4

PRAHALAD, C. K., RAMASWAMY, V., 2004, Co-creation experiences: The next practice in value creation, *Journal of Interactive Marketing*, Vol.13

RIGBY, D., 2011, *The future of shopping*. Harvard Business Review, Vol. 89

Saviolo, S., 2019, Signature Experience: Art and science of customer engagement for fashion and luxury companies. EGEA spa.

SILVERSTEIN, M.J., FISKE, N., 2003, *Trading Up to new Luxury. Opportunities for Action in Consumer Markets*, The Boston Consulting Group, USA.

TRUONG, Y., SIMMONS, G., MCCOLL, R., KITCHEN, P.J., 2008, Status and Conspicuousness - Are They Related? Strategic Marketing Implications for Luxury Brands, *Journal of Strategic Marketing*, Vol.16

TYNAN, C., MCKECHNIE, S., 2009, Experience marketing: a review and reassessment, Journal of Marketing Management, Vol. 25

VANSCOYOC, K., HONEYCUTT, E.D., KARANDE, K., MANN, J., 2015, Why do consumers continue to shop on the internet?, *Proceedings of the 2000 Academy of Marketing Science (AMS) Annual Conference. Springer International Publishing*, doi:10.1007/978-3-319-11885-7_11

VARGO, S.L., LUSCH, R.F., 2004, Evolving to a new dominant logic for marketing, *Journal of Marketing*, Vol. 68

VARGO, S.L, LUSCH, R.F., 2008, Service-dominant logic: continuing the evolution, *Journal of the Academy of Marketing Science*, Vol.36

VEBLEN, T., 1981, *La teoria della classe agiata*, Einaudi Torino

VICKERS, J.S., RENAND, F., 2003, The marketing of luxury goods: An exploratory study - three conceptual dimensions, *The Marketing Review*, Vol. 3

VIGNERON, F., JOHNSON, L.W., 2004, Measuring Perceptions of Brand Luxury, *The Journal of Brand Management*, Vol.11

WEB REFERENCES

Gartner's Unified Retail Retailer Survey (July-August 2018) https://www.gartner.com/en/newsroom/press-releases/2019-04-01-gartner-says-100-million-consumers-will-shop-in-augme

THE LUXURY VALUE IN THE AI ERA. A NEW "QUALITY GROWTH PARADIGM" IS BORN!

Ingrid VAILEANU
First PhD Thesis in France on Functional Economy
xvaluator@yahoo.com

Florin PAUN
International Society for Agilising Innovation
info@florin-paun.com

Claude PLOUVIET
Tiers-inclus
cplouviet@gmail.com

Columbia HILLEN
Columbia.hillen@gmail.com

ABSTRACT

The high prices associated with quality are a permanent barrier for the majority to access high quality and luxury, as the two concepts "democratization of luxury" and "luxury as quality and rarity" seemed to be contradiction in terms. But a new growth paradigm was identified if we apply quantic approach and functional economy approach to the analysis of the potential new "forms of luxury" ("luxury functionalities), which could be in the same time "not luxury quality" and "luxury quality" depending on the "observer", after the analogy with "the cat and the paradox of Schrodinger". But in the digital world, the "observer" is demultiplexed, the observation is in real time and continuously). Luxury domain could inspire and generalize the "augmented value creation" by "open valorization strategies" and scaled-up by national regulatory support (for example, the Law PACTE in France, the country where fashion and luxury adds to more than 42 milliards and 86% exports). New research will be conducted on this potential "augmented quality growth paradigm" inspired by the luxury new business model.

Keywords: democratising luxury, open qualification, luxuring, Impact Readiness Level (IRL), « pret-à-personnaliser », augmented luxury value, functional economy.
JEL codes: D460, D470, D230, D210, (D82, D83, D84), P420, P470, E710.

INTRODUCTION

Newly shared strategies and tools managing the evolutions of the innovation models (Chesbrough, Van Haverbeke, 2008; Paun, von Tunzelman, Richard, 2011) and the transitions towards new economic models like the "functional economy" (Du Tertre, 2007, Mont 2002, Vaileanu-Paun, 2010) accompanied by an evolution of evaluation and valorization models (Vaileanu-Paun, et Boutillier, 2012) are applied in this article for the first time in the fashion and luxury domains. This new theoretical approach of the functional economy as well as quantic approach in the measure and "open valorisation" of the "Luxury value" today integrates the digital transformations (Lemoine, 2014, 2018) and tools as well as the permanent, real time impacts of digital world on the valorization process. New approaches, tools and concepts are presented as key solutions for understanding and managing the new "forms of luxury" (like "the personalization", "the contextualisation"). The new and divers actors join the opportunities of the luxury sectors and complementary news centers of creation of the shared "augmented value" (Vaileanu, Paun, 2018) emerge in all fashion and luxury domains.

This article is thus proposing an experimental approach for the "open valorisation" together with the stakeholders of the potential clients of a constantly evolving and contextualized "luxury offer" thanks to this extending valorization process and its perimeters (in space and time). This approach allows and encourages the integration in real time and continuously the social and environmental impacts of new products, services and "Product-Services-Systems "(Mont, 2007) towards what we could call "personalized luxury functional offers". These new complementary "functional solutions" perceived under the light of the functional economy theoretical approach, are in perfect resonance with structural environmental transformations, "new urban rhythms" (Bailly, Heurgon, 2001), identifying together with the clients and their ecosystems ("Client as a System" (Vaileanu- Paun, 2010) new forms of "offers" as "Product-services systems" (Mont, 2002, du Tertre, 2007), "new forms of luxury" like "personalisation and contextualization" with a continuously renewable offer of thus perceived exclusive " luxury values".

This new approach shows that in the context of evolutions of the firms and their environment (Laperche, Uzunidis, 2012; Zeting, 2015) taking in consideration more and more the diversity of environmental and social impacts (perceived by a big diversity of "observers") on both short and long perspectives, the value of luxury is emerging even stronger while integrating *ex ante* the positive externalities perceived by all these stakeholders on extended space and time perimeters.

The luxury firms and brands are thus profoundly changing their relations with their stakeholders. The development of the domains of fashion and luxury are contested and even contestable by some of the populations exclusively protecting the environment. Some of the sectors benefiting from the impacts subject are blocked by their "path dependency" (Uzunidis, 2009) and the choices leading to industrial crisis impacts are sometimes "path dependents" and might lead to competition relations between actors having completely different (if not opposing) interests: some aiming mainly for monetary capitalistic value (entrepreneurs, multinationals) some focusing on social value (job creation, employee approach) and others aiming for the biodiversity and environment protection (including the impacted populations but also the ecologist organisations).

If the theory of stakeholders dates back to 1980 with the works of Freeman (Freeman, 2013) the terminology and concepts of "stakeholders" gets the origins in the works of Ansodd (1968) considering the evolution of the firm's role: the firm has to justify its objectives in such a manner that each group (stakeholders) might find "satisfaction". Even at this stage of the analysis, the digital tools propose a better understanding in the "degree and criteria of satisfaction" (Xvaluator, 2016). But for Ansoff, these new social and environmental responsibilities are limiting the economic accomplishments by the firm. For the Functional Economy, the capacity to integrate *ex ante* the social and environmental externalities, to co-construct value and recognition of shared value (thus observed as "augmented value") together with the stakeholders represent the new centers of profits for the firm and for its extended ecosystems of stakeholders.

"The Functional economy" is a theoretical construct whose definition is meeting general consensus (Vaileanu-Paun, Boutillier, 2012). It's about changing the transaction of the property of a product by selling the usage functionality "Product-Service-System" co-constructed with the clients by personalizing the access to the product and different services integrated *ex ante* to the process of usage of the products. The objective is no longer the sell the property of the product but the "performance" capacity to respond to specific "functionality demands". For example, instead of selling just the cars and transferring the property to the client, the automobile sector evolution tends towards a functional economy model and is already confirmed by the "functionality offers" of "mobility" (including the access to use different mix of mobility products (cars, bicycle, train, etc) and including services (insurance, maintenance adjusted for each client) as customized mobility functionalities. Several pioneers of the Functional Economy (Foundation Concorde, (2011), Michelin, Xerox, Peugeot, Renault, Electricité De France, Velib, Apple, etc.) are already engaging profound transformations of their production and commercialization in their sectors by de-sectorising and including digital innovations in the process to access to these "functionalities offers".

For example, the clients of EDF (Electricité de France) become thus potential co-producers of renewable energy (commercial offer Bleu Ciel EDF, allowing clients to sell back to EDF the locally produced energy thanks to the contract of "co-construction of the offer EDF" that could be "selling "the functionality of 20° comfort solution" in the house heating management. The commercialisation strategies of these new « functionality offers » are integrating the opinion of the user ("the observer" of the value thus co-created) and are evolving towards an integrated "smart-grid efficient transactions" within a dynamic stakeholder's ecosystem (Vaileanu Paun, 2010a, 2010b, Atelier Bepos et Smart Grids, DGALN/PUCA).

The interest for this new theoretical approach is to understand that the evolution of the industrial economic model (fordien business model, considering social and environmental externalities as cost centers), needs evolution towards different economic models like the "functional economy" which considers the same externalities as new centers of creation of "shared value": observed as "value" by the firm and its stakeholders ecosystems. Thus, the issues of compatibility with social and environmental imperatives become opportunities to create and share new "forms of luxury", thus co-constructed and co-perceived, giving the firm a greater role in the society (without reducing it to only its main economic value creation).

The luxury domains are evolving towards new experimentation fields extending the offer of a "product" (selling the product and transferring the property to the client) to an offer of a "luxury functionality" (Vaileanu, 2010, Mont. 2002) including adapted access to products, services and their personalisation and contextualisation.

Further to new examples in the luxury literature, "sensorial experience" (Holbrook & Hirschman, 1982), digital luxury experiences (Batat, 2017), specific phrases like "luxurious webmosphere" or "luxemosphere" were developed, indicating the need to adapt to new digital and open innovation dynamic to anticipate the new actors and methods of value creation. There is a need of new approach of luxury sector that might be complementary and totally different from the majority of research approaches sometimes even exclusively on the "selling of the luxury products or brands" (Lipovetsky et Roux, 2003).

1. STATES-OF-THE-ART ON THE THEORETICAL APPROACH OF THE FUNCTIONAL ECONOMY

The literature on this new desectorized approach (du Tertre, 2010) of the « functional economy (Vaileanu, Paun, 2011) focuses both on analysing the luxury offer and demand as well as the new actors and centers of value creation in the domains of fashion and luxury in France including the companies which singed in 2010 the "Chart of good practices of the fashion and luxury (Charte, 2010).

This article is bringing a new and complementary analysis of the luxury business model, both of the production and consumption processes in order to get out of the fordien approach: the gain of productivity by selling more products at a higher price and finding solutions for low production costs. The functional economy relates better to the approaches of the « service economy » (without being reduced to it) (Gadrey, 2002, Gadrey et Zarifian, 2002, du Tertre, 2006) and is focuses on "selling performance" (Stahel, 2006) of a functionality specific to the luxury domains' actors and co-constructed with their clients and their ecosystems of stakeholders: "client as system" (Vaileanu-Paun, 2010).

« The wellbeing », « the well-looking » in the fashion sector are veritable «fashion functionalities depending on a « Product- Service-System » (products and integrated services) - PSS (Mont, 2002) capable of the performance to respond the best to complexes specific needs impossible to satisfy other way by just selling products and services separately.

This functional approach looks for understandings of the impact of the counterfeiting business model and its negative effects for the luxury sector as pretends to translate luxury into its affordable version based on the fordienne mass production and distribution of less expensive low quality products other way inaccessible to a greater number of potential clients. The pretention of counterfeiting business model to democratize luxury products by simple fordien levier of cheap and low-quality products, justifying delocalization of production (Uzunidis, 2008), cannot convince on its democratisation of luxury pretention. More than it can harm the planet with polluted bad quality products produced in bad conditions by low paid workers and ignoring the costs of transport and recycling issues.

The economists (Moati, Corcos, 2009, Du Tertre, 2007) are already analysing the important impacts on the evolution from simple « transactional markets » towards « relational collaborative markets » encouraging thus the loyalty creation politics as well as more efficient collaborative innovation processes like "open innovation" (Chesbrough, Van Haverbeke, 2008) by integrating as opportunity the actors' asymmetries" in the highly collaborative and agile process (Paun, 2009, 2010, 2011) and finally engaging specific tools (DRL-TRL) (Paun, von Tunzelman, Richard, 2011) for "hybridizing of the Tech – Push (offer) and Market Pull (demand)" strategies (Paun, Mayer, 2013).

The methodology of this collective research work is resourced in practical work by the actors of the sector of luxury which in France has been gathered within a common domain « Fashion and Luxury » and bibliographical and research work on the functional economy with an exploration focus (related to the institutionalist theoretical framework micro-méso-macroeconomic) on the evolutions of the firm, of the territory and of the economic model. We thus bring this new analysis and approaches to understand and anticipate new tendencies and outputs in the most recent strategies of the actors in fashion and luxury domain in France.

Following the essentials of economic literature, we identify on a méso-economic level (fashion and luxury domain in France) the shift from an economic model based on a value depending on the mass production and consumption of standardised products and services where the role of the producer is" to create value" and the role of the consumer is" to destroy value" through the consumption process (Mont 2002), towards an economic model where the value is co-constructed together with the clients and theirs stakeholders (of course, there are different degrees of co-construction process).

The process of Co-producing the luxury value becomes as important as the luxury product or brand itself. The relation between producer and consumer is not linear, with consecutive activities leading to transaction selling the product, but embarks also the producer, the consumer and the stakeholders in a "spiral of extended value creation" (Vaileanu, Paun, 2018) including co-construction, open valorisation, personalisation, contextualization, integrating recycled materials process, recycled material resourcing, etc.

An allegoric comparison is the evolution of "art as co-created value" developed recently by the Museum Guggenheim which integrates no longer exclusively finished masterpieces but also unfinished and "in the process masterpieces" of artists like for example Marcel Duchamps: "*the Process of creation it's part of the masterpiece itself*".

To emphasise the importance of the "process" itself of creating "augmented luxury value" together with the products and services perceived and recognised as "high quality value" we propose in this article a new concept: the verb "luxuring" (in French "luxier"). "Luxuring" (Paun, Vaileanu, 2018) as highly collaborative process involving all the stakeholders that make possible the emergence of new "luxury functionalities", "luxeperience" (Batat, 2017), and allow the creation of new forms of luxury including both products and services without reducing the "luxury quality designation" to only the property of products and services but transfer it to a shared use of "Product-Service-Systems" (Mont, 2002).

More than just luxury products and services, the client's experience and its emotional and relational dimensions become more and more important for a luxury brand which are advised to better integrate their clients' needs to satisfy them on both functional and human level (Batat, 2017).

For example, tourism destinations could be transformed by local actors from different sectors in high value exclusivity luxury experiences ("luxury functionalities") which create "shared value" but "indivisible value" (du Tertre, 2010, Vaileanu, 2010) as the quality is perceived as "territorial value" only through the joint capacities of "contextualization" and shared experiences. The example of the "Ireland Writing Retreat" (https://www.irelandwritingretreat.com/artists-retreat), selected in 2019 as one of the best 10 creatives retreats in The Guardian created a new "augmented value" of Donegal as exclusive destination for writers and those looking for training to become writers (https://www.irelandwritingretreat.com/opt-in?utm_campaign=67f57c5e-8641-469e-a666-9f1e4e954f39&utm_source=so). These new potential luxury functionalities could be co-produced and co-evaluated together with all the stakeholders as their augmented value consists in their capacities and performances as collective collaborative process.

Functional economy strategies for firms consist thus in the dynamic of the process, in the capacity to "perform" selling the "usage" of the product and integrated adapted services instead of the selling of the propriety of a product or separate service pre-destined as "luxury" because of its luxury "brand'. This shift in the economic model from fordien-industrial model to functional economy structurally change the methods of production and consumption (Bourg et Buclet, 2005, du Tertre, 2006, Vaileanu-Paun, 2010) integrating *ex ante* the processes of social and environmental issues by extending the process to the recycling and relevant "productive configurations" including the value of the "immaterial collective patrimony" (du Tertre, 2007) created and developed in the dynamic of the process of "luxuring".

We discuss this new questions on the importance of a new economic model approach on the issue of value creation and value evaluation with the evolution towards "open valorisation" (Vaileanu, Paun, 2018) in the domain of fashion and luxury and the role of the digital transformations in the re-localisation in Europe of the production of new forms of luxury. The example of the relocalisation of Nike and Adidas productions in Germany thanks to AI solutions of mass consumption of high value products and "mass personalization and customisation" as complementary new economic fundamentals assuming the rarity criteria of classic luxury value (and even more than rarity, the "exclusivity" but for everyone) and thus becoming an "extended-augmented value" (incorporating all forms of value: social, ecological, economic and market values).

Facing the general tendency "of reduction the innovation cycles" (Paun, 2018), the fashion and luxury sectors create new dynamics by involving more variety of innovation actors and more of their stakeholders in highly collaborative process of open innovation leading to new "forms of luxury" thus co-constructed and co-evaluated with their clients and stakeholders in real time and continuously.

The objective at the meso-economic level (in France and in the domain - fashion and luxury) is to understand through the new "open valorisation" process the pertinence of the functional economy model for the economic growth of the luxury domain including the democratization of the access to luxury values for much more potential clients without impeaching from respecting the luxury classical determinants (rarity, quality) and from sustainable development objectives. But even more, the solution is based on these new forms of democratization of luxury by integrating new complementary fundamentals: personalisation, contextualization, integration *ex ante* of the social, ecological and economic impact solutions.

2. METHODOLOGY AND NEWS TOOLS FOR IDENTIFYING THE « AUGMENTED EXTENDED VALUE OF LUXE » THANKS TO COLLABORATIVE STRATEGIES OF "OPEN VALORIZATION"

2.1. New tool of the collaborative innovation: « Impacts Readiness Level » (IRL) (Paun, Vaileanu, 2018)

Collaborative innovation and especially the "open innovation (Chesbrough, Van Haverbeke, 2008; Paun, von Tunzelmann, Richard, 2011) is perceived as essential process for the creation and valorization integrating thus a greater number of diversity of actors and "observers' perspectives" (Xvaluator, 2016) representing not a threat (as in fordien segmentation approach) but a strength as important inputs if « the diversity of the asymmetries » (Paun, von Tunzelman, Richard, 2011) (culture asymmetries, risk asymmetries, temporality asymmetries, etc) between the innovation actors are compensated by innovative tools (DRL-TRL, Paun, 2009) in order to facilitate collaborations and "shared augmented value creation". The results of these highly collaborative interactions and tools is the "agilising innovation processes" (Paun, 2018) aiming to reinforce the capacities and capabilities (Paun, 2011) of actors to perform by integrating *ex ante* the direct and indirect (effects médiats, Du Tertre, 2007) impacts at social, ecological, economical levels.

The valorization potential of a highly collaborative innovation ecosystem depends in the same time by the number and the diversity of the actors involved in interactions, of their collaboration capacities and « capabilities » (Paun, von Tunzelman, Richard, 2011) as well as of the quality of the adaptive tools (including digital tools and new approaches) and methodologies supporting them to perceive, qualify, share and valorise the inputs of each of the actors.

The quality of a collaborative innovation ecosystem is:

- Directly proportional to the square of the number of the ecosystem actors,
- Directly proportional to the actors integrating the ecosystem with the intention to offer (respond to demands) (tech-push),
- Indirect proportional to those expressing a demand and the intention to benefit of the ecosystem (market-pull)
- Directly proportional to the specific characteristics (asymmetries) of the direct members of the ecosystem and
- Indirectly of their own external potential networks (especially their diversity and complementarity) and directly proportional to the "capabilities" (Paun, von Tunzelman, Richard, 2011) of action and success of each of the innovation actors involved. (Paun, 2018).

These "capabilities" depends of the quality, efficiency of dynamic tools and collaborative strategies (DRL-TRL, IRL, Shared Risks and Benefits Contracts, etc) (Paun, 2009) as well as of the capacity of the actors to use them and evaluate on innovation on longue trajectories not only on "one shot" innovation project or product.

The Value of a Collaborative Innovation Ecosystem = N square – N / 2 x N offer / N benefx As (Div, Compl.) x Cap (Tools, Action)

Source: (Paun, Vaileanu, 2018) Valorization of the collaborative innovation ecosystems

N = Number of the innovation actors in a collaborative innovation ecosystem

NV offer = Number of the innovation actors with the intention and resources to OFFER solutions to the other ecosystem' members

NV benef = Number of the innovation actors with the intention to benefit of the ecosystem solutions for their DEMAND

As = Specific Characteristics – asymmetries identified within the ecosystem members

Div = The degree of diversity of the ecosystem members

Compl = The degree of complementarity of the ecosystem members

Cap = Capabilities of the ecosystem

Tools = Collaboration and exchanges tools, aiming to compensate asymmetries in order to facilitate highly collaborative agile innovation processes

Act = Capability of members to be dynamic and engage RESOURCES and ACTIONS

The integration of the diversity of impacts in the collaborative innovation practices is co-substantial to the agile and highly collaborative process as more we integrate diversity at all levels (subjects of interests, topics, localisations and temporalities different in accordance to each specific context of each of the member of the ecosystem), more we increase the perimeters of competences and capabilities of all actors and thus more chances to create shared value for all the ecosystem members and even for their external indirectly impacted networks of stakeholders.

Even if at the beginning of the collaborative innovation process the impacts seem to be observed more internally to the firms (in terms of increase of competences of the human resources, new approaches, new ideas, etc.) longer we persist in "agilising the innovation ecosystems " (Paun, 2018), more we impact the stakeholders directly or indirectly even in totally different sectors to the initial collaborations and thus contribute to scale-up the evolution of the economic models in all sectors and territories (impacts registered at macro-economic level).

Figure 1: Impacts Readiness Level (IRL) measuring the degree of maturity and intensity of the highly collaborative process of innovation

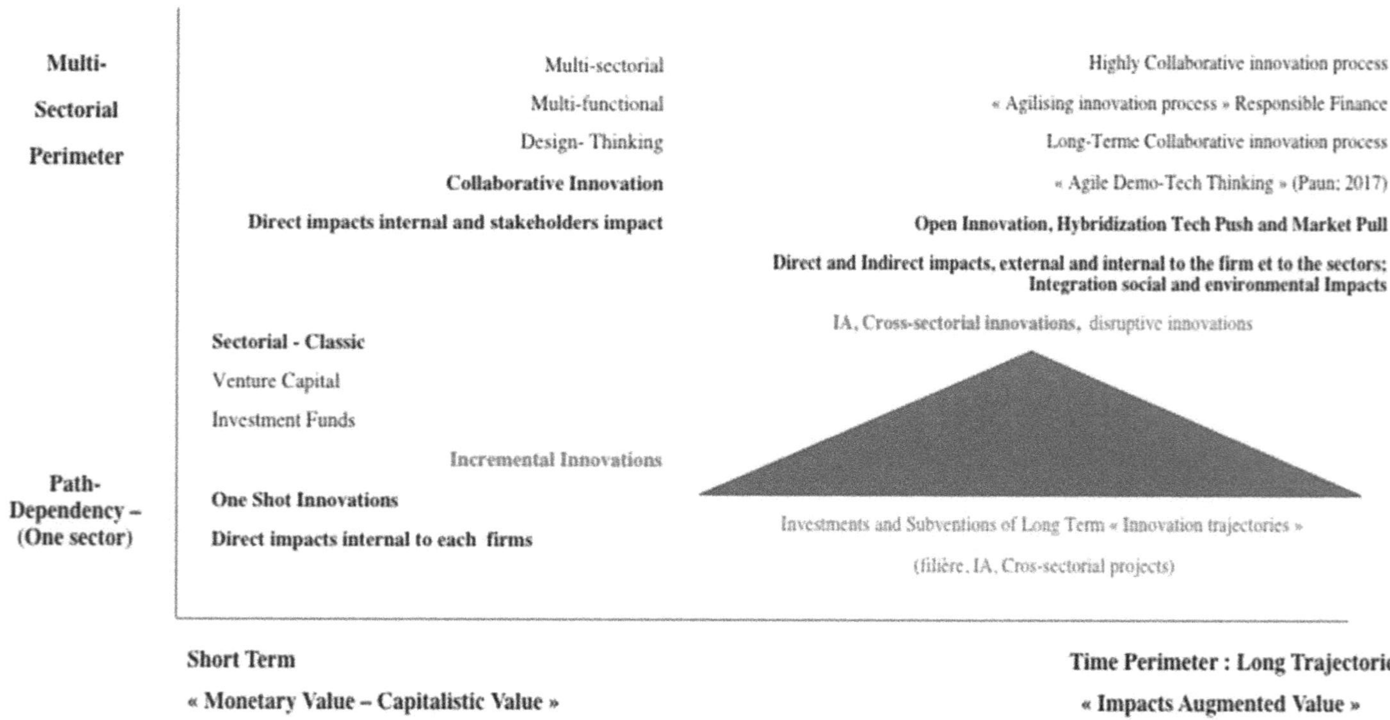

Source: Paun, Vaileanu, 2018.

While the products and brands were considered till recently, in the last years, as the only centers of value creation for the luxury domains, nowadays in the digital era the social networks there are higher expectations of compliances with social and ecological criteria. In the perspective of the AI future impacts, there are high expectations for new centers of value creation in the fashion and luxury branches. The « luxury value » expects more and more capacities to integrate in adapted services and shorter innovation cycles (shorter time to market collections) and capacity to integrate innovation from other larger domains, for example collaboration in the health issues thanks to 3D printers of luxury gadgets.

In fact, the digital innovations (IA, 3D Printers, etc) are challenging the classical fundamentals of the luxury domains which based their brands valorization on « exclusivity » (Tom et al., 1998), "social Statute" and "authenticity "(Berry, 1994; Chaudhuri, 1998).

The example of the fashion and luxury domain are facing the pressure (from social network and digital tools, constant real time evaluations « like » on the new centers of « open valorization » as GAFA (Vaileanu, Paun, 2016) to democratize the access to luxury products ("luxure" a concept promoted by Jean Paul Gautier to challenge such experimentations) experiment collaborations of "haute couture" designers like Karl Lagerfeld through his collaboration with the « fast fashion » brands like H&M.

The paradox of the democratisation of the luxury products through the fordien experimentations supported by social networks and brands, proves that in spite of the voluntarism of visionary luxury creators like Karl Lagerfeld, it is impossible to use standardised products and reduced prices to allow mass consumption of "luxury" as thus the concept itself of "Luxury" disappear behind low-cost mass consumption fundamentals.

The paradox « accessible luxury products » meaning to open access to mass consumptions of luxury products and brands cannot be solved in the fordien economic approach as luxury means "rarity" and especially "NOT mass consumption".

That's why the functional economy models provide solutions to imagine "new forms of luxury" and the possibility of democratization of access to luxury experiences involving luxury products and integrated adapted services and thus selling not the luxury product (its property) but the "luxury functionality" (usage in certain contexts and exclusive adapted conditions).

2.2. What are the values of luxury?

We consider now the question about the capacity to identify the « augmented value » or different forces and centers of value creation thanks to the interactions with the stakeholders allowing the co-evaluation and « open valorization » possible only thanks to the digital tools (Xvaluator, 2016) and decisions to integrate *ex ante* all perceived externalities.

Using the functional economy concepts and approach (Vaileanu-Paun, 2009) to analyse the value creation for the first time in the fashion and luxury domains in France by the organization and integration of externalities (material and immaterial patrimony) offers an holistic view on the relevant four forms of "perceived value" by all the stakeholders: financial and capitalistic value, market value, social – working solutions value and environmental – ecological value.

Figure 2: "Client System" is continuously defining its needs further to interactions with its stakeholders who might have contradictory objectives as aiming creating more financial, social or environmental values. The new approach in qualifying the client and its ecosystem of stakeholders revealing the "heterogeneity of each client" under the pressure of the different interest of its stakeholders. The heterogeneity of each ecosystem members (including clients) represents a potential source of « augmented value » under the functional economy approaches but a cost center under the fordien approach.

Figure 2. "Client Système" qui auto définit ses besoins en function des interactions avec ses parties prenantes

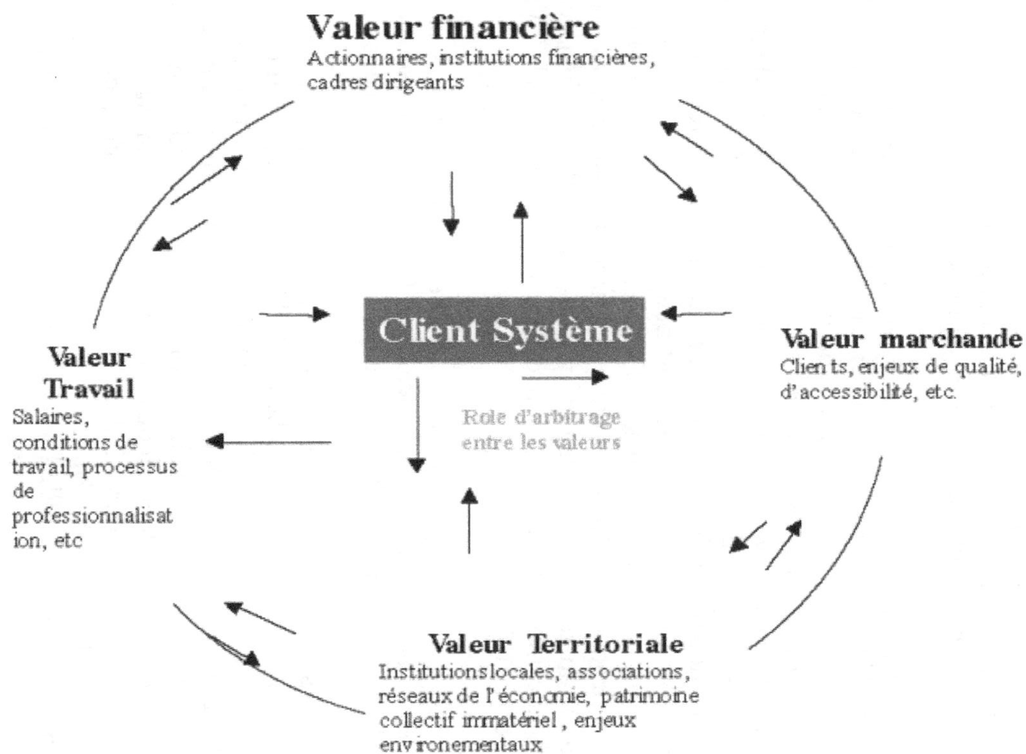

Source: *Vaileanu-Paun, 2009.*

Figure 2: Client System which is continuously defining its needs further to interactions with its stakeholders who might have contradictory objectives as aiming creating more financial, social or environmental values.

New approach in qualifying the client and its ecosystem of stakeholders revealing the heterogeneity of each client under the pressure of the different interest of its stakeholders). The heterogeneity of each ecosystem members (including clients) represents a potential source of « augmented value » under the functional economy approaches.

The luxury value (as identified as augmented value through multiple observers Client Systems) is taking in consideration the territory impacts and the evolution in real time of the perceived values potentially different and even antagonistic: *financial and capitalistic value, market value, social – working solutions value and environmental – ecological value.* Thus, the functional economy is perceived as essentially a process of concretization of territorial value which is one of the reasons that the growth of the luxury domains could find new interests and news value creation centers by re-localizing production in France, in Europe. This re-localizing tendencies of luxury production offers a counterweight to the last decades marked by delocalization following productivity gains under the fordien economic model's incentives ("Periodization of the economic models" Vaileanu, Boutillier, 2010)

In order to allow the emergence of "new creativity forms of luxury" and open valorization of these « luxury functionalities » we identified several "new fundamentals" in the fashion and luxury domains in France:

a.) The degree of « cognitive proximity » (Uzunidis, 2008) of the brands creators and their potential clients following in real time on social networks and all digital tools the evolutions of the brands and thus contributing (as multiple observers) to the creation of « luxury cultures ». More the "luxury culture" is shared on digital tools and reinforced by AI algorithms of choices' dependencies, more all these exchanges, images and comments about the brands, their inspired behaviours, create "luxury experiences" by millions of potential clients without buying yet the products or engaging in added services (as like maintenance, insurance that could be considered constraints and thus are not associated to the new "luxury culture"). Creating this "cognitive proximity" with the luxury brands and creators, a huge ecosystem of stakeholders could propose new forms of luxury: "personalized luxury products and integrated services" or "contextualized luxury products and integrated services". As example, the Fashion Show of Karl Lagerfeld who used real life topics (for creating this immaterial patrimony of "cultural proximity" shared with his potential clients): strikes, feminists or homosexual causes in accordance with the evolution of the 21st society values.

b.) The degree of impacts: social, environmental, economic impacts revealed by the stakeholders and the organisational system to identify and integrate their opinions and different criteria (bottom-up) as for example: choices of materials, of human resources, recycling solutions, etc. We can no longer think the luxury functionality without integrating *ex ante* the compliance to social, environmental and economic criteria (a new law in France "Law PACTE" is now inspiring the future laws in Europe proposing the "extended social and environmental missions of a firm") which certainly will shape the image of the "European luxury functionality", probably different from the Chinese or American ones. However, the CSR (Corporate Social Responsibility), or Sustainable Development Reports are no longer sufficient to convince the diversity of stakeholders using social network and digital tools to qualify information and new digital tools are needed (The example of Xvaluator – universal qualifier of Data "Like" aggregated from all platforms used by clients) (Tritto, 2017). These innovative digital tools are solutions for integrating and valorising the opinions « like » in real time and integrating the whole diversity of criteria (bottom-up), subjects and their participative ponderation (How much counts the « Like » from Facebook in comparison with a "Like" on Airbnb. New innovative digital tools like Xvaluator could disrupt the GAFA as offer the citizens the power to co-evaluate, to share and co-qualify even the sources of their collective « likes ". These process of "open qualification" and "Open valorization" could structurally change the models of evaluation and valorization in the fashion and luxury domains introducing for example the "Real Time CSR open evaluations" (Xvaluator, 2016). The capacity to identify the « degree of compliance to social and environmental impacts criteria (using the measure tool of the maturity of Impact compliance « Impact Readiness Level » - IRL (Paun, Vaileanu, 2018) becomes already an imperative not only a desideratum, at least for selling the "luxury functionalities" (Vaileanu-Paun, 2009, 2010, Vaileanu-Paun, et Boutillier, 2012).

c.) The Temporality of innovations (new fashion collections, products or services in the fashion and luxury domains) determined in the past by only seasonal fashion shows must integrate triple temporality levels:

- An "instant temporality" responding to the omnipresence of expectations and comments on social networks and digital platforms which evaluates (even without buying) the « luxury functionalities »
- A "sectorial temporality" following the seasonal fashion shows and collections
- A "long term temporality" (territorial) with expectation from the « luxury functionality » to comply with territorial and society long-term

objectives as expressed by all the different stakeholders and their own ecosystems.

This "Triple temporality of luxury functionalities » revealed by the concepts of the Functional economy proves that the « luxury values » are outstandingly territorial values, meaning that they are able to create local shared value without possible division of this value but accessible to all stakeholders on longue potential innovation trajectories.

This scientific approach of the evolutions of the "Luxury augmented value" thanks to the digital tools and highly collaborative innovation strategies proves the potential of democratization of "new forms of luxury" and anticipates tendencies and needs which put practically the bases of a new economic model in the fashion and luxury domain in France: "the luxury functional economy".

We are acknowledging "the resilience determinants of the new forms of fashion and luxury domains" (Vaileanu, Paun, 2018) (especially during the fordien industrial crises): first the capacity to integrate through the dynamic of the stakeholder's larger perimeters of connected sectors (like digital, 3D printing, etc) revealing the "augmented value" and secondly projecting the "luxury value" on the triple temporality not only on the present fluctuations of perceived immediate capitalistic value.

Thanks to this analysis of the economic model of luxury domains at the dawn of AI era, we can expect the increase of importance of solutions of "luxury functionalities for everybody" once we understand the possibility of decoupling of the "perceived value" from the "price" (as today the highest price is related directly with best positive impacts and high quality).

The unexpected conclusion to this research work on the subject of luxury value allow us already to affirm that the economic model of luxury functionalities profoundly transformed by digital and AI solutions, makes possible the evaluation of the quality as largely recognized as "augmented value" on larger sectorial and triple temporality perimeters and thus decoupling the "luxury high value" from "the highest Price". In the fordien model, a habit in the perception of attributing high costs to high value, the high Price is connected to the high costs and the high value of the brand. Even more, and contrary to the expectations (a wrong habit in the perceptions) we demonstrate the validity of connecting HIGH QUALITY and LUXURY VALUE with LOWER PRICE (as we associate the low costs of long term recycle processes, lower that the costs for unrecycled low quality materials charging the stakeholders and the future generations with the real huge cost of cheap and non-quality products today).

2.3. The Power of the Luxury Value as Augmented value co-constructed together with stakeholders

The importance of taking in consideration in real and continuous time the stakeholders' opinions (« consom-acteurs », « clients-systems ») in the dynamic process of open valorization of the offers of « luxury » associated with « high quality » and « augmented value » (co-constructed) by this new digital system of continuous observation and evaluation (the « value » becomes only when is « perceived value ») reminds the Platon approach of the knowledge in the "cave allegory" (du Livre VII of The Republic) projecting the men in chains, blocked in a cave and turning the back to the entry so that all what they could see is their own shadows and the projected other objects far behind them. This Platon allegory puts in light the importance of the "observation", of the projection of the reality and the "observed subject" (in Platon's case the man and the ascension condition to knowledge and its transmission) and in our case the subject is the « value of luxury functionalities » thus directly conditioned by the methods and tools of observation of the value in specific contextualization of the open observation process.

Again, the Guggenheim example reminds the importance of the process of the value creation and its observation ("perceived value) as important as the result (the observed subject).

This scientific demonstration of the conditioned perceived value of luxury as "augmented value" (through the process of co-evaluation together with the different observers in the enlarged ecosystem of stakeholders) allows us to decouple the "augmented value" of the new forms of luxury from their "Price". The quality luxury value is high but the price could be lower than the counterfeiting produces as the perceived social and environmental cost of counterfeiting is much higher than the cost of recycled quality products. A simple change in the approach of the functional economy offers unexpected solutions to the paradox (that we named "Karl's paradox") of the "democratisation of the luxury offers" demonstrating not only that the democratisation of new forms of luxury is possible without contradicting the luxury determinants (rarity, high quality) but also the Price of High quality "augmented luxury value" (new offers) should be lower than "low quality, non-recycled and anti-social production system of products" as the cost of recycling and social justice are higher and today the responsibility is diluted in time and within stakeholders including the State and tax payers' contributions.

Figure 3: « Karl Paradox - Chouppette Method » ("Karl's cat" as "Schrodinger's cat" where the question is to either be "high luxury quality" or "Not high luxury quality" during the observation process multiplied by the digital tools. The quantic approach leads to envisage the democratization of the luxury offers through "new forms of luxury": « prêt-à-personnaliser » et « prêt-à-Contextualiser » which can transform any Product-Service- System in potential "high luxury quality" only after the "observation process".

Figure 3: « Karl Paradox - Chouppette Method ». Democratization of the new forms of luxury: "ready for customization", "ready for personalization" and leading to the reindustrialization of France and Europe

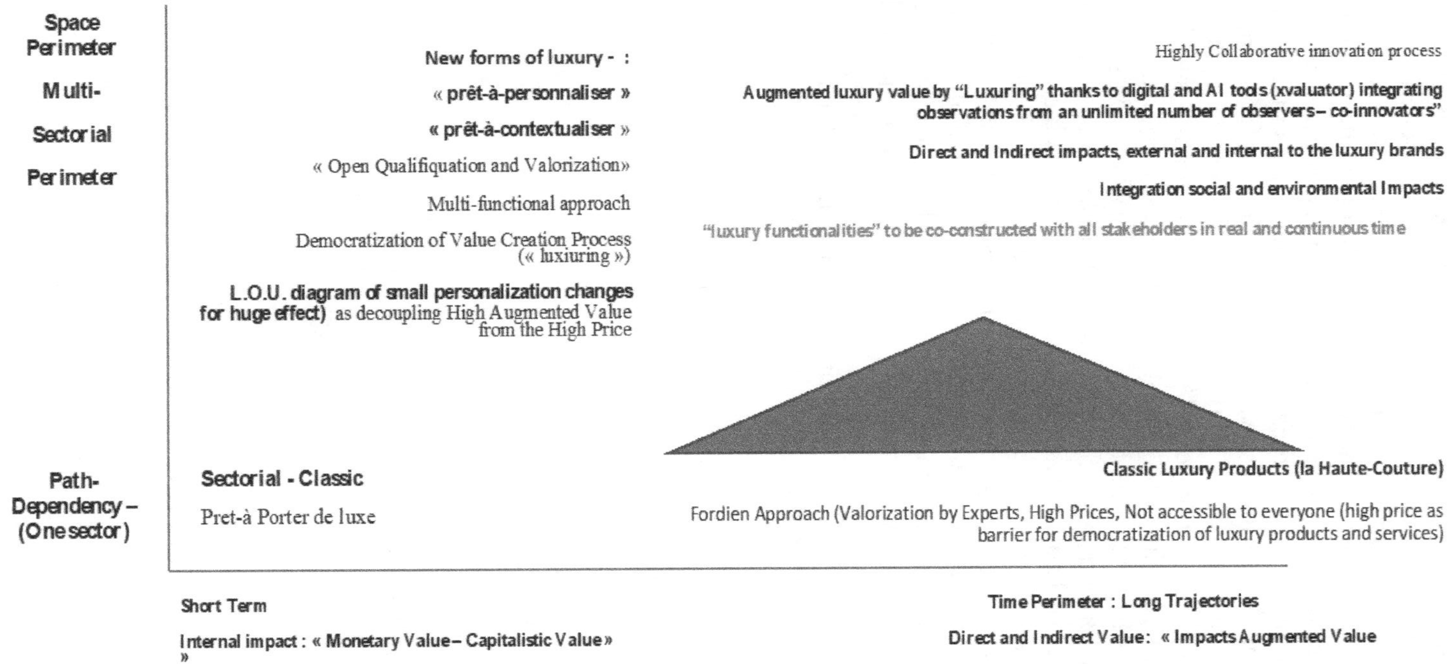

Source: Paun, Vaileanu, 2019.

The positioning on the market of the new forms of luxury offers (through personalization, contextualization, etc) depends also on the performance of digital tools allowing real time and continuous connections and interactions with the stakeholders and the integration of their Demands, immediate evaluation, aggregation of compliance with other demands, qualifying the multitude observations in order to allow to these actions ("luxuring") creating different luxury functionalities to be perceived as performant by all the observers. For example, the capacity to quickly personalize the shoes NIKE made in Germany – standardized and quality mass production complying this CSR imperatives but also personalized for each client out of millions thanks to AI solutions. The digital transformation of the fashion and luxury brands proposes new determinants of luxury value: the singularity, the exclusivity, the fast co-innovation solutions together with the client and its own stakeholders' ecosystems. Low price (as low cost of personalisation – colour, design, etc) but high-perceived value and positive impact through digital tools like Xvaluator (L.O.U. Diagram of Likes optimization use in marketing of the new forms of luxury functionalities) become the new unique collaborative solutions with the favourite brands, unique personalised experimentations, co-innovations, with high potential of becoming "luxury augmented value" is perceived as so.

Figure 4. L.O.U Diagram by Xvalautor, universal tool for “open qualification” and “open valorization” of DATA “like”

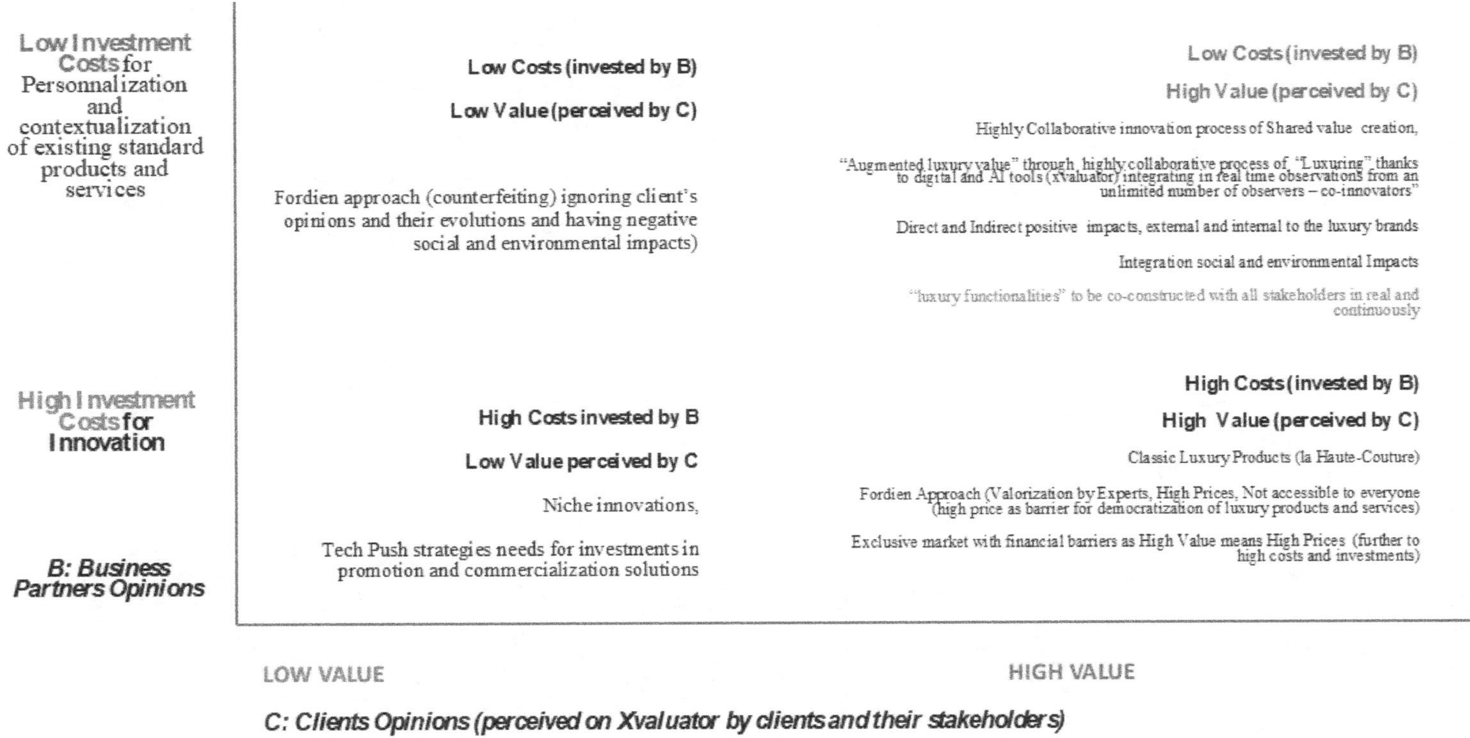

Source : Xvaluator (brevet et certificat d'utilité 2016, Paun, Vaileanu, 2018.

3. THE NEW CENTERS OF CREATION OF "AUGMENTED LUXURY VALUE"

If till recently the luxury creators have voluntarily tried to give access to luxury products or services by proposing cheaper options to some of their creations (for example Karl Lagerfeld, "haute-couture" creator and his collaboration with the fast fashion H&M) to offer opportunities for « mass consumption of several luxury products » which seems to be a paradox in terms) today, another business model is possible and could efficiently offer solutions to democratize the "new forms of luxury". In fact, instead of trying to democratize access to some of luxury products by lowering the prices, luxury brands could imagine selling different luxury functionalities: from "pret-à-porter-luxe" to « prêt-à-personnaliser » or « prêt-à-contextualiser »!

The impossible situation of trying to respond to the demand of mass consumption of luxury, push us to deny the determinants of luxury (the rarity, the exclusivity, the high prices). But the experimentations of new industrial production of quality and though low-price products like Nike re-located in Germany thanks to AI and robotization of the production opens new solutions to « personalisation » in real time and at any time of exclusive high-quality products at low prices.

The new forms of luxury of the fashion and luxury domains of the 21st century is thus capable to register economy of scale by mass standardized production associated to low-cost re-localized production thanks to high quality digital and plants robotization solutions while keeping the luxury determinants of exclusivity as options thanks to the new process like "personalization" and "contextualization", capable to renew the offers without limits without encouraging the programmed obsolescence of products (with negative environmental impacts).

The new luxury offers of the 21st century is an offer of "luxury functionality" integrating adapted services anticipated on larger sectorial impacts and taking in consideration the triple temporality of the impacts, which responds also to the capacity to retain customers' loyalty and renew the offers thanks to contextualization and recycling integrated process. It will be difficult to change the choice of the brand because of the importance of integrated services more than the brand itself. This « augmented hallow of integrated services and direct and indirect connections with the brands is the result of a different approach and evaluation of the "luxury functionalities' value" as future luxury offers creating both local and multisectorial values.

As a first conclusion to this research work, if the fashion and luxury domains are doing their revolution it is not against digital and AI transformations, but is to embark them in the highly collaborative process like the "open valorization" in order to find solutions to the paradox of democratization of some of the luxury forms: the "mass consumption for exclusive luxury functionalities.

Thus, the fashion is making its revolution by evolving the new forms of luxury to change from
« prêt-à-porter » (which produces much unsold products and is perceived as aggressive « fast fashion » and unreasonably consumerist (in the sense of « situationists » and « lettristes » movements already in the sixties) towards the commercialisation of the « prêt-à-personnaliser » (ready to personalize) or « prêt-à-contextualiser » (ready to contextualize) solutions which demand direct relation with the consumer, long term collaborations to transform and reuse the same product but redesigned exclusively for each of the millions of mass customers.

This new dynamic of the sectors is offering all brands the opportunity to use these new centers of value creation thanks to 3D printers and digital tools to reconnect producer and customer together with their unique ecosystems of stakeholders loyal to their « luxury culture » and « experimentations thanks to communication through social networks and related digital platforms.

Thanks to the digital transformations, the capacity to perceive and integrate *ex ante* the estimations of the "augmented value" through its estimated impacts confirmed by the ecosystems of stakeholders (direct or indirect impacts of the "luxury functionality") allows the comparison with "counterfeits" and "low quality products" which through their estimated costs generated for the ecosystems become "more expensive than quality products because of integration of future induced costs of recycling, public health, social issues, etc.

A second conclusion_of this research work is that "high quality luxury functionality" could cost LESS thank basic "low-quality products" as the "augmented value" is integrating future induced social and environmental costs.

Brands like L'Oréal (source: T-Day, Bercy, the 13th of February 2019) is integrating the advantages of this « digital innovation era: « era of innovation and of the engineers ») as their more thank 7 million products commercialised all over the world are potentially personalized to respond to individual desires for each of the clients thanks to digital connectivity tools. The stars of luxury in fashion in France like Karl Lagerfeld (to whom we offer tributes and respects by this research work on his Desir to democratise the luxury) allow evolutions in the fashion and luxury domains in France witnessing profound transformations.

4. STRATEGIES TO DEMOCRATIZE THE ACCESS TO LUXURY. DEDICATION TO KARL LAGERFELD WHO VOLUNTARY EXPERIENCED NEW WAYS TO OPEN ACCESS TO LUXURY FASHION OFFERS

The approach of the "luxury value" by Karl Lagerfeld seems to be in perfect adequation with the new approach of functional economy concerning the extended centers of value creation including other functionalities and sectors or other contextualisation than just the sale of the products: his haute-couture fashion shows are contextualized with real life and important social and environmental issues (Lagerfeld is dressing the luxury offer with a situation, he presents the history of strikes in Paris, or renewable energy imperative to create " a situation" "inspire an emotion" and offer the "experience of luxury value". Karl Lagerfeld joined Chloé in 1964 in the accessories departments, one of the fashionable brands in the sixties and first to evaluate on the new market: « le prêt-à-porter de luxe ».

Gaby Aghion, the founder of the Haute Couture brand commented about Karl Lagerfeld approach as « being on all the fronts », plentiful in ideas » and in journal Liberation in 2014 Karl himself proposes to enlarge the limits of the fashion sector "to everything else" integrating services and new and unexpected contexts: "*this corresponds to my profound nature [...] I love being everywhere, I love doing everything, participate to everything, knowing everything. The ubiquity of the fashion and its different categories is my destiny freely chosen and consented*".

More the presence of the "Selfie Generation", with a society raising the individualism and personal entertainment, and more Karl Lagerfeld is becoming a singularity, a tutelar personality in the luxury domains more and more internationalized and thus transforming him in one of the key emblems of the mondialized capitalism.

In 2004 H&M a giant of the « fast fashion » is developing collaborations with the best fashion names and the first was Karl Lagerfeld with a collection of low prices created by him which is a brand and a logotype perfectly fitting the expectations of the "Selfie Generation" where "everything must become somebody ready to transform in something". Karl Lagerfeld was the luxury and all its excessiveness together with a certain idea of ant conformism who putted the basis of new strategies of value creations and sharing the luxury experience.

5. TOWARDS NEW FORMS OF LUXURY AND THEIR DEMOCRATISATION

Consequently, to the research work, the question is how to use the new forms of luxury which are integrating the « augmented value" co-constructed with the stakeholders (extended in time and within different other impacted sectors and revealing the « extended eventual estimated costs or savings » (recycling, social costs) which are not initially determined but could be determinable and in evolution according to the perceived values. Especially the issue of identifying these interactions and co-evaluations, « open valorization and qualification process » (method Xvaluator) is possible thanks to the digital transformations and AI innovative solutions for a constant and in real time participative valorization by all the stakeholders.

These new forms of luxury do not rely anymore only on the classical evaluation by the sectorial experts (using experts evaluation criteria « top-down » and managed by the leaders of the fashion and luxury domain) as for example the specific fashion codes in "haute-couture" different form criteria of "fast fashion".

These new forms of luxury (which construct the luxury value based on new determinants like « personalisation in real time », continuous « contextualisation ») could emerge at all time and in all regions or connected sectors thanks to the unprecedented connectivity with customers and the capacity to quickly integrate their opinions and needs for personalized solutions.

Thus, these new forms of luxury are conceivable and perceivable thanks to digital tools (like Xvaluator) but also thanks to new « quantic approaches » (anticipating maybe the future quantic computer's impacts on luxury offers).

Different cognitive related concepts like « tiers inclus" » (Lupasco, Nicolesco, 1987, Nicolesco, Plouviet, 2018), cross-fertilisation in the highly collaborative process of open innovations « mangrove forest » (Paun, 2016) replacing simple "value chain", or the « recursive causality » (Morin, 2011) as well as the AI strategies of « open valorisation" and "open qualification" of Data "like" in real time (Xvaluator, 2016) supports the increase in capacities of observations and collaborative valorization process. Thus, new luxury values could emerge unexpectedly further to the observations, qualification and connectivity of different brands with their stakeholders. There is this probability of creation of new centers of luxury value (initially "not-luxury" previous to observations), so initially undetermined yet but potentially determinable as "luxury augmented value".

The old philosophical problem of the objective existence of phenomena independently of our observations is now revisited in the specific context of the luxury, high quality products, services and luxury experiences. Based on the quantic approach (including Bohr's Copenhagen interpretation) we could envisage the question if the observation is producing the observed attributes, in our case if the open valorization ("like") by multiple "observers" is in fact producing the "high quality" attributes of new forms of luxury which are not predestined initially beginning (before the observation – valorisation) to become luxury.

More different actors become « observers » of subjects « potentially having luxury value » more the process of observation-evaluation (for example, giving « likes » on different digital platforms) could have a bigger probability to allow the emergence of "luxury values" of the products and integrated services under observation process ("open valorisation") made possible by the digital innovative tools (Xvaluator, 2016).

This research approach of the « subject luxury value » reminds the analogy with the experiment « the cat or the paradox of Schrödinger » (Schrödinger, 1992) which gives new ways to foresee the existence of luxury value or of a potential luxury functionality or centre of augmented value creation depending on the observation conditions (emerging luxury value corresponds to the observation of the cat as alive and the lack of luxury value during the observation corresponds to the observation of the cat as dead).

As well as for the Nobel Prize Physician Erwin Schrödinger, the question is about the issue of measurement (observation of the cat or evaluation, valorization in the case of "luxury value probability). During a measurement activity the « quantic subject » (in our case is « the subject potentially having luxury value ») will be found in one of the determined status: for the Cat of Schrodinger the determined state is either alive or dead and in our analogical case the subject has either "luxury value" or "no luxury value".

What is important to be acknowledged is that « the measure itself » (in our case the observation and evaluation by millions of potential customers of the subject and their stakeholders – with for example the simple evaluation « like ») which disturbs the system and push it out of its superposed quantic state (where both luxury and "non-luxury" values could emerge) towards a determined, measured state: either “luxury value” or “not-luxury value”.

The conclusion is that this status of « luxury value » do not pre-exists before the « measure ». The observation, the “open valorization” highly collaborative process » seems to determine the « luxury value » emergence.

The paradox of Schrödinger describes a cat in a box with the mortal gas bottle and radioactive source. If a Grieger measures a certain radiation the bottle breaks and the cat dies. After the Copenhagen interpretation the cat is in the same time alive and dead. But if we open the box, we can observe the cat and determine either that it’s alive or dead. The statement “the cat is dead and alive » (and adapted to our case « the subject is luxury value and in the same time « not luxury value ») is actually confusing as each of the phrase is the denial of the other. In fact, there is a third possibility: the cat could be in a state of superposition cumulating more states usually incompatible, in our case « the subject is in the same time « luxury value » and « no luxury value ». In fact, a quantic subject (in our case the « observed luxury subject ») could have properties contradicting our experiences and perceptions.

This new quantic approach (which we entitled « Karl paradox– Chouppette method after the name of the cat of Karl Lagerfeld) of any « subject » potentially being « luxury value » is even more reinforced by the use of concept « tiers inclus » meaning « luxury » and in the same time « non luxury » especially thanks to luxury creators - personalities integrating the both dimensions in their works: « testing everything », « being everywhere » (haute-couture but also « fast fashion », pret-a porter-luxe, etc).

“ The cat or paradox of Schrödinger » (Schrödinger, 1992) becomes with this research work for luxury new economic model and solutions for democratizing luxury (and thanks to digital transformations and the quantic approach of the « subject which is potentially luxury value), the « Chouppette method or Karl paradox » (Vaileanu, Paun, 2019): the luxury value (or non – luxury value) is thus revealed only once the observation of the subjects accomplished by all the stakeholders of the fashion and luxury domain.

In this respect, the digital transformation of luxury domains and its innovative tools are also transforming the evaluation (observation) methods and increase the numbers of observers as well as the timing (real time and continuously) which demands further research on impacts of results from “open vaporization” processes of a “luxury value” perceived as outstandingly collaborative, territorial, evolving in real time (Vaileanu, 2011, Vaileanu, Von Niel, 2013, Vaileanu et Paun, 2019).

This new observation-evaluation approach of « open valorization » succeeds not only to integrate continuously more and more diversities at all levels (subjects, criteria, sources of criteria etc) but is source of new qualified data which could be a collective augmented value (Xvaluator, universal open qualification tool).

As example, the Xvaluator method (patented in 2019 "XVA1 FR") of open valorization and open qualification of data « likes » integrates an infinite source of "likes", criteria of "likes" (bottom-up), sources of "likes" weight factors, contextualisation of data « likes » (comparisons) opening the new possible centers of value creation for new actors integrating the determinants of the new forms of luxury: the degree of personalization and of dynamic.

In fact, the democratisation of luxury (a fodien paradox and a desiderata for some luxury brands) seems now possible but just for the new complementary forms of luxury having different fundamentals from the classical once, selling the "property" not "the usage functions": high price, the reputation of the brand, the costs of quality materials, the rarity, etc.

Some of the new fundamentals of the new complementary forms of luxury are:

- The capabilities to co-produce, co-innovate with the potential customers and their stakeholders in continuous evolutions
- Integration of the highly collaborative process of co-construction of "luxury functionalities" based on "recursive causality" (Morin, E.) integrating the fact that the results are both causes and the effects
- Multisectoral, multifunctional approaches, interconnectivity between sectors and their offers, "mangrove forest "approaches allowing the values chains to interconnected each other's integrating *ex ante* the social, environmental, economic impacts and more and more stakeholders' collaborations.
- Integrate "in the same time" (« en meme temps ») processes like « tiers inclus » inspiring the strategy of non – contradiction (applied to "open valorisation" process of the "new forms of luxury") and capacities to integrate, aggregate more and more diversity and even « opposing attributes ». For example, « luxury value » and « low price » could be justified by the « extended augmented value » (decoupling "value" from the "high pricing" in order to allow general access to high quality, and thus democratize access to luxury values).

- Integrate quantic logic in the processes of open collaborative valorization by all the stakeholders in real time and continuously. In fact, the new forms of production and consumption of luxury functionalities (experimentations) do not wait to be claimed as luxury but propose the « potentiality of luxury » related to certain situations or contexts creating links between different actors having an important role as « observers » about the state of the « observed subject » as being luxury value or not. We could say that Karl Lagerfeld was in a quantic approach and compatible with "tiers inclus" concept: "in the same time" in the "haute couture" and in the "pret-à porter-luxe" for fast fashion. The homage to Karl Lagerfeld (the article has been written in the day of his death) is to name the paradox of democratization of luxury after him and his cat Chouppette) as emblematic solution thanks also to the digital transformation and open valorisations and open qualification tools (Xvaluator). The observation and open valorization of clients and stakeholders could create through their common observation (like) the attribute of "luxury "for the new forms of luxury (experiences) that become valued only after these observations that embody both potentialities ("luxe" and "non luxe" attributes).

The reasoning of « tiers incus » means to recognize in the world of irrefutable interconnections (as in the quantic approach) a cut from the reel world affecting the real world itself. The real entity can thus show contradictories aspects appearing as absurd from the point of view of postulate "either this or that". Theses even aspects stop to be absurd in a reasoning based on "this and that". At the beginning of its book entitled "The principle of antagonism and the logic of the energy" Stephan Lupasco presents the postulate which links a phenomenon to its "anti-phenomena reasoning" through negation recognizing thus the terms of contradictories at Aristotle, the dynamic of the contradictory reasoning: **the negation of a term gives the antagonist term so that if one becomes active, the other becomes possible (potential).** The expression « in the same time" is the sign of the complexity thinking transcending the division of a binarity meaning also that each true thinking implies an interior dialog associating arguments necessarily controversial.

The expression "in the same time" is not a juxtaposition of contradictions and neither a synthesis, resulting in a contradiction creating the necessary dynamic as Bassarab Nicolescu explains (Nicolesco, preface," Principe d'antagonisme et logique de l'énergie, de S. Lupasco). The capacity to identify "luxury functionalities" and in the same time "their contradiction" (non-luxury value) depends especially on the observers and on the quality of "open valorisation" collaborative process and related digital tools.

6. THE AUGMENTED OR EXTENDED VALUE (INCLUDING SOCIAL AND ENVIRONMENTAL VALUES) OF PERFORMANTS SUBJECTS. EXAMPLE OF FUTURE PACTE LAW IN FRANCE.

The importance of compatibility between economic, social and environmental performances by the firms have not always been an imperative in the fordien economic model in the last 60 years. Taking in consideration the different forms of impacts of the productive system affecting the environment, the social and societal values were gradual and marked by different transformation dynamics while successively challenged by different crisis (resources, energetic, ecologic, financial or trust crisis).

Since the fifties, the economic model of the firms registers an important evolution for coping with different impacts of crisis exhaustion of resources, geopolitical conflicts, intensification of international competition, generalisation of digital solution and undergoing digital transformation of firms (Du Tertre, 2009).

In the case of luxury domain, as well as in all sectors engaging in the new functional economy model, the maintenance, repairing, recycling services are integrated *ex anté* in the strategies of co-conception, co-production and co-evaluation of the « functionally augmented value ». In the reasoning of functional economy, the focus has shifted towards more dematerialized processes and value creation allowing the shift from selling the property of separate products and standardized services towards the selling of "unities of usage of the "PSS - Product Service Systems which have the capacity to decouple the economic growth from the flux (selling) of materials (Van Niel, 2006; Steinberger, J.K., van Niel, Bourg, 2009).

The counterfeiting is a fordien alternative (highly dependent on mass consumption and devouring resources – based on disposable cheap and copied products) negatively affecting the luxury margins. However, the developing of strategies to re-use, repair, the luxury products as well as the newly personalised and contextualized forms of democratisation of luxury could support both the margins of the luxury sector and the sustainable development solutions to democratize luxury.

6.1. Examples of the pertinence of the functional economy in certain sectors in France

In France, the functional economy is experimented in some sectors proving that the advantages of this economic model renewal seam to by both performant and stable.

The working group 6 in the Debate Grenelle de environment (Grenelle 1) retained as definition for the functional economy: the modern model designating the commercial transactions related in the same time on the usage of a product or equipment and not anymore on the selling of the property of the product and experiencing positive effects in terms of sustainable development by reducing the consumption of materials / energy resources.

The Functional economy has already successful experimentations in certain fields by multinationals and SMEs and succeeds to be an alternative to the fordien economic model (based on the programmed obsolescence of products and equipment).

The « fleet solution » created by Michelin proposes to the clients in the transportation (since 1920) an integrated pneumatic service including adapted other services like maintenance, substitution if necessary. The client is paying the usage of the products – equipment's measured in terms of km. performed or in tone / km performed; Michelin has thus transformed its strategies and activities related to the centre of value creation: the functionality of km. performed! This allows the clients to use less energy and use the tyres 2,5 times longer than with classical tyres considering the integrated functionality of maintenance allowing longer product life cycles and especially by benefiting of permanent innovations while **paying less.** The Concorde Foundation (2011) is already proposing in its report on emerging functional economy model in France a presentation the determinants of an economic sector ready to shift to the functional economy:

1. Know-how in selling associated services to the sold product or equipment
2. Products / services easy to be qualified and measured
3. Important exploitation costs
4. Critical market size
5. The products and services sold are not in the core business of clients
6. The feasibility of the functional economy depends on the capacity to transform the investment costs in functional costs.

The transition towards the functional economy depends on structural changes (du Tertre, 2010) which take in consideration the interdependencies (micro-meso-macro strategies) between: the strategies of the firms, local territorial strategies and economic and development models of the society. The functional economy is used in different fields but only a law like the Law PACTE generalizing the importance of social and environmental compliance of the firms could generalize the use of the functional economy in France and in Europe.

6.2. Example of the Law PACTE in France and the importance of the extended evaluation of the firms

In France the Law PACTE (Action Plan for Growth and Transformation of the Firms) proposed an evolution of the firms' status aiming to connect social and environmental mission to rentability. This status entitled 'firm with mission » met the French directors consensus quoting a recent opinion poll (Prophil/HEC/Viavoice (*Étude Prophil sur les entreprises à mission et sondage téléphonique en février 2018.*)

"*We want to engrave the principle that the firm's mission is not only to serve the shareholders and their short-term results expectations but also to support social and environmental values as part of its average and long-term running activities* » considered Nicole Notat and Jean- Dominique Senard co- authors of the Governmental Report Notat-Senard. On the subject of the « general interest firms » after having auditioned more than 200 persons in France.

« The 6300 companies' members of FACE, including the 1000 participants in 2018 at the international conference organized by The Foundation for the Transformations about the « mission firm » en 2018 per La Foundation pour les Transformations (or recent conferences by l'AG du future initiated by Geneviève Ferone) proved that the firm has an important role, that we need its innovation capacities and that its employees have often a social and societal engagement (Berhault, G., 2018).

Different initiatives of think and act tanks, professional networks like Mooveje, IME, SOS-Groupe, IE-Club and Conferences on functional economy at Cerisy (du Tertre, 2006) or the Forums and conferences focusing on the energy sector and innovations organized by Revue Passages leaded by Emile Malet getting together all the key stakeholders of the energy sector and its clients in different other important sectors (like the mobility) or the Le annual Forum Convergences, the conferences of Fondation des Transitions, (Berhault, G., 2018), the Debates of the Cercle of the economists prepare the structural transformations of firms for integrating more missions especially the social mission.

This common research work by practitioners of fashion and luxury domains and economists of the functional economy focus on the understanding of the conditions of luxury value creation (augmented value » through the co-evaluation together with the stakeholders the firms ready to integrate the material and immaterial externalities (Vaileanu-Paun, 2009, 2010, 2011, (Tertre, 2008) in order to make possible the emergence of new forms of luxury integrating social and environmental impacts aiming of more resilient firms in France and in Europe (Vaileanu, 2009).

In France the Law PACTE is an opportunity to enlarge the experimentations of « firms of mission » and scale-up the good practices of extended evaluations to more interconnected sectors, regions and temporalities by integrating more stakeholders in the process of « open valorization » in real time and continuously as complementary actions to the Classique experts' evaluations.

6.3. Opportunities for evolutions of the luxury model in France. Example of the « fashion and luxury"

On the 8th of January 2019, Bruno Le Maire, the Minister of Economy and Finance in France together with Franck Riester, Minister of Culture, and Guillaume de Seynes, the President of the Strategic Committee for the fashion and luxury domains signed the Strategic Contract for the development of the Fashion and Luxury Domains.

« *The French fashion and luxury sectors are a permanent reason of pride. There are firms that know how to renew continuously, and to gain new market shares, which are conquering and which spread out the French know-how all over the world. The projects in the strategic contract signed today are in perfect coherence with the challenges of the fashion and luxury domains and will thus lead to even more French Excellency all over the world."* declared Bruno le Maire who initiated also the Law PACTE.

Organized in 6 structuring actions, the Strategic contract should allow the Fashion and luxury sectors in France to maintain its preeminence and also give resources for growth:

1. Developing the domains attractivity: Creation of innovative course and a communication campaign about the technical jobs of the fashion and luxury domain with the objective to increase the learning process with 20% during the next two years
2. Assuring an ecosystem priority on the higher-level education and research in the fashion: starting in 2020 the French Fashion Institute will welcome 800 students. The fundamental and applied research will be related to the future 4.0 fashion and luxury industries.
3. Improving the competitiveness of the ecosystem of providers and guide them on their transformational strategies towards the industry of the future: a 360° diagnostic of the identified growing firms will be done by BPIFRANCE which will guide them in the sectorial
4. Accompanying and financing emerging fashion companies: guiding solutions by BPIFRANCE of the brands that register strong development within the sectorial accelerator. The resources of the Institute l'IFCIC will be reinforced
5. Elaborating a traceability device for the fashion and luxury domain with the development of an efficient and secured technological solution

for the whole production value chain programmed to be tested on volunteers' firms in 2021.

6. Inspiring a virtuous dynamic of circular economy with the launching of two technological demonstrators of recycling processes in the textile sector

« *Our fashion and luxury domain are the first exporter of France. I also preside over Colbert Committee gathering 82 luxury groups. Their collective value adds up to 42 milliards euros, with 86% exports. France is ready to act in order to reinforce the exports we want this challenge but if all sectors would have 86% of exports this problem would not exist anymore*" declared Guillaume de Seynes in November 2018.

These recent objectives and actions by the actors of the fashion and luxury domain in France are reinforcing exactly the ecosystems of stakeholders anticipating the development of resources talents and know how assuring long-term evolution of the sectorial growth and of the shared value production.

CONCLUSIONS AND FUTURE RESEARCH PERSPECTIVES

In the light of functional economy approach and quantic approach, this article is relevant for the evolution of the fashion and luxury domains towards new growth and « augmented value creation together with the stakeholders.

The luxury functionality value of the 21st century is an augmented value obtained not by just the selling of the property of rare and expensive products and services but also by new luxury forms of experimentation, the personalized and contextualized products allowing the democratisation of luxury experience by decoupling the quality and high value of the classical pricing. By integrating larger perimeters of evaluation 'in time and in different sectors with different exported impacts, the new forms of luxury have both high perceived quality and lower prices as lower recycling and social impacts estimated costs together with the stakeholders.

More important, the new profit centers and luxury value creation change the viability of the fordien economic model and under the functional economy approach and impacts of digital and AI tools, the re-localisation of the luxury domain productions in France and Europe becomes efficient and effective. All actors including new SMEs could benefit of the solutions of democratisation of luxury access: through capacities to personalise in real time and produce contextualized "luxury product and services systems" and gain customer loyalty through "luxury culture" experimentations on social networks and dedicated platforms.

Instead of fordien segmentation of markets, the fashion and luxury new forms take in consideration the « heterogeneity » of the "clients as systems" and their needs for exclusivity and personalized solutions, the ultimate exclusivity criteria associated with lower prices for higher quality solutions including the use of luxury products and adapted integrated luxury personalized services.

The offer of personalization 4.0 is still not on the market but the ingredients to assist to an impressive transformation of the luxury sectors by integrating the "paradox of Karl" (chouppette method) of democratization of access to luxury functionalities and in the same time protecting the classical model of "haute-couture" codes.

New practices to co-innovate in the luxury functionalities are under experimentations together with the potential clients of brands both high quality and low acceptable prices are in train to transform simple "like" opinions on social networks in « like to buy » behaviours thanks also to innovative digital tools (Xvaluator, universal qualifier of "likes" through the open qualification and open valorisations methods (Vaileanu, Paun, 2016)

Thanks to this new scientific approaches (functional economy but also the quantic approach) of the necessary augmented value (including even opposing or contradicting values perceived by different stakeholders) it becomes possible the integration *ex ante* of the expected impacts perceives on larger perimeters of sectorial and time perspectives. This might explain the resilience of the luxury domains during crises (the triple temporality of evaluation of the luxury perceived values). More than this, the possibility to offer access to everybody at the luxury functionality responds to the « paradox of Karl » of trying to democratize the luxury but also could penalize the lack of compliance with social and environmental values (for the low-quality products the costs of negative externalities should increase the price of the counterfeits and all low-quality products (including huge costs for depollution or recycling issues).

From now on, the equation of « augmented luxury value » is the following: greater the quality and perceived value by larger ecosystems of stakeholders and on longer periods of time, less costy the externalities and lower the price for democratization of access to quality luxury solutions. Lower the quality and value (with polluted materials and process and negative social impacts) higher the accessibility price (as the costs for recycling, depolluting and social justice will be incorporated ex ante in the co-evaluated value".

The complementary « Chouppette method – the Karl paradox) aiming the democratization of the luxury functionalities and new forms of luxury in complementarity with the classic codes and experts evaluations for the classic luxury products and services allows the emerging of new economic growth models for high quality co-production and re-localisation of luxury industries in Europe. This means that the fashion and luxury domains and their resilience could inspire the whole new economic growth model of the 21st century that could be centred on HIGH QUALITY and LOW (accessible) PRICES, (democratization and mass consumption of high value functionalities). This could become a new "quality growth paradigm" (Paun, Vaileanu, 2018) compliant ex anté with the sustainable growth (the quality for everybody) thanks also to the "open valorisation" and "open qualification" highly collaboratives process accessible through the digital solutions (Xvaluator, Vaileanu, Paun, 2016).

The luxury quality has no Price and the lack of quality costs us all for long periods of time !

REFERENCES

ATWAL, G. & WILLIAMS, A., 2009, Luxury Brand Marketing – The Experience is Everything! Journal of Brand Management, 16, 5/6, pp. 338-346.

BAILLY J.-P., HEURGON E., 2001, Nouveaux rhythms urbains : quels transports ? Éditions de l'Aube.

BATAT, W., 2017, Luxe et Expérience client, Dunod, Paris.

BERHAULT, G., 2018, Métamorphose numérique. Ed. Alternative Gallimard, livre collectif avec Gilles Berhault, Carine Dartiguepeyrou, Thierry Gaudin, Francis Jutand, Bernard Stiegler, Henri Verdier.

BERRY, J.W., 1994, Acculturation and Psychological Adaptation. In A.- BOUVRY, M., VAN DE VIJVER, F.J.R. and SCHMITZ, P. (Eds.), Journeys into Cross-cultural Psychology (pp. 89-125). Lisse, Netherlands: Swets and Zeitlinger.

BIC (Business Innovation Center, Indonesia), 2018, "*110 Indonesia's innovations - 2018*": goo.gl/A562NE, Indonesia's eleventh annual publications since 2008 (pages on Dr. Paun's thesis on the Hybridization of Tech Push and Market Pull: DRL-TRL) pp. 44-45.

BOURG, D., BUCLET, N., 2005, L'économie de la fonctionnalité : changer la consommation dans le sens du développement durable, Futuribles, Nr. 313, novembre, 27-37.

BOUTILLIER, S., UZUNIDIS, D., 1999, La légende de l'entrepreneur. Le capital social, ou comment vient l'esprit d'entreprise, Éditions La Découverte et Syros, Paris, p. 18, 1999.

CHAUDHURI, A., 1998, Product Class Effects on Perceived Risk: The Role of Emotion. International Journal of Research in Marketing, 15(2), pp.157–168.
« Charte de bonnes pratiques de la filière mode et luxe » (2010). signé par le Président de la Fédération Francaise de Couture, du prêt à porter des couturiers et des créateurs de mode, M. Didier Grumbach, par le Président de l'Union Francaises des Industries de l'Habillement et par le Ministre chargé de l'Industrie, M. Christian Estrosi
DE BORLODOT, A., HERBAYS, M., 2016, Mémoire- recherche : Le Prix du temps est-il un frein à l'économie de la fonctionnalité ?, 2016, Université Catholique de Louvain.
CHESBROUGH, H., VAN HAVERBEKE, W., WEST, J., 2008, Open Innovation: Researching a New Paradigm, OUP Oxford, p. 400, 2008.
DU TERTRE, C. (2006). Economie de la fonctionnalité, développement durable et innovation institutionnelle, ARTEMIS-GERME.
DU TERTRE, C., 2006, Économie de la fonctionnalité, performance et Développement Durable, colloque de Cerisy des 15–19 juin 2006.
DU TERTRE, C., 2007, Investissements immatériels et patrimoine collectif immatériel, in C. Laurent et C. du Tertre (éditeurs), Secteurs et territoires dans les régulations émergentes, Editions L'Harmattan, Paris.
DU TERTRE, C., 2008, Ouvrir le champ de l'évaluation de la performance au registre des externalités » - une condition des coopérations entreprises / collectivités territoriales.
HEURGON, E. (coord.), 2000, Le développement durable, c'est enfin du bonheur ! Éditions de l'Aube, pp. 104-120.
FONDATION CONCORDE, 2011, Nouvelles visions pour une société de la connaissance : L'économie de la fonctionnalité, vers un nouveau modèle économique durable, Paris
FREEMAN, E., 2013, R. Edward Freeman, Alexander Moutchnik (2013): Stakeholder management and CSR: questions and answers. In: UmweltWirtschaftsForum, Springer Verlag, Vol. 21, Nr. 1. https://link.springer.com/article/10.1007/s00550-013-0266-3.
GUGGENHEIM MUSEUM, The unfinished works of Marcel Duchamps. (2019). The Proces of art's creation is part of the artists' masterpiece.
HOLBROOK, M., ELIZABETH, B., HIRSCHMAN, C., 1982, The experiential Aspects of Consumption: consumer fantasies, feelings and fun, Journal of Consumer Research, September, 9(2) 132-140.
LAPERCHE, B., UZUNIDIS, D., 2012, Eco-Innovation, Knowledge Capital and the Evolution of the Firm, The IUP Journal of Knowledge Management, Vol. X, No. 3, July 2012, pp. 14-34
LEMOINE, P., 2014, RAPPORT LEMOINE : La nouvelle grammaire du succès La transformation numérique de l'économie française, Rapport gouvernamental, NOVEMBRE 2014 (https://www.economie.gouv.fr/files/files/PDF/rapport_TNEF.pdf)

LEMOINE, P., 2018, Une révolution sans les Français ? Action citoyenne et transformations à l'age numérique, éditions l'Aube.
LIPOVETSKY, G., ROUX, E., 2003, Le Luxe Eternel - De L'âge du Sacré au Temps des Marques, Paris : Le Débat, Gallimard.
LUPASCO, S., NICOLESCO, B., 1987, Le principe d'antagonisme et la logique de l'énergie, Ed. l'esprit et la matière, Le Rocher, P71 (repris par http://tiersinclus.fr/hommage-a-stephane-lupasco-dehors/)
MOATI, P., CORCOS, A., 2009, Des marchés transactionnels aux marchés relationnels une approche théorique pour repenser l'impact des politiques de rétention de la clientèle.
MONT, O., 2002, Clarifying the Concept of Product-Service System, Journal of Cleaner Production.
MORIN, E., 2011, La Voie, Pour l'avenir de l'humanité. Paris, Fayard.
NICOLESCO, B., 2010, Qu'est-ce que la réalité ", Réflexions autour de la pensée de Stéphane Lupasco, Ed Liber
NOTAT, N., SENARD., J-D., 2018, L'entreprise, l'objet d'interet collectif, Rapport aux Ministres de la Transition écologiques et solidaire de la Justice, de l'Economie et des Finances, du Travail.
PAUN, F., 2011, From managing information asymmetries towards systemic asymmetries approach in technology transfer and innovation strategies: An economic analysis of the SME strategy at ONERA – the French Aerospace Lab, IUP Journal of Knowledge Management, vol. IX, n° 4, October, 2011b.
PAUN, F., 2012, The Demand Readiness Level Scale as New Proposed Tool to Hybridize Market Pull with Technology Push Approaches in Technology Transfer Practices, in Technology Transfer in a Global Economy, Springer series: International Studies in Entrepreneurship, vol 28, 397 p, 2012.
PAUN, F., VON TUNZELMAN, N., RICHARD, P., 2012, Asymmetries and dynamic interactive capabilities in technology transfer between ONERA – the French Aerospace LabTM and SMEs, Journal of Innovation Economics & Management, 1, p. 103-137, 2012.
PAUN, F., 2013, Technological Entrepreneurship and Asymmetries », dans Carayannis E. (Ed.) Encyclopedia of Creativity, Invention, Innovation and Entrepreneurship: 2013, p. 224-229, 2013.
PAUN, F., 2013, Technology Push and Market Pull Entrepreneurship », dans Carayannis E. (Ed.) Encyclopedia of Creativity, Invention, Innovation and Entrepreneurship: Springer, 2013.
PAUN, F., MAYER, H-A., 2013, L'innovation par les outils d'hybridation des approches Technology Push et Market Pull, dans Business & Innovation, L'innovation, Analyser, anticiper, agir, edition Peter Lang, p. 175-195.
PAUN, F., 2014, Conference Parlementaire Sur L'innovation Ouverte. Innovation au cœur de la relance économique française, Pour une

industrie française de l'innovation ouverte. 2014. http://www.rivington.fr/media/conference_pg_30.pdf.
PAUN, F., 2014, J'innove, donc je suis ! Visionnaires du XXIe siècle. Editions L'Harmattan, p. 27-92. http://www.ubifrance.fr/0019782343020051+j-innove-donc-je-suis-.html, 2014.
PAUN, F., 2014, Du TRANSPORT à la MOBILITE. Une innovation sociétale qui démultiplie la création de valeur partagée, Sommet International de l'Innovation, http://www.utc.fr/intervenants-sommet-international-innovation.php, 2014.
PAUN, F., 2014, TOUS ENTRE-PRENEURS. La croissance du XXIe siecle a l'heure entrepreneuriale. ENTREPRENEURIAL AGE. Éditions L'Harmattan, Paris, (en français et en anglais, repris par UBIFRANCE = http://www.ubifrance.fr/0019782343037400+tous-entre-preneurs-.html), 2014.
PAUN, F., LAUDIER, I., 2015, dans INNOVER OU PERIR. Éditions L'Harmattan, Paris, 2015
PAUN, F., 2018, Raccourcir les cycles d'innovation, dans TECHNOLOGIE ET INNOVATION, Nr. Dynamiques d'innovation dans les industries aérospatiale et de défense, Volume 3, 2018.
PLOUVIET, C., 2018, www.Tiersinclus.fr (cercle de tiers-inclus et de la mésologie)
SCHRÖDINGER, E., 1992, Physique quantique et représentation du monde », Le Seuil, coll. « Points-Sciences », 1992, 184 p., poche (ISBN 2-02-013319-9)
STAHEL, W., 2006, The Performance Economy, Palgrave Macmillan
Tom, G., Garibaldi, B., Zeng, Y., Pilcher, J. (1998) Consumer demand for counterfeit goods, Psychology & Marketing, Vol. 15, Issue 5, pp. 405-421.
TRITTO, G., CARROLL D., KAROUBI N., A, TRITTO M, MARSH-DRIKOS, VAILEANU I. (Xvaluaror), 2017, Health technomics and social determinants in global health – strategies for health providers, operators and target populations for human safety and homeland security – The 2017 World congress in computer science computer engineering & applied computing | CSCE'17, July 2017, Las Vegas.
UZUNIDS, D., 2008, Proximity and Innovative Milieu, Forum The Spirit of Innovation III, Tacoma, Seattle, May, 2008.
UZUNIDIS, D., 2009, Crise industrielle et renouveau économique des territoires : reconversion et dépendance de sentier »
VAILEANU-PAUN, I., 2009a, Stratégies des entreprises et des territoires dans l'économie de la fonctionnalité. Le Cas EDF, Thèse de sciences économiques en cours, Université Paris Diderot (présoutenance en 2009).
VAILEANU-PAUN, I., 2009b, Colloque RRI à Grenoble, Travail, capital savoir dans la mondialisation : « La valeur entrepreneuriale comme construit institutionnel encastré dans le territoire dans le contexte de globalisation,

http://www.colloque.wesford.fr/index.adml?l=111&r=1368
VAILEANU-PAUN, I., 2010, Vers une évaluation territoriale des entreprises, Collège énergie climat du Conseil général de l'Environnement : http://extranet.college-energie.cgedd.developpement-durable.gouv.fr/IMG/pdf/These_Ingrid_Valeanu_Paun_cle2523a7.pdf)
VAILEANU-PAUN, I., 2010, Economie de la fonctionnalité et Smart Grids, Atelier Bepos et Smart Grids, DGALN/PUCA
VAILEANU-PAUN, I., 2011, Le luxe : une valeur éminemment territorialisée : Une lecture de l'économie de la fonctionnalité du business modèle du luxe par rapport aux enjeux développement durable. Le cas de la filière mode et luxe en France. LUXE et CONTREFACON : enjeux, dé s et perspectives. (2011). Geneve, Suisse. 2011. (<halshs-00634053>). Charte de bonnes pratiques de la filière mode et luxe signé par le Président de la Fédération Francaise de Couture, du prêt à porter des couturiers et des créateurs de mode, M. Didier Grumbach, par le Président de l'Union Francaises des Industries de l'Habillement et par le Ministre chargé de l'Industrie, M. Christian Estrosi, 2010).
VAILEANU-PAUN, I. et BOUTILLIER, S., 2012, Développement durable. Du Paradigme de l'économie industrielle à l'économie de la fonctionnalité, dans Business &Innovation, « Innovation verte ». De la Théorie aux bonnes pratiques, 2012, éditions Peter Lang, Bruxelles, 31-63.
VAILEANU-PAUN, I. et VAN NIEL, J., 2013, Modèles d'innovation dans l'économie de la fonctionnalité. Business & Innovation, L'innovation, Analyser, anticiper, agir, édition Peter Lang, p. 439 – 459.
VAN NIEL, J., 2007, Economie de la Fonctionnalité. Définitions et Etat de l'Art, 2007 (http://www.economiedefonctionnalite.fr/wp-content/uploads/2010/04/definition_et_etat_de_lart-Johan-Van-Niel.pdf)
XVALUATOR, 2016, Brevet et Certificat d'utilité, (www.xvaluator.co).
ZETING, L. et LAPERCHE, B., 2015, The knowledge capital of SMEs: The French paradox, Journal of Innovation Economics & Management 2/2015 (n°17), p. 27-48 URL: www.cairn.info/revue-journal-of-innovation-economics-2015-2-page-27.htm.DOI:10.3917/jie.017.0027, 2015.

LE ROLE DES REPRESENTATIONS DANS LE VECU EMOTIONNEL DE « L'EXPERIENCE DU LUXE » ET SON EVALUATION : UNE ETUDE EXPLORATOIRE AUPRES D'UNE CIBLE JEUNE GRAND PUBLIC

Candy KOLENC
Université Bordeaux IV
Laboratoire IRGO
candy.kolenc@u-bordeaux1.fr

Mouna BOUNAOUAS
Institut Supérieur d'Informatique & de Gestion à Kairouan
mouna.bounaouas@gmail.com

ABSTRACT

This qualitative study explores the valorization of experiences perceived as luxurious by young consumers (26 biographical stories). Four main categories have been identified. 1) The luxury offer: In the two cases (direct and indirect experience), the respondents described components of mix marketing (product, price, place and promotion). However, the luxury experience is not always produced or controlled. 2) Feelings: experiential living implies individual emotions and feelings described by respondents during the consumption experience. The authors noticed that negative emotions were likely to appear when the contact employees seem unpleasant. 3) Individual representations: Luxury representations make consumers able to evaluate their own experience. However, positive or negative experience can affect individual representations. 4) Consumer values: They appear to be more generated by the experiential context than luxury products possessions. They also seem to be closely linked to individual representations. The findings provide first insights about the understanding of the luxury experience and highlight the role of individual representations in its valorization.

Keywords: luxury, consumer values, experience.

RESUME

Cette étude qualitative exploratoire porte sur la valorisation de l'expérience perçue comme relevant du luxe auprès d'une cible jeune grand public (26 récits biographiques). Après une analyse du champ théorique mobilisé et les conditions de l'échantillonnage, nous montrons quels sont les liens entre les composantes de l'expérience et les émotions générées. L'étude montre que les composantes de l'expérience concernent quatre niveaux de perception. 1) L'offre de luxe : les répondants sont en mesure de décrire les variables du mix, sans toutefois que l'expérience du luxe apparaisse comme toujours contrôlée. 2) Le vécu expérientiel : l'expérience perçue comme « luxueuse » génère un vécu mémorable et des émotions intenses. De l'étude se dégage nettement que les émotions négatives sont susceptibles d'apparaître lorsque le personnel de contact semble désagréable. 3) Les représentations individuelles : les répondants sont susceptibles de modifier leurs représentations en fonction de leurs vécus. 4) Les valeurs consommateurs : elles apparaissent davantage liées aux contextes expérientiels et aux représentations individuelles qu'à la possession d'objets de luxe. Les résultats obtenus présentent des premiers éléments de compréhension de l'expérience du luxe et mettent en évidence le rôle des représentations individuelles dans sa valorisation auprès d'une cible jeune grand public.

Mots-clés : Luxe, expérience de consommation, valeurs des consommateurs
JEL codes: M30, M31.

INTRODUCTION

Cette étude exploratoire vise à comprendre ce que peut être une expérience perçue comme relevant du luxe auprès des jeunes (17 à 24 ans) ayant consommé au moins une fois un bien ou un service de luxe. La démocratisation du secteur (Truong et al., 2009), notamment au travers des stratégies d'extension des marques (Roux, 1995), réoriente l'industrie du luxe vers une cible plus large et permet l'accès, notamment aux jeunes, de plus en plus tôt au monde du luxe.

Ainsi, ce travail porte sur les premières expériences qualifiées comme luxueuses par des jeunes issus de classes moyennes à un moment de vie où se forgent les représentations : Quelles sont donc les expériences qualifiées comme luxueuses et quelles en sont les composantes ?

1. « L'EXPERIENCE DU LUXE » AU CROISEMENT DE DEUX CHAMPS DE LITTERATURE EN MARKETING

L'approche expérientielle (Hirschmann et Holbrook, 1982) n'est pas complètement étrangère au luxe. La littérature propose des exemples de marques de luxe ayant eu recours à l'approche expérientielle au travers de la mise en scène, la reconstitution des univers de leurs créateurs ou la mobilisation de l'histoire de la marque de luxe (Hetzel, 2002 ; Adham in Allérès, 2006). Par ailleurs la récente littérature sur le luxe suggère que le marché du luxe est passé d'un modèle de consommation ostentatoire traditionnel à une sensibilité expérientielle marquée par le changement de la manière dont les consommateurs définissent aujourd'hui le luxe (Dion, 2007 ; Atwal et Williams, 2009 ; Wiedmann et al., 2009 ; Bauer et al., 2011).

S'agissant du luxe, la littérature s'accorde sur le manque de consensus sur sa définition (De Barnier et al., 2005 ; Lallement, 1999 ; Dubois, 1991). Il est donc essentiel de chercher à comprendre la perception de cette valeur luxe lors d'une expérience de consommation en tenant compte des différences individuelles. Les consommateurs développeraient un sens du luxe pour leurs marques, en se basant sur leurs interactions (avec le produit, l'environnement ou autrui) mais aussi en fonction de leur passé socioéconomique (Vigneron et Johnson, 1999). Toutes ces interactions se déroulent sur deux axes perceptuels : une dimension sociale et une dimension personnelle (Vigneron et Johnson, 2004 ; Wiedmann et al., 2007).

Dans une perspective expérientielle, la perception de cette valeur luxe de la marque résulterait de cette multitude d'interactions entre le consommateur, l'objet de consommation et les éléments de son environnement (Aurier, Evrard et N'Goala, 2004). Par conséquent, le cadre théorique de cette recherche repose sur l'interrogation conjointe de deux champs conceptuels de la littérature relatifs à l'expérience d'une part, et au luxe d'autre part.

1.1. Des valeurs luxe aux valeurs consommateur

Bien que les travaux sur la valeur luxe s'intéressent plutôt à la valeur générée par l'interaction avec la marque de luxe (Vigneron et Johnson, 1999, 2004), la littérature marketing suggère l'existence d'expériences vécues sans contact avec la marque voire même, en dehors de dispositifs expérientiels (Filser, 2002 ; Ladwein, 2003). En ce qui concerne les valeurs consommateur, on retrouve des typologies de valeurs établies sur la base de dimensions similaires à celles du luxe (Holt, 1995 ; Holbrook, 1999 ; Aurier, Evrard et N'Goala, 2004, Pulh, 2002), à savoir les orientations vers soi (but autotélique, orientation vers soi de la consommation) ou vers les autres (but interpersonnel, orientation vers autrui).

Les valeurs seront ainsi abordées selon leur orientation plutôt que selon leur origine disciplinaire, de manière à appréhender les spécificités d'une offre de luxe et surtout de définir les contours de l'expérience de luxe au travers de la littérature.

a. Les valeurs personnelles et les valeurs orientées vers soi

La littérature sur le luxe offre une palette de valeurs consommateur orientées vers soi qu'elles soient intrinsèques et associées au plaisir ou qu'elles soient extrinsèques et générées par des composantes utilitaires de l'offre.

- L'hédonisme : les recherches sur la consommation du luxe suggèrent que les produits de luxe sont aussi consommés pour leur dimension hédonique (Dubois et al., 2001, Renand et Vickers, 2003) de part leurs caractères à la fois hédoniste et symbolique (Dubois et al., 2005). D'ailleurs la valeur hédonique est également reconnue dans la perception des marques de luxe (Vigenron et Johnson, 1999, 2004 ; Wiedmann et al., 2007, 2009). Des réponses émotionnelles sont associées à la consommation du luxe telles que la beauté esthétique ou les plaisirs sensoriels (Kapferer, 1997 ; Benarrosh-Dahan, 1991 ; Allérès, 1991 ; Fauchois et Krieg, 1991 ; Roux et Folch, 1996). Le concept du luxe même est lié à cette expérience sensorielle et aux plaisirs (Castarède, 1992 ; Dubois et al., 2001)

- La qualité : la qualité excellente est la première association spontanée au luxe chez les répondants (Dubois et al., 2001). Un produit de luxe est un produit parfait (Allérès, 2006) ou de très bonne qualité (Lipovetsky et Roux, 2003). Elle est associée à la supériorité technique et technologique des produits (Lombard, 1989), à un effet de perfectionnisme recherché par les consommateurs chez les marques de luxe (Vigneron et Johnson, 1999) et justifie le prix élevé par deux indicateurs : la nature des ingrédients ou du processus de l'élaboration plus la délicatesse, et l'expertise de la production du service (Dubois et al., 2001).

Trois autres valeurs orientées vers soi sont introduites dans le modèle de Wiedmann et al. (2009) :

- La facilité de l'utilisation : elle dépend, de par sa dimension fonctionnelle, à la fois des caractéristiques propres au produit de luxe et des besoins des consommateurs. Son évaluation peut être objective ou subjective, en fonction des objectifs de l'utilisation.

- Le matérialisme : cette valeur est introduite dans la dimension individuelle du luxe. Elle se réfère à l'importance que représente la possession de l'objet du luxe dans la vie du consommateur. Plus ce dernier est matérialiste, plus il développe une attitude positive à l'acquisition du produit.

- L'identité de soi : elle fait partie de la dimension individuelle et se réfère à un aspect privé de la perception de la marque de luxe. Elle permet de mesurer la congruence de l'image de soi avec l'image perçue du produit ou du service de luxe. De ce point de vue, les produits de luxe permettent d'attribuer un sens symbolique à sa propre identité et peut alors influencer l'achat.

b. Les valeurs sociales/interpersonnelles et les valeurs orientées vers autrui

Trois composantes principales de l'orientation sociale de la valeur luxe dans la consommation ont été identifiées dans les recherches en marketing.

- L'ostentation : La consommation ostentatoire (Veblen, 1899) a longtemps dominé la littérature sur le luxe. Elle s'est développée avec les recherches centrées sur l'influence des groupes de référence sur la consommation des marques de luxe (Bourne, 1957). Cependant, la valeur ostentatoire ne peut expliquer qu'en partie la consommation dans le luxe, puisque les produits ou services peuvent aussi être consommés en privé (Bearden et Etzel, 1982 ; Vigneron et Johnson, 1999 ; Berry, 1994). Dans une perspective de consommation ostentatoire, il a été démontré que le prix joue un rôle positif dans la perception de la qualité (corrélation positive), et qu'il est donc un indicateur discriminant de la valeur luxe. C'est une conséquence logique de l'excellente qualité, devenue une caractéristique intrinsèque au luxe et garantit un sentiment de confort et de sécurité (Dubois et al., 2001).

- L'unicité : également associée à la rareté (Catry, 2007) et à l'exclusivité du produit ou de la marque et garantit de ce fait un effet de snobisme (Leibenstein, 1950). L'unicité est complexe à cause de son ambivalence liée à la fois aux effets personnels et interpersonnels. D'une part, elle est considérée comme une valeur fonctionnelle : plus le produit est rare, et unique, plus le désir de le posséder est grand. L'unicité renforce donc le désir de posséder le produit de luxe (Wiedmann et al., 2007, 2009). D'autre part, fortement liée à un effet de snobisme (Leibenstein, 1950), elle prend en compte les désirs personnels et émotionnels lors de l'achat ou de la consommation et influence et est influencée par le comportement des autres (Vigneron et Johnson, 1999). Elle répond donc à un désir à la fois personnel, celui de posséder et social celui de se différencier.

- La valeur sociale : la consommation du luxe est révélatrice d'appartenance à un groupe social et/ou de différenciation avec les autres groupes non consommateurs de luxe. Elle est fortement liée au concept d'extension de soi (Belk, 1988) qui suggère que la possession fait partie de l'identité d'une part. D'autre part, elle est liée au prestige, qui est une valeur déterminante pour la marque de luxe (Vigneron et Johnson, 1999), puisqu'elle sert de signe symbolique et distinctif de l'appartenance à un groupe (Wiedmann et al., 2009).

Les valeurs luxe interrogent les motivations des consommateurs ainsi que leurs comportements. La littérature s'est principalement attachée à décrire et expliquer les segments de consommateurs sur le marché du luxe.

1.2. Le comportement des consommateurs du luxe au prisme de l'approche expérientielle

L'intérêt pour le consommateur du luxe dans la littérature aborde deux orientations majeures : managériale d'une part et comportementale d'autre part. Dans une orientation managériale, les travaux sont plutôt destinés à :

- Mieux comprendre la valeur luxe qui distingue une marque de luxe de celle qui ne l'est pas (Nueno et Quelch, 1998 ; Kapferer et Bastien, 2009 ; Vigneron et Johnson 1999, Wiedmann et al., 2007).
- La mesure de la valeur luxe des marques (Vigneron et Johnson, 2004 ; Christodoulides et al., 2009) et le positionnement des marques de luxe (Kapferer et Bastien, 2009).

Dans une perspective comportementale de la consommation, les auteurs s'attachent à comprendre et expliquer les motifs et les modalités de la consommation :

- Les comportements vis-à-vis des produits de luxe (Vickers et Renand, 2003), les motivations de consommation (Truong, 2010) et la comparaison des motivations entre les sociétés asiatiques et occidentales (Wong et Ahuvia, 1998).
- Les attitudes, mesures des attitudes et les profils – issus de segmentations - des consommateurs (Dubois et Duquesne, 1993 ; Dubois et Laurent, 1993, 1996 ; Dubois et Paternault, 1997 ; Dubois et al., 2001, 2005 ; Wiedmann et al., 2009).

a. Valeur consommateur et motivations individuelles

Dans une perspective expérientielle, fondée sur l'interaction objet/individu, la valeur perçue est considérée comme ni totalement subjective (de par l'interprétation subjective de l'individu), ni totalement objective (de par les caractéristiques objectives de l'objet) (Holbook, 1996 ; Aurier, Evrard et N'Goala, 1998, 2004). Ainsi, deux dimensions de la valeur sont généralement retenues, une orientation intrinsèque versus extrinsèque de la valeur de l'objet et une orientation vers soi versus vers autrui concernant l'individu qui valorise l'objet (Aurier, Evrard et N'Goala, 2004). Les études sur les motivations des consommateurs de luxe (Truong, 2010) confirment également cette double orientation (vers soi versus vers autrui) des buts de consommation combinés avec des buts intrinsèques versus extrinsèques dans les pratiques de consommation (Holt, 2005).

- Une orientation sociale : motivation extrinsèque, reflète le désir d'impressionner les autres. Ses antécédents ont été présentés dans les recherches en référence au concept classique de Veblen (1899) de la théorie de consommation ostentatoire. Dans le cadre d'une consommation de produits ou de marque de luxe (Vigneron et Johnson, 1999 ; Wiedmann et al., 2007), les valeurs extrinsèques orientées vers autrui, déjà établies dans le cadre d'une consommation expérientielle (Holbrook, 1994 ; Richins, 1994 ; Holt, 1995 ; Lai, 1995), vont apparaître.

- Une orientation personnelle : la motivation est intrinsèque et reflète des buts d'accomplissement de soi. Ici la consommation du luxe est personnelle, et les valeurs intrinsèques orientées vers soi dominent (Holbrook, 1994 ; Richins, 1994 ; Holt, 1995 ; Lai, 1995).

b. Variables de segmentation et profils des consommateurs de luxe

Quelle que soit la dénomination des profils, la segmentation des consommateurs du luxe repose sur des valeurs attendues et/ou perçues. Les valeurs consommateur identifiées permettent de distinguer quatre profils attitudinaux à l'égard du luxe (Dubois et Laurent, 1993 ; Dubois et al., 2001, 2005).

- Une attitude réserviste : où la valeur prix élevée est perçue comme indécente, tout comme la valeur ostentatoire. La valeur qualité n'est pas reconnue comme déterminante du niveau de luxe.
- Une attitude distante et un sentiment de malaise : ici on note le manque d'expérience dans le luxe qui crée un malaise vis-à-vis des produits et des marques de luxe.
- Une implication plaisir : les valeurs hédoniques (plaisir, passion, bien être) priment et engendrent une forte implication et un fort intérêt pour le luxe.
- La valeur du signe : les valeurs symboliques priment sur les valeurs intrinsèques. La consommation des produits de luxe permet de révéler la personnalité.

Dans les mêmes travaux, trois profils principaux de consommateurs sont identifiés à partir de ces profils attitudinaux.

1) Les élitistes : la consommation est basée sur la valeur exclusivité/unicité. La valeur prix élevé est fortement appréciée et permet de distinguer le consommateur.
2) Les démocrates : favorables à une distribution intensive des produits de luxe, le luxe doit être accessible à tous.
3) Les distants : les valeurs superfluité et prix élevé entrainent une forte distance vis-à-vis du monde du luxe qui peut se transformer en un rejet.

Plus récemment, Wiedmann et al. (2009) ont élaboré une segmentation à partir des valeurs luxe proposant quatre profils de consommateurs.

1) Les matérialistes : la consommation est orientée vers les valeurs personnelles comme l'hédonisme ou vers la valeur fonctionnelle comme la facilité de l'utilisation ou encore la qualité.
2) Les fonctionnalistes rationnels : la valeur extrinsèque orientée vers soi (la qualité) permet la satisfaction des besoins personnels.

3) Les extravagants : c'est la valeur prestige (extrinsèque orientée vers autrui) qui prime sur la valeur qualité ou encore sur la valeur hédonique.

4) Les hédonistes introvertis : attirés par les valeurs intrinsèque (hédonisme) ou extrinsèque (qualité) orientées vers soi.

Les travaux portant sur le luxe sont plutôt orientés vers la segmentation des consommateurs, et la perception de la valeur luxe, néanmoins il nous semble que la perception du concept luxe évolue en fonction des expériences vécues. Face à l'accessibilité croissante du luxe au grand public, et notamment auprès de cibles jeunes, nous nous intéressons au vécu des premières expériences perçues comme relevant du luxe et aux interactions génératrices de valeurs.

2. CHOIX ET MODALITES DE L'ENQUETE EXPLORATOIRE

Rappelons que l'objet premier de l'approche étant de répondre à la question « Quelles sont les expériences qualifiées comme luxueuses et quelles en sont les composantes ? ».

Pour explorer les premières expériences qualifiées comme expérience de luxe, une approche qualitative a été privilégiée. En effet, peu de recherches se sont intéressées au vécu expérientiel dans l'expérience du luxe auprès de la cible jeune grand public.

Une première étape de l'enquête a été effectuée à l'aide d'entretiens face à face. Cette première démarche s'est révélée infructueuse, les répondants manifestaient une gêne, un malaise et de nombreuses difficultés d'expression orale sur le concept luxe. Une autre méthode de recueil a été ainsi mise en place au moyen de récits biographiques écrits. Trois groupes d'étudiants en première année universitaire (I.U.T. GACO) à Agen ont été interrogés. Ces derniers disposaient de deux heures pour répondre librement à une série de questions ouvertes (Annexe 1). Ce sont par nature des récits autobiographiques (Pineau et Legrand, 1992 in Rouleau, 2003). Au total 73 étudiants (44 jeunes femmes et 29 jeunes hommes) ont été interrogés par écrit. Cette dernière démarche s'est révélée plus fructueuse et a permis de faire apparaitre des premiers résultats.

Après une première lecture flottante destinée à effectuer un premier repérage des thèmes récurrents, une sélection des récits les plus pertinents a été effectuée. Les récits sélectionnés traitent au moins d'une expérience de produit et/ou service ou de marque de luxe, perçue et qualifiée comme une expérience de luxe par les répondants. Le corpus final se constitue de 26 récits biographiques de jeunes âgés de 17 à 24 ans (médiane à 19 ans) de sexe féminin pour la grande majorité (voir annexe 2 : liste des répondants).

Les récits sélectionnés ont été analysés selon un processus inductif de classification (Spiggle, 1994). L'approche exploratoire étant libre de toute hypothèse a priori, les auteurs ont opté pour une analyse thématique de contenu. Pour réduire les biais, les deux chercheurs ont procédé selon les étapes suivantes : 1) lecture individuelle minutieuse des récits sélectionnés, pour découper et classer le texte selon des thèmes et des sous-thèmes ; 2) codage indépendant des catégories récurrentes (accord sur 11 des 13 sous-catégories construites avant la codification finale ; 3) discussion des catégories et confrontation des résultats de l'enquête avec la littérature (Bardin, 1977 ; Miles et Hubermann, 1984).

3. PRINCIPAUX RESULTATS DE L'APPROCHE EXPLORATOIRE

L'enquête a conduit à l'identification de quatre catégories distinctes mais inter-reliées entre elles. Comprendre ce qui permet à l'expérience d'être qualifiée comme relevant du luxe chez les répondants passe ainsi par la prise en compte de quatre niveaux de perception qui fondent les catégories identifiées : caractéristiques de l'offre et/ou du contexte expérientiel, vécu expérientiel (émotions et sensations), représentations individuelles et évaluation de l'expérience (valeur luxe).

3.1. La perception du contexte expérientiel

Pour relater le vécu d'une expérience de luxe, les répondants décrivent en détail les différentes variables du marketing mix et/ou du contexte expérientiel.

Prix/Produit : le couple prix/produit, conformément à la littérature, est souvent cité conjointement et confirme la corrélation positive : la qualité justifie le prix du produit. De même, les résultats confirment les valeurs existantes dans la littérature au niveau du produit, service ou la marque, telles que l'unicité, l'exclusivité, la qualité, la durabilité.

Lieu/distribution : s'agissant du lieu, l'expérience est perçue comme relevant du luxe de par son dispositif expérientiel mémorable, les répondants détaillent ainsi la décoration, les couleurs, la disposition des produits, la mise en scène ou encore l'ambiance du magasin. Ces éléments relèvent typiquement de la stimulation des sens (Schmitt, 1999 ; Hetzel, 2002). Les expériences contrôlées sont davantage perçues comme relevant du luxe lorsque le contexte est fortement enclavé (Carù et Covà, 2007) et que les répondants le décrivent comme un endroit « fermé » (Marion, 18 ans) voire « interdit » (Cédric, 23 ans).

De manière moins attendue, certaines expériences vécues en dehors de dispositifs contrôlés sont considérées comme relevant du luxe. Dans ce cas, les répondants décrivent majoritairement les éléments de l'environnement tels que les villas de luxe, les habitants, et le personnel de maison, les bâtiments, les édifices et demeures privées et/ou publiques, susceptibles d'être considérés comme des éléments non contrôlables mais déclencheurs d'une expérience de luxe. A ce titre, déambuler dans une ville prestigieuse comme Paris ou Monaco est perçu comme une expérience de luxe, dans la mesure où elle génère un vécu expérientiel : « Mes expériences directes en rapport avec le luxe ont été des séjours dans les villes de Saint-Tropez et Monaco. » (Julie, 18 ans).

Personnel de contact : Quelle que soit l'évaluation de l'expérience perçue comme relevant du luxe, les répondants mettent l'accent dans un premier temps sur la description du personnel : « La personne qui me faisait le soin ne parlait pas j'entendais juste sa respiration. Sa peau des mains était très douce. » (Priscilla, 18 ans) ; « Les vendeurs étaient en costume et étaient attentifs aux moindres désirs des clients. » (Claire, 17 ans).

Ces éléments, de manière indépendante ou combinée, vont générer un vécu expérientiel décrit dans les récits.

3.2. Le vécu expérientiel

Les résultats permettent de distinguer les éléments déclencheurs d'émotions lors d'une expérience perçue comme relevant du luxe. Celles-ci seront abordées selon leur caractère contrôlé ou non contrôlé dans le cadre d'un dispositif expérientiel.

a. Les émotions générées par un dispositif expérientiel contrôlé

Quatre éléments clés du dispositif expérientiel sont susceptibles de déclencher des émotions lors d'une expérience de luxe chez les répondants : le prix, le lieu, le personnel de contact et le produit.

- Le prix : l'expérience du luxe est fortement marquée par la perception du prix. Ce dernier (affiché ou pas en vitrine ou indiqué dans un encart publicitaire) peut à lui seul, susciter de brèves émotions relatées dans les récits, à commencer par la surprise, mais également des réactions de « stupeur » (Cécile, 20 ans) ou de « choc » (Julie, 19ans) devant des sommes considérées comme exorbitantes. Le prix peut même susciter des sentiments de frustration, d'autant plus lorsqu'il est comparé à celui de produits non luxueux.

« Une simple poudre compacte Dior ou Chanel coûte en moyenne 45€ alors que la marque Sephora en propose en moyenne à 16€. Voir cette différence de prix entraîne un sentiment de frustration et d'ébahissement, une poudre compacte qui coûte le prix d'un pantalon ou d'une paire de chaussures. Il est frustrant de se dire que des personnes peuvent se les acheter sans pour autant culpabiliser en pensant à ce qu'ils auraient pu faire avec cet argent » (Mélissa, 18 ans).

- Le lieu : lorsque l'expérience est directe (par exemple dans l'enseigne d'une marque de luxe), le lieu et ses éléments de théâtralisation abordés précédemment par rapport à une perspective descriptive est évidemment générateur d'émotions. « De plus, l'atmosphère avec ses grands rideaux rouges ses dorures ces loges personnelles me donnaient une impression de grandeur, de fierté. » (Héléna, 19 ans).

- Le personnel de contact : comme cela a été souligné précédemment, fait partie intégrante du dispositif expérientiel. A ce titre, la compétence et/ou le professionnalisme des vendeurs génère du « bien-être, de la confiance, envie de posséder le produit » (Priscilla, 18ans). En revanche, encore une fois le rôle du personnel de contact s'avère déterminant puisqu'il peut également générer des émotions négatives et influencer ainsi le vécu de l'expérience. « Lors d'un voyage à Paris, je suis rentré dans les galeries Lafayette et je ne portais pas de grandes marques (comme Chanel, Guess…) et toutes les vendeuses m'ont immédiatement dévisagé. Je me suis senti mal à l'aise mais j'étais aussi énervé car je voyais ça comme de la discrimination. Puis j'ai regardé autour de moi et j'ai vu un décor magnifique. […] J'ai trouvé ça très dommage car cette ambiance gâchait le décor. » (Cédric, 23 ans).

- Le produit : qu'il s'agisse d'un bien (produits cosmétiques, vestimentaires et accessoires de marques de luxe pour notre cible) ou d'un service (hôtellerie-restauration, instituts de soins), le produit est à lui seul générateur de plaisir. « C'était un jour inoubliable que j'ai passé avec ma famille. Pour moi c'était sympa car on était tous réunis dans un restaurant où je ne pensais pas un jour y rentrer. La saveur du buffet était délicieuse, il y avait même un groupe de musiciens qui mettait de l'ambiance. L'acoustique était super ! » (Yaudrey, 23 ans).

b. Les vécus expérientiels non contrôlés

Les résultats soulignent les influences de l'environnement, notamment le contexte social et le comportement des autres individus sur le vécu de l'expérience. En ce sens, le vécu d'une expérience même contrôlée (visite d'enseigne) peut être influencé par l'interaction avec d'autres individus, perçus comme représentatifs du luxe. Les émotions négatives générées par des interactions « non contrôlées » avec autrui sont plutôt de l'ordre de « sentiments d'infériorité » (Justine, 19 ans), d'« intimidation » (Claire, 17 ans), et de « malaise » (Marion, 18 ans). Les comportements perçus comme positifs en revanche (simplicité, sympathie, bienveillance d'individus riches) engendrent avant tout de la surprise, et sont même susceptibles d'amener à une reconsidération des représentations.

« Elle a pu me prouver que ce que je pensais impossible : que l'argent ne tourne pas toujours la tête aux gens que certains savent rester eux-mêmes malgré qu'ils vivent dans le luxe, certains aiment aussi en faire profiter ceux qui leur sont proches. » (Julie, 18 ans)

3.3. Les représentations individuelles

Les représentations du luxe concernent quatre niveaux de lecture : l'offre de luxe (le couple prix/produit), l'univers du luxe en général (l'immatériel et le symbolique), les pratiques de consommation et enfin les comportements (perçus ou imaginés) des membres de l'univers luxe.

- L'offre du luxe : c'est le couple prix/produit en particulier qui est souvent évoqué. Le prix, perçu comme très élevé, permet aussi de situer l'accessibilité de l'offre (accessible, intermédiaire ou inaccessible). De même, la théâtralisation et la mise en scène fastueuses sont typiquement associées à l'offre du luxe, et garantissent certaines valeurs expérientielles (sensations). Cependant, elles évoquent également des associations négatives pour les individus. Cela les conduit, par exemple, à considérer la superfluité de la situation : « Même si j'ai passé une soirée agréable, consommé du champagne, un vin excellent et que j'ai apprécie le buffet, j'ai trouvé que toute la mise en scène qui accompagnait cette soirée était vraiment superflue » (Aïcha, 23 ans).

- L'univers luxe : il est souvent associé à un « autre monde » (Fanny, 20 ans) et rejoint la littérature dans la mesure où il est marqué, pour l'ensemble des répondants, avant tout par la richesse et la possession. Il est également symbole de liberté, d'une vie sans contraintes financières permettant de satisfaire ses moindres désirs (achats impulsifs). Toutefois, certains répondants insistent également sur les stéréotypes négatifs associés à l'univers du luxe comme le caractère superficiel ou éphémère. « Le luxe reste quelque chose d'éphémère qui n'a pas de réelle nécessité mis à part un plaisir passager. » (Ottavia, 18 ans).

- Les pratiques de consommation : les stéréotypes associés aux pratiques de consommation luxueuses se composent, pour les répondants, de styles de vie et de modes de consommation spécifiques. Ils sont étroitement liés aux représentations de l'univers du luxe : la « liberté de consommation et d'achat permise par un budget quasi illimité » (Héléna, 19 ans). Ces pratiques se traduisent aussi par les choix de consommation qui portent « exclusivement sur des grandes marques » (Julie, 18 ans), quelle que soit la catégorie du produit concernée. Malgré une certaine fascination pour l'univers du luxe en général, les répondants ne manifestent que peu d'attrait pour les modes de vie évoqués. Les stéréotypes négatifs alimentent largement les récits et amènent les individus interrogés à justifier leur distance vis-à-vis du luxe.

- Les comportements : les individus vivant dans le luxe sont souvent perçus par les répondants comme « maîtrisant les règles de la bienséance, le langage parlé, la tenue (l'éducation), la posture droite, tête haute (avoir une confiance), la démarche ou attitude physique et bien sur l'attitude, la morale, liées à un niveau d'éducation élevé » (Priscilla, 18 ans). Néanmoins, la perception des consommateurs de luxe est fortement marquée par des stéréotypes négatifs ; ils sont décrits comme « arrogants » (Mylène, 18 ans), « imbus de leur personne » (Eva, 18 ans), « hautains » (Julie, 19 ans) voire « dédaigneux » (Marion, 18 ans).

Les résultats obtenus à propos des représentations individuelles semblent étroitement liés aux émotions mais également à la valorisation plus générale de l'expérience du luxe.

3.4. La valorisation de l'expérience

Les valeurs perçues lors d'une expérience qualifiée comme relevant du luxe, sont générées chez les répondants par deux composantes majeures : le produit et l'environnement.

a. Les valeurs générées par le produit

Au-delà des valeurs utilitaires du produit telles que « la performance » (Christelle, 20 ans) ou « le niveau de qualité élevé » (Laura, 19 ans), la valorisation de l'expérience du produit peut passer chez les répondants par une forme « d'estime de soi » (Fanny, 20 ans), « d'amélioration de la confiance en soi » (Héléna, 19 ans) ou encore de « fierté » (Eva, 18 ans). Ces résultats rejoignent la littérature sur l'orientation personnelle de la consommation du luxe et les valeurs orientées vers soi (Truong, 2010). En revanche, si les valeurs orientées vers autrui apparaissent dans les récits, elles ne sont pas liées à l'expérience des répondants, mais plutôt à une projection de soi ou à une situation imaginée.

« Mais pouvoir parfois s'offrir un vêtement ou accessoires ou autres de grandes marques procure du plaisir, celui d'abord de le posséder mais aussi celui de pouvoir le porter et le montrer. » (Julie, 18 ans).

« Au niveau social je trouve que posséder un article de luxe procure une certaine fierté (enfin pour l'instant pour moi c'est plus un rêve qu'autre chose). » (Claire, 17 ans).

b. Les valeurs générées par l'environnement

L'expérience du luxe est souvent interprétée chez les répondants comme la découverte « d'un autre monde inconnu parfois qui nous demande d'apprendre les règles à appliquer dans ces circonstances. » (Ottavia, 18 ans). Cependant, l'inaptitude à se comporter de manière appropriée ou à paraître compétent dans la situation théâtralisée peut contribuer à détériorer l'aisance durant l'expérience.

« On ne se sentait pas à notre place, on ne savait pas comment se comporter. J'avais envie de saucer mon assiette mais mon copain m'a arrêté en me disant « Non, ça ne se fait pas ! ». On ne sait pas comment se comporter, on regardait les gens à coté de nous pour voir quel couvert utiliser, à quel rythme il faut manger, comment se tenir sur sa chaise, comment essuyer sa bouche. [...] On n'osait même pas parler » (Alexa, 18 ans).

Par ailleurs, les évaluations de certaines expériences font intervenir des valeurs morales altruistes (éthique, égalité), qui amènent les répondants à considérer l'injustice perçue quant à l'inaccessibilité voire l'incongruité du dispositif expérientiel, plutôt que le vécu expérientiel : « Cela m'a apporté une image très négative en situant le domaine du luxe comme privilégié même vis-à-vis de la société de la justice de l'égalité entre les individus… » (Charlotte, 18 ans). Enfin, certaines expériences peuvent amener à une remise en question positive par la modification des représentations acquises auparavant : « C'était pour moi une expérience humaine très enrichissante et elle m'a remise en question sur la vision que j'avais des personnes vivant dans un environnement luxueux. » (Justine, 19 ans). En ce sens, la valorisation de certaines expériences peut alors conduire à une reconstruction des représentations.

Néanmoins, il est à souligner que toutes ces valeurs semblent éphémères chez les répondants, puisqu'elles sont à la fois générées par un contexte expérientiel spécifique et liées à une situation vécue perçue comme extraordinaire.

CONCLUSIONS ET POURSUITE DE L'ENQUETE

L'objet de cette première approche exploratoire auprès d'une cible jeune grand public (ayant consommé au moins une fois un produit, service ou marque de luxe), est de comprendre ce que perçoit la cible comme une expérience relevant du luxe. Les résultats obtenus, nous permettent de mettre en évidence des premiers éléments de compréhension de l'expérience du luxe auprès d'une cible jeune grand public. Premièrement, il apparaît que les situations perçues comme des expériences de luxe par nos répondants relèvent principalement soit, de consommations extraordinaires de prestations de services (hôtels ou restaurants de luxe), soit d'expériences non contrôlées (visite de lieux et de villes mythiques, séjours chez des particuliers possédant et consommant des produits de luxe, participation à des soirées « branchées »). De manière moins attendue, l'expérience est qualifiée comme luxueuse chez les répondants même en l'absence de marque de luxe. Deuxièmement, même lorsque ces derniers consomment des produits de marques de luxe (généralement des accessoires), ils semblent davantage marqués par la théâtralisation du point de vente plutôt que par l'acquisition de l'objet. Troisièmement, pour nos répondants, le vécu émotionnel apparaît plutôt généré par l'interaction avec le lieu et les individus faisant partie de l'environnement, que par la possession d'un objet de luxe.

Par ailleurs, cette recherche a permis de souligner le rôle majeur des représentations individuelles dans la valorisation de l'offre. Les représentations apparaissent comme des « outils de décryptage » de l'expérience, dépendant notamment de la familiarité avec l'univers du luxe et influençant le vécu, et donc la valorisation de l'expérience. Néanmoins, le vécu émotionnel peut contribuer au changement ou à l'évolution des représentations individuelles. C'est pourquoi, le rôle des représentations dans le vécu émotionnel et dans la valorisation de l'expérience perçue comme relevant du luxe, amène à s'interroger quant à l'évolution des représentations au fil des expériences. Il est donc envisagé d'une part, de réinterroger la cible sur leurs expériences futures. D'autre part, l'enquête sera recentrée sur les expériences avec des produits de marques de luxe situés dans des degrés accessible et/ou intermédiaire auprès de la cible jeune grand public.

ANNEXE 1 : LISTE DES QUESTIONS FOURNIES AUX REPONDANTS.

1) Qu'est-ce que le luxe pour vous ?

2) Quels sont les éléments les plus représentatifs du luxe selon vous ? (cela peut concerner des individus, des objets, des comportements, des styles de vie, des habitudes et/ou des modes de consommation, des rituels, des tendances…)

3) Décrivez en détails vos différentes expériences directes (vous-même) ou indirectes (par un intermédiaire : individu, média - par exemple publicité dans des magazines, à la télé ; luxe incarné par des stars…) des produits (biens ou services) de luxe ?

Précisez pour chaque expérience, que vous la considériez comme bonne ou mauvaise :

- S'il s'agit d'une marque ou d'un produit de luxe, dont vous donnerez le nom ou la catégorie (produit),
- A quel moment et dans quel contexte celle-ci s'est déroulée (lieux, ambiance, autres individus, décoration, mise en scène…),
- Ce que cela vous a procuré en termes de sensations ou d'émotions,
- Ce qui vous a marqué (caractéristiques du produit ou de la marque : couleurs, odeurs, sons et/ou musique, goûts, …),
- S'il y a lieu, l'interaction avec le personnel de contact (qualité de l'accueil par exemple),
- Un titre résumant cette expérience.

4) Pour l'ensemble de vos expériences, expliquez ce que cela a eu comme conséquences :

- Au niveau personnel (satisfaction ou pas, estime de soi, émotions et sensations, plaisir, sentiments…),
- Au niveau social (appartenance, expression d'un statut, fierté, réalisation de soi…).

ANNEXE 2 : LISTE DES REPONDANTS

N° Récit	Prénom Initiale du Nom	Sexe	Age	Bac	Profession père	Profession mère	Ville des parents	Boursier
1	Marion W.	F	18	ES	Recherche emploi	Auxiliaire de vie	Marmande (47)	Non
2	Laura G.	F	19	STG	Chef d'entreprise	Chef d'entreprise	Montfaucou-montigné (49)	Non
3	Aïcha T.	F	23	L	Chauffeur pois lourd	Au foyer	Houailou (98)	Oui
4	Priscilla S.	F	18	Pro.	Chef d'entreprise	Comptable	Sainte colombe (47)	Non
5	Julie R.	F	18	ES	Commerçant	pharmacienne	Marmande (47)	Non
6	Justine D.	F	19	ES	Chauffeur de bus	Secrétaire de gestion	Villenave-d'ornon (33)	Non
7	Héléna S.	F	19	ES	Commerçant	Intervenante en anglais	Nérac (47)	Non
8	Ottavia A.	F	18	STG	Plombier	Aide soignante	La réole (33)	Non
9	Yaudrey T.	F	23	Pro	Chimiste	Au foyer	Canaia (98)	Oui
10	Claire L.	F	17	S	Militaire	Au foyer	Bon -encontre (47)	Non
11	Alexa M.	F	18	STG	Facteur	Vendeuse	Laroque (47)	Non
12	Audrey R.	F	18	STG	Militaire	Au foyer	Bourges (18)	Oui
13	Mylène S.	F	18	ES	Mécanicien agricole	Secrétaire	Layrac (47)	Oui

N° Récit	Prénom Initiale du Nom	Sexe	Age	Bac	Profession père	Profession mère	Ville des parents	Boursier
14	Fanny G.	F	20	STG		Agent de la poste	Noailan (93)	Oui
15	Christelle L.	F	20	ES		Assistante logistique	Bon-encontre (47)	Oui
16	Cédric C.	H	23	ES	Instituteur	Au foyer	Agen (47)	Non
17	Audrey M.	F	19	STT	Formateur	Au foyer	Houailou (98)	Oui
18	Lisa J.	F	19	STG	Cuisinier industriel	Aide soignante	Agen (47)	Oui
19	Charlotte L.	F	18	ES	Ingénieur	Préparatrice en pharmacie	Ploudalmézeau (29)	Non
20	Sébastien L.	H	19	STG	Bijoutier	Assistante de direction	Agen (47)	Non
21	Cécile D.	F	20	L	Technicien bancaire	Secrétaire	Vianne (47)	Oui
22	Ingrid K.	F	24	STG	Retraité	Retraitée	Poindimie (98)	Oui
23	Thomas V.	H	18	ES	Directeur commercial	Responsable formation continue	Villenave d'ornon (33)	Non
24	Mélissa G.	F	18	STG	Prothésiste dentaire	Rédactrice en chef	Aussevielle (64)	Non
25	Eva B.	F	18	STG	Agent de maitrise	Secrétaire médicale	Sainte colombe (47)	Oui
26	Julie C.	F	19	ES	Chauffeur routier	Formatrice	Prayssas (47)	Non

REFERENCES BIBLIOGRAPHIQUES

ADHAM, L., 2006, 'La boutique du luxe : un espace théâtralisé' in Allerès (ed.) Luxe…Métiers et management atypiques, Economica.

ALLERES, D., 1991, Spécificités et stratégies marketing des différents univers du luxe, *Revue Française de Marketing*, 132/33, pp.71-95.

ALLERES, D., 2006, Luxe…Métiers et management atypiques, Economica, Paris.

ATWAL, G., & WILLIAMS, A., 2009, 'Luxury brand marketing-the experience is everything!', *Journal of Brand Management*, vol. 6, n° 5, pp. 338-346.

AURIER, P., EVRARD, Y. & N'GOALA, G., 1998, 'La valeur du produit du point de vue du consommateur', Actes du congrès des IAE, Nantes.

AURIER, P., EVRARD, Y. & N'GOALA, G., 2004, 'Comprendre et mesurer la valeur du point de vue du consommateur', *Recherche et Applications en Marketing*, vol. 19, n° 3, pp. 1-20.

BARDIN, L., 1977, L'analyse de contenu, Presses Universitaires de France, Paris.

BEARDEN, WO. & ETZEL, MJ., 1982, 'Reference group influence on product and brand purchase decisions', *Journal of Consumer Research*, vol. 9, n° 2: pp. 183–194.

BELK, RW., 1988, 'Possessions and the Extended Self', *Journal of Consumer Research*, vol. 15, n°. 2, pp. 139-153.

BENARROSH-DAHAN, E., 1991, 'Le contexte lexicologique du luxe', *Revue Française du Marketing*, 132/133, pp. 45–54.

BERRY, CJ., 1994, The idea of luxury, a conceptual and historical investigation, Cambridge University Press, Cambridge.

BOURNE, FS., 1957, 'Group influence in marketing and public relations', in Rensis L & Hayes SP (ed.), Some Applications of Behavioral Research. Basil, Switzerland, UNESCO.

CARÙ, A. & COVA, B., 2007, 'Consumer immersion in an experiential context', in A Carù & B Cova (ed.), Consuming experience, Routledge, New York, pp. 34-47.

CASTAREDE, J., 2003, Le luxe, Que sais-je ?, Paris.

CATRY, B., 2007, 'Le luxe peut être cher, mais est-il toujours rare ?', *Revue Française de Gestion*, vol. 2, n° 171.

CHRISTODOULIDES, G., MICHAELIDOU, N. & LI, CH., 2009, 'Measuring perceived brand luxury: An evaluation of the BLI scale', *Journal of Brand Management*, vol. 16, n° 5/6, pp. 395-405.

DION, D., 2007, 'Processus de sacralisation des magasins de luxe', 12emes Journées de Recherche en Marketing de Bourgogne, Dijon.

DE BARNIER, V. & RODINA, I. & VALETTE-FLORENCE, P., 2005, 'Which luxury perceptions affect most consumer purchase behavior? A cross-cultural exploratory study in France, the United Kingdom and Russia', Congrès Paris-Venise des Tendances Marketing, Venise.

DUBOIS, B., 1991, 'Qu'est ce que le luxe ? Une analyse exploratoire de visuels publicitaires', *Revue Française du Marketing*, 132/33, pp. 55-64.
DUBOIS, B. & LAURENT, G., 1993, 'Y a-t-il un euro consommateur de luxe ? Une analyse comparative des profils sociodémographiques des acheteurs européens', *Recherche et Application en Marketing*, vol. 8, n° 4, pp. 107-124.
DUBOIS, B. & DUQUESNE, P., 1993, 'The Market for Luxury Goods: Income Versus Culture', *European Journal of Marketing*, vol. 27, n°1, pp. 35-44.
DUBOIS, B. & LAURENT, G., 1996, 'Le Luxe par-delà les Frontières : Une Etude Exploratoire dans Douze Pays', *Décisions Marketing*, vol. 9, pp. 35-43.
DUBOIS, B. & PATERNAULT, C., 1997, 'Does Luxury have a Home Country? An Investigation of Country Images in Europe', *Marketing and Research Today*, vol. 25, pp. 79-85.
DUBOIS, B., LAURENT, G. & CZELLAR, S. 2001, 'Consumer rapport to luxury: Analysing complex and ambivalent attitudes', *Les cahiers de Recherche du groupe HEC*, n° 736, pp. 1-56.
DUBOIS, B., CZELLAR, S. & LAURENT, G., 2005, 'Consumer segments based on attitudes toward luxury: Empirical evidence from twenty countries', *Marketing Letters*, vol. 16, n° 2, pp. 115-128.
FAUCHOIS, A. & KRIEG, A., 1991, 'Le discours du luxe', *Revue Française du Marketing*, 132/133, pp. 23–39.
FILSER, M., 2002, 'Le marketing de la production d'expérience : statut théorique et implications managériales', *Décisions Marketing*, vol. 28, pp. 13-22.
HETZEL, P., 2002, 'La mise en scène de l'identité d'une marque de luxe sur son lieu de vente : L'approche expérientielle des magasins Ralph Lauren', *Revue Française du Marketing*, vol. 2, n° 187.
HOLBROOK, MB. & HIRSCHMAN, EC., 1982, 'The Experiential Aspects of Consumption: Consumer Fantasies, Feelings and Fun', *Journal of Consumer Research*, vol. 9, n° 2, pp. 132-140.
HOLBROOK, MB., 1994, 'The nature of customer value: an axiology of services in the consumption experience', in R Rust & RL Oliver (ed.), Service quality: new directions in theory and practice, Thousand Oaks, Sage Publications, pp. 21-71.
HOLBROOK, MB., 1996, 'Customer Value - A Framework For Analysis and Research', *Advances in Consumer Research*, vol. 23, n° 1, pp. 138-142.
HOLBROOK, MB., 1999, Consumer Value. A framework for analysis and research, Routledge, London and New York.
HOLT, DB., 1995, 'How Consumers Consume: A Typology of Consumption', *Journal of Consumer Research*, vol. 22, n° 1, pp. 1-16.
Kapferer, JN., 1997, 'Managing luxury brands', *Journal of Brand Management*, vol. 4, pp. 251–260.

KAPFERER, J. & BASTIEN, V., 2009, 'The specificity of luxury management: Turning marketing upside down', *Journal of Brand Management*, vol. 16, n° 5/6, pp. 311-322.
LADWEIN, R., 2003, Le comportement du consommateur et de l'acheteur, 2ème édition, Economica, Paris.
LAI, AW., 1995, 'Consumer values, product benefits and customer value: a consumption behavior approach', *Advances in Consumer Research*, vol. 22, pp. 381-388.
LALLEMENT, O., 1999, 'Caractéristiques des éléments spécifiques de la marque de luxe dans l'esprit du consommateur. Une étude des images mentales associées à un visuel publicitaire', Actes du XVe congrès de l'A.F.M, Strasbourg.
LEIBENSTEIN, H., 1950, 'Bandwagon, Snob, and Veblen Effects in the Theory of Consumers' Demand'. *Quarterly Journal of Economics*, vol. 64, pp. 183-207.
LIPOVETSKY, G. & ROUX, E., 2003, Le luxe éternel, Gallimard, Paris.
LOMBARD, M., 1989, Produits de luxe, Economica, Paris.
MILES, MB. & HUBERMAN, MA., 1984, Qualitative data analysis: an expanded sourcebook, 2ème édition, Sage Publications, Thousand Oaks.
Nueno, JL. & Quelch, JA., 1998, 'The mass marketing of luxury', *Business Horizons*, vol. 41, n° 6, pp. 61-68.
PULH, M., 2002, 'La valorisation de l'expérience de consommation d'activités culturelles : le cas des festivals d'arts de la rue', Thèse de doctorat en Sciences de Gestion, Université de Bourgogne.
RICHINS, ML., 1994, 'Valuing things: the public and private meanings of possessions', *Journal of Consumer Research*, vol. 21, n° 3, pp. 504-521.
ROULEAU, L., 2003, 'La méthode biographique', in Y Giordano (ed.), Conduire un projet de recherche. Une perspective qualitative, Editions Management & Société, Paris, pp. 133-171.
ROUX, E., 1991, 'Comment se positionnent les marques de luxe ?', *Revue Française du Marketing*, 132/33, pp. 111-118.
ROUX, E., 1995, 'Consumer Evaluation of Luxury Brand Extensions', EMAC Conference, ESSEC, Paris.
ROUX, E., 2002, 'Le luxe au-delà des chiffres : quelles logiques d'analyse ?', *Revue Française du Marketing*, n° 187.
ROUX, E. & FLOCH, JM., 1996, 'Gérer L'Ingérable : La Contradiction Interne de toute Maison de Luxe', *Décisions Marketing*, vol. 9, pp. 15-23.
SCHMITT, B., 1999, 'Experiential Marketing', *Journal of Marketing Management*, vol. 15, n°1/3, pp. 53-67.
SPIGGLE, S., 1994, 'Analysis and interpretation of qualitative data in consumer research', *Journal of Consumer Research*, vol. 21, n° 3, pp. 491-503.
TRUONG, Y., MCCOLL, R. & KITCHEN, PJ., 2009, 'New luxury brand positioning and the emergence of Masstige brands', *Journal of Brand Management*, vol. 16, n° 5/6, pp. 375-382.

TRUONG, Y., 2010, 'Personal aspirations and the consumption of luxury goods', *International Journal of Market Research*, vol. 52, n° 5, pp 653-671.
VEBLEN, TB., 1899, The Theory of the Leisure Class. Boston, MA: Houghton Mifflin.
VICKERS, JS. & RENAND, F., 2003, 'The Marketing of Luxury Goods: An exploratory study – three conceptual dimensions', *The Marketing Review*, vol. 3, n°. 4, pp. 459-478.
VIGNERON, F. & JOHNSON, LW., 1999, 'A review and a conceptual framework of prestige-seeking consumer behavior'. *Academy of Marketing Science Review*, vol. 1999, n° 1, pp. 1–15.
VIGNERON, F. & JOHNSON, LW., 2004, 'Measuring perceptions of brand luxury'. *Journal of Brand Management*, vol. 11, n° 6, pp. 484-506.
WIEDMANN, KP., HENNIGS, N. & SIEBELS, A., 2007, 'Measuring consumers' luxury value perception: A cross-cultural framework'. *Academy of Marketing Science*, vol. 11, pp. 1–21.
WIEDMANN, K., HENNIGS, N. & SIEBELS, A., 2009, 'Value-based segmentation of luxury consumption behavior', *Psychology & Marketing*, vol. 26, n° 7, pp. 625–651.
WONG, NY. & AHUVIA, AC., 1998, 'Personal Taste and Family Face: Luxury Consumption in Confucian and Western Societies', *Psychology and Marketing*, vol. 15, n° 5, pp. 423-441.

BOOK REVIEW

Wided BATAT, 2019, *Digital Luxury: transforming Brands & Customer Experiences*, London, Sage Publishing, 280 p.
Wided BATAT, 2017, *Luxe et Expérience Client*, Paris, Dunod, 248 p.

More than in any other sector, luxury consumption is a response to a search for emotions, pleasure, uniqueness, consideration, and greatest services. The luxury consumer wants to live experiences – not just buy luxury products or services. To meet the new demands of customers, in these two books, Wided Batat offers a concrete vision of the new luxury experience and digital tools that will help luxury brands create an ultimate luxury experience, both online and offline. Although it is one of the most traditional industries, the luxury sector is very dynamic and changes rapidly under the influence of new ideas, technologies and generations. One of these influences is the pervasiveness of digital technology and social media. Digital luxury experiences, as stated by Batat in the following two books, differ from their offline counterparts. Despite the growing centrality of luxury brands and products, few studies have been conducted to identify important antecedents and determinants of the customer experience in luxury goods and services. That is why, the content offered in these two books provides luxury businesses with a practical, contemporary, and multidisciplinary expertise that is useful to create suitable and profitable luxury experiences that are tailored to the emotional and functional needs of luxury customers. Using a theoretical and practical approach as well as expert opinions, figures, and illustrations of several examples of luxury brands, the reader can understand the theoretical foundation, the implementation process, and the emerging challenges related to the new experiential luxury marketing and the digital strategies that address the functional, emotional, hedonic, and relational needs of the new luxury consumer.

In the first Book "*Luxe et Expérience Client*" (Dunod, 2017), the logic presented by the author is based on the idea of approaching the consumption of luxury through a perspective centered on the customer experience and its subjective, emotional, relational, human, digital, rational, and functional dimensions. This book is aimed at luxury retailers and marketing directors by providing them with an innovative glance and insight into the marketing approach, customer relationship management, and communication strategies to be put in place to satisfy their customers functionally and emotionally. The principal contribution of this book is to provide an in-depth analytical review of the key trends and case studies of the customer experience, thus addressing two main issues: changing behaviors and the advent of a new customer characterized by expectations and needs that go beyond the merely functional benefits and the idea of the possession of luxury. This book is indeed the first to offer a concrete and analytical vision of the customer experience and its offline and online application in various luxury domains such as hotels, restaurants, retail, events, etc. through a multidisciplinary literature review. The reader can then understand the theoretical foundation, the implementation and the new challenges related to the new luxury marketing based on the customer experience and its "luxury experience wheel." The luxperiential marketing is, in fact, in phase with the functional, emotional, hedonic, and relational needs of the new consumer.

The first chapter explores the emergence and development of luxury consumption, moving from the ostentatious and statutory dimensions of luxury consumption to the rise of the emotional luxury. This chapter contributes to the luxury realm by offering a new definition of luxury that integrates the customer experience to explain the transition from the traditional luxury marketing that reflects ostentatious consumption to the experiential luxury marketing. Chapter 2 proposes to question the notion of "experience" and its application in the field of marketing before analyzing its contribution to the luxury and traditional marketing sector used today by luxury brands. In Chapter 3, a new concept "luxperience," which is a contraction of two words "luxury" and "experience" is proposed. Through the concept of "customer luxperience," this chapter attempts to explore the customer experience in luxury, its components, and its foundations through the presentation of all the actors and factors of the "Luxury experience wheel" that are involved directly or indirectly in the luxury experience bubble. Chapter 4 proposes starting from the limits of traditional luxury marketing by developing the experiential approach as a whole. This approach helps to better understand the elements that make up the "customer luxperience", a central notion in this book. The objective of Chapter 5 is to question the relevance of traditional studies to understand and analyze the customer experience. The challenge is to go beyond classical methodologies by introducing alternative, immersive, and more appropriate marketing research tools for the study of the customer experience and its "luxury experience wheel." Finally, chapter 6 closes the book by presenting the interest for luxury brands to extend their experiential offerings to the virtual world on websites, but also in connected concept stores, creating immersion, and involving customers in exchanges with real and virtual socialization agents. These interactions are facilitated by immersive technologies such as 3D, avatars, augmented reality, 3D printing, connected objects, etc. This chapter responds to this question by explaining the main components of the digital customer experience or the e-luxperience needed to turn websites into a functional, creative, emotional, and interactive experiential space.

In the second Book "*Digital Luxury: transforming Brands & Customer Experiences*" (Sage, 2019), the author develops a theory of the digital luxury experience. Specifically to conceptualize what a digital luxury experience is, how it differs from offline luxury experiences, how it is organized, and what its drivers are. This book gathers recent research articles on two literatures: digital luxury and customer experience as well as luxury case studies to explore open questions regarding the luxury brand consumption experience in the digital era. Luxury consumption experiences typically involve elements of craftsmanship, rarity, modern art, and timeless quality. Taking a step beyond traditionally investigated brand experiences, this book underlines the idea that digital media are democratic, allowing anybody to engage with the brand from anywhere, which lessens the sense of exclusiveness associated with luxury. Many luxury brands have successfully developed social media communication strategies, e-shopping platforms, and digital products and luxury consumers have embraced the digital environment. All of this raises the question of what the digital luxury experience is. The author of this groundbreaking book questions its main characteristics, derivers, and consequences and aims to identify the underlying mechanisms for consumer experience of luxury brands on social media. The book explores novel approaches to study the digital luxury experience and investigates how technologies can enhance the luxury retail and phygital consumption experience.

In this book, the author explores avenues for future research to explain and predict the evolution of luxury consumption behavior and effective means of brand communication in a new phygital context merging physical and digital consumption experiences. Furthermore, this book provides a comprehensive picture of brand experience transformation by exploring the digital luxury experience from two perspectives: luxury industry through examples and case studies and interdisciplinary luxury literature analysis. Indeed, for a long time, traditional luxury brands have been reluctant to accept the opportunities provided by digital technologies. Some of the major concerns have included the increased accessibility of brands online, which might dilute the scarcity and perceived exclusivity of brands; new design technologies that could undermine the heritage, craftsmanship, and sensory experiences that consumers have with brands; and the co-creation and close interaction between the customer and brands that could undermine the aspirational dimension and the distance between the creator and the consumer. In the meantime, anecdotal evidence shows that some luxury brands have already seized the opportunities made possible by digital channels and have integrated them into their strategy without harming the brand's values. For example, Burberry has been recognized as the pioneer of digital collaboration for its work with Snapchat, Google, and YouTube. Because social media increase the visibility of luxury experiences, some research indicates that luxury experiences derived from services may have assumed the role of luxury products in conspicuous consumption. Therefore, the digital context raises two questions: What is the meaning of a digital luxury experience? What are the technologies and devices that luxury companies can use to create pleasurable and profitable digital brand experiences? Therefore, the objective of this book is to explore novel approaches to the study of the digital luxury experience as well as to investigate how technologies can enhance or inhibit the luxury industry and consumption experience.

The first part of this book, "The Digital Luxury Experience Revolution," explores the contributions that the concept of customer experience has made to digital luxury marketing in addition to the main challenges that luxury companies are facing when trying to shift or transform their brand experiences. In Chapter 1, the author questions the meaning of the digital luxury experience and what it represents. It explains the transition from luxury as a product to luxury as experience, and then, as an experience within the digital era. It also highlights the contributions that the concept of customer experience and its tangible and intangible dimensions has made to digital luxury marketing. In the second chapter, the author explains the digital transformation of luxury businesses and describes the evolution of digital marketing in the luxury sector. Chapter 2 addresses the challenges of this digital transformation in the luxury sector and offers a new digital marketing strategy: "Blue Sunflower Marketing," a disruptive strategy through the use of an innovative tool, the "Digital Luxury Triangle" (DLT), that luxury companies can implement to design successful brand experiences. Chapter 3 examines the way in which luxury companies can connect with digital natives and share luxury experiences with them. The objective of this chapter is to identify how digital natives are taking ownership of blogs and developing new relationships with luxury brands. The author also discusses how the members of this digital generation use social media to develop their online *person-branding*; how they connect with luxury brands as influencers, Instagramers, and bloggers; and how these young people share luxury brand experiences with their followers.

The second part of this book, "Realms of the Digital Luxury Experience," explores, throughout five chapters, the technologies used by luxury brands to access the five main digital luxury experience realms. Chapter 4 presents the first realm: the immersive digital luxury experience. In Chapter 5, the author introduces the second digital luxury experience realm: the connected digital luxury experience where she explaines how connected objects and the Internet of Things (IoT) can be regarded by luxury companies as new databases to be taken into account in order to design highly customized connected luxury experiences. Chapter 6 focuses on the third digital luxury experience realm: the playful digital luxury experience. This chapter introduces the reader to the concept of gamification and its related technologies that luxury businesses can implement to design immersive, emotional, and enjoyable brand experiences. Chapter 7 presents the fourth realm of the digital luxury experience: the humanized digital luxury experience. Artificial intelligence

(AI), virtual agents, chatbots, and robots represent some of the future fundamentals of digital luxury experience design. This chapter presents a thoughtful analysis of the technologies related to AI, virtual assistants/agents, chatbots, and robotics in order to understand how luxury professionals in different sectors can use them to design humanized and emotional experiences. Chapter 8, the last chapter in Part II of this book, introduces the fifth realm: the prototyped digital luxury experience. In this chapter, the author introduces the 3D printing technology and answers the following questions: How is 3D printing used in fashion and luxury today? And, what advantages does it offer when compared to traditional processes?

The third part of this book, "Digital Luxury Experience: What's Next?" explores the future innovations and considerations regarding digital luxury marketing. This part includes three main chapters. In Chapter 9, the author introduces the first challenge that luxury companies face when designing the ultimate digital luxury experience and switching to a new experiential marketing mix that goes beyond the traditional use of the mix by addressing the 7Es: Experience, Exchange, Extension, Emphasis, Empathy capital, Emotional touchpoints, and the Emic/etic process. Chapter 10 focuses on the transition from big data to immersive smart data for developing insights into the digital luxury experience by using complementary and alternative market research tools. Finally, Chapter 11 concludes by addressing the third challenge, linked to the emergence of a new paradigm: the "phygital" luxury consumption experience. The author explores the notion of the phygital context, a new environmental setting combining both physical places and digital spaces in the luxury sector.

Wided Batat, Associate Professor – American University of Beirut
wided.batat@bnc-consulting-group.com

A PROPOS DE M&O

Marché et Organisations

Marché et Organisations est une revue d'économie et de gestion par thème, visant, outre un lectorat relativement large, à promouvoir la recherche relative aux liens et dynamiques entre le marché et les organisations (entreprises, institutions publiques, associations, etc.). Si le marché repose sur un mode d'allocation des ressources et sur la coordination des activités économiques au moyen de règles et au travers d'une combinaison de décisions individuelles et collectives, il se structure aussi en lien avec les organisations, dont les intérêts peuvent être divergents, complémentaires, convergents, et il touche divers enjeux autour de la coordination des acteurs. Comment les marchés sont-ils coordonnés autour de problématiques sectorielles, nationales, locales mais aussi internationales ? Comment les organisations tissent-elles leurs liens au travers et en référence au marché ?

Marché et Organisations questionne ainsi l'actualité économique et de gestion en révélant ces liens et les dynamiques, marchands et non marchands, entre le marché et les organisations. Son ambition est d'apporter aux chercheurs et aux praticiens, une réflexion rigoureuse et novatrice en économie et en gestion sur ces questions. Elle souhaite, en outre, diffuser ces recherches à l'ensemble de la communauté scientifique internationale. Ainsi, les contributions peuvent être en langue française et anglaise.

Market and Organizations

Market and Organizations is an academic journal in Economics and Management by themes, aiming, beside a relatively wide readership, to promote research on the links and dynamics between the market and organizations (companies, public institutions, associations, etc.). Whether the market is based on an approach of allocating resources and on the coordination of economic activities via rules and through a combination of individual and collective decisions, it is also structured in the relation with organizations, whose interests are perhaps divergent, complementary, convergent, and it involves several issues surrounding the coordination of actors. How are markets coordinated around the issues at level of sector, nation, local as well as international? How do organizations build their linkage through and in relation to the market?

Market and Organizations, thus, presents the questions on economic and management actuality by revealing these links and the dynamics, both market and non-market, between market and organizations. The ambition of the journal is to offer researchers and practitioners a rigorous and innovative reflection on economics and management on these issues. It also desires to disseminate these researches to the whole international scientific community. Therefore, the contributions can be in French and in English.

Les articles proposés : - 45 000 - 50 000 caractères (espaces compris), incluant les notes de bas de page, la bibliographie, les tableaux, les figures et les annexes, - soumis par email à : Dimitri Uzunidis et Justine Manier, uzunidis@univ-littoral.fr, justine.manier@univ-littoral.fr Les domaines de recherche acceptés pour évaluation sont principalement en économie et en gestion. Sous réserve que le sujet du Cahier le justifie et que la ligne éditoriale de la revue soit respectée, des articles en droit, sociologie et histoire peuvent être acceptés. Les articles publiés peuvent être mono ou multidisciplinaires. *Marché et Organisations* est une publication sous la responsabilité éditoriale du Réseau de Recherche sur l'Innovation : http://2ri.eu La revue est diffusée par Cairn : https://www.cairn.info/revue-marche-et-organisations.htm Site de la revue : https://www.rrifr.univ-littoral.fr/editions/marche-et-organisations/	*The article submission* should: - comprise 45 000 – 50 000 characters (with spaces), including footnotes, references, tables, figures and appendices. - submit by email to Dimitri Uzunidis and Justine Manier (uzunidis@univ-littoral.fr, justine.manier@univ-littoral.fr) The research domains accepted for evaluation are mainly in economics and management. Provided that the topic of Special Issue justifies it and that the editorial line of review is respected, articles in law, sociology and history can be accepted. Published articles can be single or multi-disciplinary. *Market and Organizations* is a publication under the editorial responsibility of the Research Network in Innovation: http://2ri.eu. The Review is distributed by Cairn: http://www.cairn.info/revue-marche-et-organisations.htm Web site: https://www.rrifr.univ-littoral.fr/editions/marche-et-organisations/

MARCHE ET ORGANISATIONS
L'HARMATTAN

Numéros précédemment parus

N°1 : Artisanat. La modernité réinventée, 2006
N°2 : La petite entreprise, elle a tout d'une grande. De l'accompagnement aux choix stratégiques, 2006
N°3 : Tourisme et Innovation. La force créative des loisirs, 2007
N°4 : Le travail. Formes récentes et nouvelles questions, 2007
N°5 : Les universités et l'innovation. L'enseignement et la recherche dans l'économie des connaissances, 2007
N°6 : Entrepreneuriat et accompagnement. Outils, actions et paradigmes nouveaux, 2008
N°7 : Développement durable des territoires. Economie sociale, environnement et innovations, 2008
N°8 : Développement durable et responsabilité sociale des acteurs, 2009
N°9 : Gouvernance : exercices de pouvoir, 2009
N°10 : Le travail collaboratif. Une innovation générique, 2009
N°11 : Economie sociale et solidaire. Nouvelles trajectoires d'innovations, 2010
N°12 : Relations à la marque et marques de la relation. Regards croisés sur le management relationnel de la marque, 2010
N°13 : Les contrats au service de la recherche ?, 2011
N°14 : Le potentiel économique de l'Afrique subsaharienne, 2011
N°15 : Management de la distribution, 2012
N°16 : Territoire Vert. Entreprises, Institutions, Innovations, 2012
N°17 : Eco-conception, conception et innovation. Les nouveaux défis de l'entreprise, 2013
N°18 : Intelligence économique : entreprises et territoires, 2013
N°19 : La finance globale. Un monde fini, 2013
N°20 : La crise du « développement », 2014
N°21 : La Chine innove. Politiques publiques et stratégies d'entreprise, 2014
N°22 : Go East! Nouvelles Economies de Marché, 2015
N°23 : L'économie du changement, 2015
N°24 : Le temps des artisans. Permanences et mutations, 2015
N°25 : Innovations de proximité et esprit d'entreprise, 2016
N°26 : L'avenir des économies du Maghreb, 2016
N°27 : Le sport aux frontières du marché du travail, 2016
N° 28 : Dynamiques internationales des entreprises, 2017
N° 29 : L'univers du risque, 2017
N° 30 : Petites entreprises dans l'histoire industrielle, 2017
N° 31 : Economie sociale et *Social Business* ? Au défi d'entreprendre et se financer, 2018
N° 32 : Education et fertilisation des économies africaines, 2018
N° 33 : L'entrepreneuriat innovant dans les pays du Maghreb, 2018
N° 34 : L'entrepreneuriat scientifique : institutions et innovation, 2019
N° 35 : Le champ économique de la culture, 2019
N°36 : Economie sociale et solidaire ? Modèles d'innovation et modes de gouvernance, 2019

Structures éditoriales du groupe L'Harmattan

L'Harmattan Italie
Via degli Artisti, 15
10124 Torino
harmattan.italia@gmail.com

L'Harmattan Hongrie
Kossuth l. u. 14-16.
1053 Budapest
harmattan@harmattan.hu

L'Harmattan Sénégal
10 VDN en face Mermoz
BP 45034 Dakar-Fann
senharmattan@gmail.com

L'Harmattan Cameroun
TSINGA/FECAFOOT
BP 11486 Yaoundé
inkoukam@gmail.com

L'Harmattan Burkina Faso
Achille Somé – tengnule@hotmail.fr

L'Harmattan Guinée
Almamya, rue KA 028 OKB Agency
BP 3470 Conakry
harmattanguinee@yahoo.fr

L'Harmattan RDC
185, avenue Nyangwe
Commune de Lingwala – Kinshasa
matangilamusadila@yahoo.fr

L'Harmattan Congo
67, boulevard Denis-Sassou-N'Guesso
BP 2874 Brazzaville
harmattan.congo@yahoo.fr

L'Harmattan Mali
Sirakoro-Meguetana V31
Bamako
syllaka@yahoo.fr

L'Harmattan Togo
Djidjole – Lomé
Maison Amela
face EPP BATOME
ddamela@aol.com

L'Harmattan Côte d'Ivoire
Résidence Karl – Cité des Arts
Abidjan-Cocody
03 BP 1588 Abidjan
espace_harmattan.ci@hotmail.fr

L'Harmattan Algérie
22, rue Moulay-Mohamed
31000 Oran
info2@harmattan-algerie.com

L'Harmattan Maroc
5, rue Ferrane-Kouicha, Talaâ-Elkbira
Chrableyine, Fès-Médine
30000 Fès
harmattan.maroc@gmail.com

Nos librairies en France

Librairie internationale
16, rue des Écoles – 75005 Paris
librairie.internationale@harmattan.fr
01 40 46 79 11
www.librairieharmattan.com

Lib. sciences humaines & histoire
21, rue des Écoles – 75005 Paris
librairie.sh@harmattan.fr
01 46 34 13 71
www.librairieharmattansh.com

Librairie l'Espace Harmattan
21 bis, rue des Écoles – 75005 Paris
librairie.espace@harmattan.fr
01 43 29 49 42

Lib. Méditerranée & Moyen-Orient
7, rue des Carmes – 75005 Paris
librairie.mediterranee@harmattan.fr
01 43 29 71 15

Librairie Le Lucernaire
53, rue Notre-Dame-des-Champs – 75006 Paris
librairie@lucernaire.fr
01 42 22 67 13

www.ingramcontent.com/pod-product-compliance
Lightning Source LLC
Chambersburg PA
CBHW071435230926
51846CB00001B/236
* 9 7 8 2 3 4 3 1 9 4 1 8 9 *